STUDIES IN RUSSIA AND EAST EUROPE
formerly Studies in Russian and East European History

Chairman of the Editorial Board: M. A. Branch, Director, School of Slavonic and East European Studies.

This series includes books on general, political, historical, economic, social and cultural themes relating to Russia and East Europe written or edited by members of the School of Slavonic and East European Studies in the University of London, or by authors working in association with the School. Titles already published are listed below. Further titles are in preparation.

Phyllis Auty and Richard Clogg (*editors*)
BRITISH POLICY TOWARDS WARTIME RESISTANCE IN YUGOSLAVIA AND GREECE

Elisabeth Barker
BRITISH POLICY IN SOUTH-EAST EUROPE IN THE SECOND WORLD WAR

Richard Clogg (*editor*)
THE MOVEMENT FOR GREEK INDEPENDENCE. 1770–1821: A COLLECTION OF DOCUMENTS

Olga Crisp
STUDIES IN THE RUSSIAN ECONOMY BEFORE 1914

D. G. Kirby (*editor*)
FINLAND AND RUSSIA. 1808–1920: DOCUMENTS

Martin McCauley
THE RUSSIAN REVOLUTION AND THE SOVIET STATE. 1917–1921: DOCUMENTS (*editor*)

KHRUSHCHEV AND THE DEVELOPMENT OF SOVIET AGRICULTURE

COMMUNIST POWER IN EUROPE: 1944–1949 (*editor*)

MARXISM-LENINISM IN THE GERMAN DEMOCRATIC REPUBLIC: THE SOCIALIST UNITY PARTY (SED)

THE GERMAN DEMOCRATIC REPUBLIC SINCE 1945

Martin McCauley and Stephen Carter (*editors*)
LEADERSHIP AND SUCCESSION IN THE SOVIET UNION, EASTERN EUROPE AND CHINA

Martin McCauley and Peter Waldron
THE EMERGENCE OF THE MODERN RUSSIAN STATE, 1855–81

Evan Mawdsley
THE RUSSIAN REVOLUTION AND THE BALTIC FLEET

J. J. Tomiak (*editor*)
WESTERN PERSPECTIVES ON SOVIET EDUCATION IN THE 1980s

Series Standing Order

If you would like to receive future titles in this series as they are published, you can make use of our standing order facility. To place a standing order please contact your bookseller or, in case of difficulty, write to us at the address below with your name and address and the name of the series. Please state with which title you wish to begin your standing order. (If you live outside the UK we may not have the rights for your area, in which case we will forward your order to the publisher concerned.)

Standing Order Service, Macmillan Distribution Ltd, Houndmills, Basingstoke, Hampshire, RG21 2XS, England.

The Emergence of the Modern Russian State, 1855–81

Martin McCauley
Senior Lecturer in Soviet and East European Studies
School of Slavonic and East European Studies
University of London

and

Peter Waldron
Lecturer in Modern History
University College, Cork

MACMILLAN PRESS

in association with the
School of Slavonic and
East European Studies
University of London

© Martin McCauley and Peter Waldron 1988

All rights reserved. No reproduction, copy or transmission of this publication may be made without written permission.

No paragraph of this publication may be reproduced, copied or transmitted save with written permission or in accordance with the provisions of the Copyright Act 1956 (as amended).

Any person who does any unauthorised act in relation to this publication may be liable to criminal prosecution and civil claims for damages.

First published 1988

Published by
THE MACMILLAN PRESS LTD
Houndmills, Basingstoke, Hampshire RG21 2XS
and London
Companies and representatives
throughout the world

Filmsetting by Vantage Photosetting Co. Ltd
Eastleigh and London.
Printed in Hong Kong

British Library Cataloguing in Publication Data
The Emergence of the modern Russian State.
1856–81. — (Studies in Russia and East
Europe)
1. Soviet Union — Social conditions —
1801–1917 — Sources 2. Soviet Union —
History — Alexander II, 1855–1881 — Sources
I. McCauley, Martin II. Waldron, Peter,
1956– III. University of London, School
of Slavonic and East European Studies
IV. Series
947.08'1   HN523
ISBN 0–333–38469–5

Contents

Preface	ix
Dates and Measurements	x
Map 1 Russia, Austria, and the Balkans, 1856–1914	xi
Map 2 The Provinces of European Russia in the late nineteenth century	xii
Introduction	1

DOCUMENTS

1. **Government Structure and Personnel** — 61
   - 1.1 The Impact of Autocracy — 61
   - 1.2 Provincial Administration — 62
   - 1.3 The Marshal of the Nobility — 62
   - 1.4 Local Self-Government — 64
   - 1.5 Autocracy and Popular Representation — 71
   - 1.6 The Law and Legal Reform — 76

2. **Mechanisms of Control** — 83
   - 2.1 The Army — 83
   - 2.2 Policing — 88
   - 2.3 The Exile System — 92
   - 2.4 Censorship — 94

3. **The Rural Scene** — 99
   - 3.1 The Need for Reform — 99
   - 3.2 The Impact of Serfdom — 101
   - 3.3 Emancipation and the Nobility — 103
   - 3.4 Emancipation — 106
   - 3.5 The Implementation of the Emancipation — 115
   - 3.6 Emancipation and Household Serfs — 117
   - 3.7 The Peasant Commune — 118
   - 3.8 The Impact of Emancipation — 119
   - 3.9 Rural Medicine — 121
   - 3.10 Peasant Life — 123

4. **Urban Growth** — 126
   - 4.1 Some Basic Statistics — 126
   - 4.2 A Working Class Emerges — 127
   - 4.3 Working Conditions — 129
   - 4.4 Urban Change — 132

Contents

5.	Society and the Regime	140
	5. 1 The Social Elite	140
	5. 2 Herzen on Russia and Europe	140
	5. 3 'Young Russia'	142
	5. 4 Pisarev and 'Realism'	144
	5. 5 Karakozov's Assassination Attempt, 1866	145
	5. 6 Bakunin's Anarchism	149
	5. 7 The Moscow Municipal Duma Asks for Reform	150
	5. 8 Populism: 'Going to the People'	152
	5. 9 Land and Liberty	154
	5.10 Black Repartition	156
	5.11 *Narodnaya Volya* – The People's Will	158
6.	Foreign Policy	162
	6. 1 The End of the Crimean War	162
	6. 2 Poland and Foreign Relations	162
	6. 3 Gorchakov's Renunciation of the Treaty of Paris	164
	6. 4 European Security	166
	6. 5 Forward Policy in the Balkans	170
	6. 6 The Balkan War, 1877–78	171
	6. 7 Expansion in Central Asia	175
7.	Education and Culture	178
	7. 1 Educational Statistics	178
	7. 2 Education and the Zemstva	179
	7. 3 Universities	179
	7. 4 Secondary Schools	184
	7. 5 Katkov on Education	186
	7. 6 Women's Education	188
	7. 7 Book Production	189
	7. 8 The Nature of Literature	189
	7. 9 Art Theory: Three Views	190
	7.10 A New School of Painting	193
	7.11 The Tretyakov Gallery	194
	7.12 Russian Music	195
	7.13 The Orthodox Church	197
8.	Nationalities	200
	8. 1 The Polish Rebellion, 1863	200
	8. 2 Roman Catholicism	203
	8. 3 The Baltic Germans	204

8.4	Finland	206
8.5	The Ukraine	208
8.6	The Jews	210
8.7	Central Asia	211

Selected Bibliography 213
Index 217

Preface

The quarter-century for which Alexander II was the ruler of the Russian Empire was one of enormous change for the country. The problems of modernising a rural state were tackled by an autocratic regime which found itself assailed by revolutionary groups drawn largely from the social elite of the empire. Alexander's assassination in 1881 was the climax of the confrontation between the Russian state and its opponents; a confrontation which was to be renewed in the decades after his death.

This volume is intended to provide a guide to contemporary perceptions of the difficulties facing Russia and the ways in which they might be solved, through a selection of documents. The introduction places the documents in a wider context.

Warm thanks are due to those who suggested material which might be included as documents, particularly to Olga Crisp, John Keep, Dominic Lieven and David Saunders. They must not, of course, be held responsible for any shortcomings or errors. All translations are our own. We are also deeply grateful to Steve Kirk who has been unstinting in his hospitality during the preparation of this work, and to Charlotte Wiseman who has typed and retyped the manuscript with skill and efficiency.

The author and publishers wish to thank the following who have kindly given permission for the use of copyright material: Cambridge University Press, for the map (Map 1) from R. E. F. Smith and David Christian, *Bread and Salt* (1984); and the Longman Group, for the map (Map 2) from Hans Rogger, *Russia in the Age of Modernisation and Revolution, 1881–1917* (1983).

MARTIN McCAULEY
PETER WALDRON

Dates and Measurements

All dates dealing with events inside the Russian Empire have been given according to the Old Style (Julian) calendar which during the nineteenth century was twelve days behind the Western (Gregorian) calender. Dates referring to events outside the empire have been given in both styles, e.g. 18/30 March 1856.

    1 pud = 16.3 kilograms
    1 verst = 1.06 kilometres
    1 desyatina = 1.09 hectares

Map 1 The provinces of European Russia in the late nineteenth century

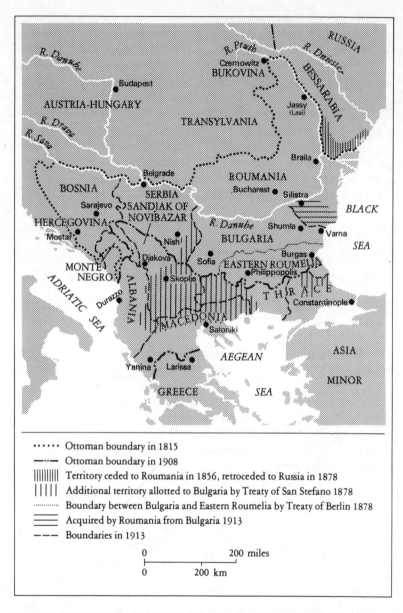

Map 2　Russia, Austria and the Balkans, 1856–1914

Introduction

In February 1855 Tsar Nicholas I died, dispirited by Russian reverses in the Crimean war. For a generation Russia had been recognised as a leading European power whilst at home Nicholas resisted change and presided over a society which was showing increasing signs of tension. The following quarter century, however, saw major shifts in Russia's situation: her international status was severely reduced whilst reform at home became a recognised instrument of policy.

The most immediate problem which faced the new Tsar, Alexander II, was the defeat which Russian forces were suffering in the war in the Crimea. France and Britain had declared war on Russia in March 1854, ostensibly to prevent Turkey from becoming a Russian satellite, but also with the intention of restoring the balance of power in Europe by dealing a blow to an over-mighty Russia. War against Russia was also seen as a means of combating tyranny and asserting the virtues of Western liberalism. Although Russia possessed the largest army in Europe and despite the fact that she was fighting a war on her own door-step, she underwent successive defeats. The death of Nicholas I did nothing to halt this trend. Sevastopol fell in September 1855, and by the beginning of 1856 Russia was ready to negotiate for peace. The first year of the new Tsar's reign thus saw a humiliating defeat inflicted upon Russia: her military commanders had been shown to be incompetent, her troops ill-trained and poorly equipped and her system of supply inadequate. It had been Russia's military might which had raised her standing amongst European powers and her defeat meant a substantial reduction in her prestige and weight. High on the agenda for the new ruler, therefore, was the need to reconstruct the armed forces so that they could cope successfully with war and provide a reliable guarantee of Russia's status as a Great Power.

Many contemporaries saw Russia's dismal military performance as a direct result of her economic and social structure. Although there had been an increase in economic activity during the reign of Nicholas I, Russia still lagged far behind Western Europe. Heavy industrial production in particular remained stagnant, with the coal and iron industries developing slowly. Transport was difficult inside Russia: by 1860 there were only 1600 km of railway in the country. Russia remained dependent on imports for the materials necessary for railway construction and this obstacle to the provision of better transport facilities was in itself a substantial hindrance to the expansion of the Russian industrial sector. Industrial growth had taken place mainly in the consumer-goods sector and it was the textile industry which benefitted most from this.

Russia was an overwhelmingly rural country for the whole of the nineteenth century and agrarian questions dominated the thinking of the government and of both its supporters and critics. Russian agriculture produced very low yields compared to its counterparts elsewhere in Europe; machinery was little used and techniques of cultivation remained generally primitive. The very structure of cultivation also contributed to the problems of agriculture: strip-farming was still widely practised and almost half the land was worked by serfs. By the 1850s the existence of serfdom in Russia was perceived as a major reason for her economic backwardness. It was argued that the enserfed peasant had no incentive to work harder or to use more advanced agricultural methods since any benefit which was obtained would go not to the peasant himself, but to the landowner. If Russian industry was to expand, increased agricultural production was a prerequisite: this was the government's major problem.

Serfdom was not solely an economic problem, for it also had significant social and political dimensions. The continued existence of a system of serfdom inside Russia served to emphasise Russia's backwardness and demonstrated to contemporaries that Russia still had a long way to go before she reached the level of the West. Questions of self-regard thus played a part in the determination of many educated Russians to see serfdom abolished, but serfdom was also believed to have a deadening effect on the political and military resources of the state. The internal political importance of the system was huge, for serfdom was the centrepiece of the methods of control which the Russian state had evolved over the centuries. As serfs, the peasants were tied to the land and encountered difficulties in trying to move away; policing was undertaken by the landowner, be it the imperial family or members of the nobility. This gave enormous responsibility to a very small number of individuals in the countryside and could prove to be fragile if peasant disturbances became widespread. The rise in rural discontent experienced during the 1850s gave the government cause for concern and showed the need for a more reliable means of controlling the rural population.

The intermediary between the private serf and the state was the noble landowner and his position also gave the government cause for concern. By the 1850s many of the Russian gentry were heavily in debt and showed very little interest in introducing any sort of improvements to their estates. The conservatism of the peasant in agricultural matters was reflected in the attitudes of the landlords; few of them took steps to improve their economic position and the decline of their agricultural fortunes was not marked by any corresponding increase in interest by the gentry in commercial or industrial matters. The stagnation of the agricultural system affected the landlords as much as it did the peasant and this too provided problems for the government: without a strong landowning class able to control the peasanty effectively, the state could find itself without guaranteed means to quell any discontent. The reduction in the economic power of the private landlords was accompanied by a decline in their political influence in the St Petersburg bureaucracy: state service was increasingly becoming the domain of men who owned little or no land and were highly educated. The landowning nobility were keen to hold on to whatever power remained to them, and the state therefore faced a further problem in trying to reconcile the aspirations of the gentry with its own perceptions of the path most suitable for Russia's development.

The picture which Russia presented in 1855 was one of a country which, by West European standards, was backward. In economic terms she was saddled with the system of serfdom, discarded and discredited elsewhere in Western Europe. Russia had hardly begun to industrialise and her economy remained almost completely based on agriculture. As a result, it was peasants who made up the majority of the population, with a relatively small proportion of noble landowners controlling them. Russia's very limited industrial base and the dominant position of the state in the economy meant that she was bereft of a sizeable middle class able to invest in industry and stimulate its further growth. Socially, therefore, Russia retained the characteristics of the type of society which was fast disappearing in the states to her West. To cap this antiquated social and economic structure, Russia was ruled by an autocracy, a regime which under Nicholas I had shown itself to be oppressive and was out of step with the liberal political philosophies developing elsewhere in Europe. By 1855 Russia was an anachronism in Europe.

During the quarter century which followed the death of Nicholas I Russia underwent a series of changes which set the pattern for the remainder of the imperial regime's existence. The temptations of European models proved irresistible early in the reign of Alexander II and reform was made in many fundamental areas of Russian life. In the political arena, the principle of elected self-government was introduced,

Numbers in square brackets [ ] refer to the section of documents.

albeit only at a local level, through the introduction of elected local councils in both city and countryside [I.4]. A second vital borrowing from Western practice came in a major legal reform which removed judicial decisions from the competence of the Tsar and those directly responsible to him and instead instituted an indpendent judiciary and jury trials [I.6]. In the economic sphere, Tsarism bowed to the inevitable in 1861 and formally abolished the institution of serfdom in the hope of stimulating the agrarian sector and providing circumstances more conducive to the development of industry [3.4]. Serfdom's disappearance was also intended to produce political results by allowing for the development of a more efficient and better-selected army and thus to allow Russia to regain her prestige as a European Great Power. Western influence was also seen during the 1860s in educational reform and in moves to relax somewhat the impact of the censorship. On one hand, therefore, Russia appeared to be following the European patterns which were believed to be responsible for the West's superiority to Russia, a superiority which had been all too clearly demonstrated during the Crimean War.

The Russian autocratic regime did not, however, make a wholehearted commitment to Western forms during the 1860s and 1870s, for traditional Russian concerns remained an important part of its thinking. Paramount amongst these was the regime's determination to retain as much of its absolute power as possible and to ensure that it could maintain direct control over the entire population of the Russian Empire. Attempts were made to improve the functioning of those institutions directly concerned with law and order: the army was reformed, both the ordinary and secret police underwent changes to try to improve their efficiency and censorship reform was intended both to relax some of the most irksome restrictions and to make the workings of the institution more effective.

This desire to retain as much authority as possible with the autocracy was also seen in the reforms which, at first sight, appear to be based on Western models. All of them include elements of compromise with the autocrat's aspiration to remain in full control of his empire. The serfs were emancipated from the power of the private landlords, but remained subject to the rural commune's authority; local councils were severely restricted in their area of jurisdiction; methods remained available for the government to reduce the scope of juries; secondary education was extended, but the curriculum was tightly controlled from the centre. The modern state which was emerging in Russia under Alexander II was therefore a hybrid; the contradictions between Western notions of political and social organisation were never reconciled with Russian conditions and the individualistic theories and innovations introduced by many of the reforms remained in constant tension with the state-centred native Russian practices. This fundamental difference in approach reached its tentacles into almost every sector of Russian life. Education was bedevilled by it and this had its effect on the formation of public opinion, whilst plans to promote economic development were restricted by the state's insistence on being able to control its population. The unwillingness of the autocracy to make any changes to its fundamental political structure served to increase the tensions which faced it, for it aroused more opposition by its refusal to introduce any political compromises in St Petersburg and the presence of such opposition meant that the state felt it had to increase further its own authority. A vicious circle had come into existence by which calls for change led to greater repression which in turn led to further calls for change.

MECHANISMS OF CONTROL

The institutions by which the Russian Empire was governed were centred on the person of the Tsar: the first article of the Fundamental Laws of the Empire declared the Tsar to be 'an autocratic and unlimited Monarch' and law emanated from him. There was no fixed procedure though which a measure had to pass before it could become law, other than to receive the Tsar's sanction. Two bodies existed which could offer advice on legislative matters, but the Tsar was under no obligation to seek their advice, or if he did ask for their views, to accept them. The State Council had been established in 1810 to act specifically as a consultative body on legislation; by the 1850s it was composed of some 60 of the most senior officials of the Empire, appointed by the Tsar. In practice, many items of legislation were never examined by the Council and Nicholas I himself wrote that 'the Council exists, in my view, to provide conscientiously for me its opinion on questions which I put before it, no more, no less'. The Committee of Ministers was the supreme executive body of the Empire, consisting of the ministers themselves together with senior members of the State Council – a total of twenty men. The Committee was in no sense akin to a Western Cabinet since its chairman had no power to determine the overall thrust of government policy and each individual minister retained the right to report directly to the Tsar. Collective responsibility was not part of the structure of the

Committee and its members recognised its fundamental impotence; its legislative actions were infrequent whilst its administrative duties were largely formal. Law could be enacted as a result of advice offered by either of these two bodies, but it could also result from a ministerial report or regulation: the only feature which all laws had in common was that they were confirmed by the Tsar – and this confirmation could come, in certain circumstances, orally.

When the Tsar had issued a law it was then passed to the Senate for examination as to whether it conflicted with existing legislation and for publication, but significant areas of law remained outside the Senate's jurisdiction. Measures declared to be of especial secrecy were not dealt with by the Senate and it had no real power to test the legality of enactments. The senators were recognised as being uninterested in their work and they had no independent authority with which they could challenge a decision of the Tsar, since they could be dismissed and appointed at his will. It was the Tsar who determined the membership of all three bodies which could have some effect on the legislation which governed the Russian Empire – State Council, Committee of Ministers and Senate – so that there was no authority which existed independently of the monarch which had any influence on the laws which governed the empire. Whilst the Fundamental Laws stated that the empire was governed 'on the firm basis of . . . laws', it was the Tsar alone who was responsible for law; his power as an autocrat overrode every other authority.

The arbitrary way in which the monarch could issue laws was reflected in the way in which Russia was administered at all levels of its government. Centrally, the country was governed by ministries located in St Petersburg which had local agencies in each province of Russia. The most significant of central government departments was the Ministry of Internal Affairs: it bore the main burden of provincial administration, controlled the police and played a large part in the affairs of the rural economy. Its staff of over 20 000 civil servants in the 1850s was by far the largest of any ministry. The head of each provincial administration was the governor, responsible to the Ministry of Internal Affairs, and he and his staff were grossly over-burdened with work; towards the end of the century it is estimated that each governor had to deal with over 100 000 pieces of paper annually [1.2]. Whilst the duties of the governor ranged across the whole spectrum of provincial life, the inadequate resources placed at his disposal in terms of staff and finance meant that it was impossible for him to exercise his power to the full. If provincial administration was inefficient, the level below was even worse. The districts into which each province was subdivided lacked any form of central administration: there was no figure equivalent to the governor, and the nearest approximation came in the person of the district Marshal of the Nobility [1.3]. He was the elected chairman of the local Noble Assembly and thus responsible only to his peers and not to the government. The government had, however, gradually loaded more and more responsibility onto him so that by the latter half of the nineteenth century he served on over twenty separate committees and was the linch-pin of district administration. The links which the marshal provided between the various district committees were purely personal; he had no institutional back-up and many marshals proved to be uninterested in their work. There was no unified district administration; the marshal did not occupy any official government position and therefore could not be disciplined by St Petersburg authorities. His lack of responsibility to the government meant that it had no control over him.

The situation in the district is only the worst example of the fact that, by 1855, Russia was chronically under-governed. The Russian empire had only 1.3 public employees per thousand of population, compared to 4.1 per thousand in Britain and 4.8 per thousand in France. There had thus emerged the paradoxical situation that whilst the autocrat was able to exercise immense authority, at the local level government was ineffective and weak. The Russian state had been unable to find ways of effectively devolving authority across the immense distances of the empire; the concentration of all theoretical authority at the centre resulted in excessive centralisation of government functions. This did not, however, mean that decisions taken in St Petersburg were efficiently carried out in the provinces, for the arbitrary legislative procedure, combined with a local bureaucracy which was grossly inefficient, resulted in the development of an administrative ethos which laid little stress on effective implementation of government decisions and equitable administration of the law, but instead was notorious for operating in an arbitrary manner and being exceptionally prone to bribery and other forms of corruption. Communications inside the Empire were extremely difficult, thus making it even more difficult to supervise the activities of the local authorities. By 1855 it was widely recognised that reform was needed to create a proper system of provincial and district administration and to try to remove the paradox whereby the exceptional power of Russian government at the centre resulted in local authorities having substantial leeway in the decisions which they took and the way in which they were implemented.

Reform in all spheres after 1855 was encouraged and prepared by important groups of the senior officials who staffed the bureaucracy. During the first half of the nineteenth century the composition of the bureaucracy had been changing, so that by 1855 a civil service was emerging with members whose primary loyalty was to the institutions in which they served and not to any single social group. Whilst over 75 per cent of the 350 most senior civil servants in the 1850s were of noble status, this conceals the fact that many of these nobles came from families which had acquired nobility through state service and were not large serf- or landowners. Nearly 60 per cent of these officials had inherited no serfs and over 80 per cent of them remained serfless throughout their careers. At the same time as landownership was in decline as a prerequisite for becoming a senior official, the educational patterns of these men were changing. The numbers who had only received instruction at home dropped to nothing and there was an enormous increase in the proportion of civil servants who had undergone a higher education, either in a university or else in a professionally orientated institute. Almost seventy per cent of civil servants entering the service in the 1840s had this latter background. These changes in the social and educational backgrounds of senior civil servants were reflected in the views which they espoused. Whilst Nicholas I continued to reject reform as an option for his government, an increasing number of middle-rank and senior civil servants were coming to see it as the only way for Russia to progress. Men such as N. A. Milyutin, later to head the Economic Department and Statistical Committee of the Ministry of Internal Affairs and A. V. Golovnin, who became Minister of Education in the early 1860s, and others stood at the centre of the 'enlightened bureaucrats' who were to play a key role in the implementation of the reforms of the 1860s.

Whilst these changes were taking place in the St Petersburg bureaucratic milieu, their influence was much less evident in the provinces. Landownership remained more common amongst provincial governors, and some 60 per cent of them owned property, whilst their educational level was far below that of their St Petersburg colleagues. Less than 20 per cent had a higher education and over 60 per cent were products of a home education. These trends were even more evident in the careers of marshals of the nobility: only 11 per cent of those entering service before 1860 had a university education, although nearly a third of them had had a military education. Very few marshals were serfless and over a quarter of them owned more than 1000 serfs – these were men from the very top layer of the Russian nobility. This more traditional

Introduction

service background of provincial officials and their greater military emphasis combined to provide a definite divergence of views between the reform-minded bureaucrats who were dominant in the capital in the 1860s and provincial officials who had been brought up in a climate more in line with the traditional autocratic concern of control.

The haphazard and ineffective institutional structure of the Russian Empire made it very difficult to utilise the resources of the country to their full extent, whilst the complete exclusion of the public from having any say in decision-making both produced resentment amongst the growing numbers of educated and informed Russians and was becoming recognised by the government as being an obstacle to the effective perception of provincial needs by the central administration. Administrative reform was therefore aimed in two directions: decentralisation of authority from St Petersburg to the provinces and self-government through the involvement of some sections of the population in local councils. Discussions took place during the late 1850s about ways of giving the provincial governor more independent power, and in 1865 governors were given extended authority over local agents of all government ministries and were able to act without the need to refer back so frequently to their superiors in the capital. At the same time as these moves were being made, preparations were taking place to introduce a system of elected local councils into European Russia. During 1857 and 1858 central government sought the views of the provincial nobility on the serf question through the medium of provincial emancipation committees, but many of these committees went much further and produced calls for local self-government as an essential accompaniment to agrarian reform. The government was itself working to produce an administrative reform and in 1860 Alexander II, together with S. S. Lanskoy and P. A. Valuev, successive Ministers of Internal Affairs, accepted the principle of local self-government. It took four years to work out the details of the new structure, the legislation eventually being issued in January 1864 [I.4].

Local councils (*zemstva*) were to be established in the majority of the provinces and districts of European Russia, with their members to be elected directly by nobles and townsmen, and indirectly by peasants. The electoral system was designed to produce noble preponderance in the zemstvo assemblies: the first elections resulted in 42 per cent of district zemstvo seats being occupied by nobles, and 38 per cent by peasants, whilst in the provincial assemblies, elected by and from the members of the district zemstva, the nobility occupied 74 per cent of seats, and peasants only 10.5 per cent. Zemstva began to be introduced into the provinces of European Russia in 1865 and by 1870 had reached 34 provinces. Their powers were extensive, since in addition to various duties being laid upon them by the government, such as road maintenance and the organisation of military conscription, they were able to take measures for 'the improvement of life'. This allowed zemstva to set up schools, organise medical services, provide agricultural advice and the like; expenditure on non-obligatory items made up 43 per cent of total zemstvo spending in 1871, increasing to 50 per cent by 1875. To enable the zemstva to carry out such tasks, they were allowed to levy local taxation on agricultural and forest land, a source which provided 75 per cent of their income, as well as to impose levies on other property and duties on trade and industry. The zemstva thus came to play a most important part in Russian provincial life: they provided services which had often not been available before the 1860s, and in doing so they employed a substantial number of professional people, such as doctors, statisticians and surveyors – the so-called 'Third Element' – who were to be important in pressing for further local autonomy and improvements in rural conditions. By allowing the principle of freely elected assemblies to become established in Russia the government was, however, surrendering a significant portion of its own authority. The zemstva had their own source of income and they were allowed wide discretion in the activities they could engage in, activities which it was difficult for the central government to control and which proved embarrassing to it. Furthermore, the introduction of zemstva gave the population as a whole a formal say for the first time in the government of Russia, albeit at a local level.

The consultation which the government had engaged in whilst preparing for emancipation in the late 1850s, together with the introduction of local councils appeared to mark an important shift in the state's attitude to participation in government. Many educated Russians hoped that these concessions would lead to the opportunity for the public to play a part in government at the national level [1.4]. In 1862 the Tver noble assembly declared itself in favour of a 'consultative assembly of representatives elected by all classes', a move which the Tsar condemned as being outside the competence of the assembly. The Tver proposal was not, however, the only call for such a step, for inside the government itself proposals were prepared for constitutional reform among these lines. P. A. Valuev, Minister of Internal Affairs between 1861 and 1868, suggested in 1863 that a consultative congress of state deputies could be established, with representatives from the zemstva, and that sixteen of its members could sit in the State Council. The idea was rejected by Alexander II who argued, in the aftermath of the Polish rebellion, that Russia was not yet ready for such a move, but this was far from being the end of such proposals.

Gentry pressure for a greater role in government continued to be felt, whilst discontent grew with Alexander II and his policies. Reform had not proved to be the cure-all which many had anticipated, whilst the concessions which the government had made were regarded as inadequate and further change was believed to be necessary by many educated Russians to complete the work which the government had begun. The assassination attempt on the Tsar by Karakozov in 1866 prompted some of the most senior officials of the Empire to argue that the causes which underlay such vivid manifestations of unrest could be removed by allowing the most responsible section of society to participate in the work of legislation. Only in this way declared the Tsar's brother, Grand Duke Konstantin Nikolaevich, could central government be made more aware of local conditions and legislate to take them into account [1.4]. This proposal of 1866, somewhat less radical than Valuev's in that it envisaged the creation of an advisory body based on the traditional noble assemblies, was also turned down by the Tsar. Both Valuev and the Grand Duke believed that representation would act to strengthen the autocracy, and this theme was continued in 1873 and 1874 by P. A. Shuvalov, chief of the Third Section – the secret police. He saw the way forward for the autocracy as being to regenerate the landed nobility, both by increasing their agricultural prosperity and by involving them in legislative work. By providing the gentry with renewed economic strength and new political influence, Shuvalov and his associates intended to provide the autocratic regime with a solid base of support. His proposals were heavily opposed inside the government where they were seen as not so much enhancing the power of the state, but as providing for its destruction by launching an unwarranted attack on the powers of the autocracy.

The stumbling-block in all these moves towards bringing about a fundamental political reform in Russia was the concept and person of the autocrat: for most of his reign Alexander II was unwilling to allow the introduction of any form of national assembly which would reduce his authority. The situation changed, however, at the end of the 1870s: an increase in terrorist activity and the evident failure of the autocratic regime to construct a stable society in Russia prompted the Tsar to appoint Count L. T. Loris-Melikov to investigate the reasons for these outbreaks and to suggest ways in which they could be halted. As head of this Supreme Executive Commission from February to August 1880, and then Minister of Internal Affairs until April 1881, Loris-Melikov saw his task in very broad terms and made proposals to reform the institutional structure of the autocracy. He firstly suggested a reorganisation of ministerial jurisdictions which would result in the Ministry of Internal Affairs being given much increased power, especially in its control of provincial affairs, and secondly, the introduction of a three-tiered system of representative assemblies [1.5]. Ministerial reform did take place, especially through the unification of all police affairs inside Loris-Melikov's ministry, and Alexander II gave his approval to the plan to introduce consultative legislative assemblies – by 1881 it was clear even to the Tsar that public opinion and especially the gentry had interests which needed to be taken into account if the regime was to be able to count on their whole-hearted support. On 1 March 1881, before the Tsar could finally sign the bill into law, he was, however, assassinated and his successor, Alexander III preferred to use more conservative and repressive measures to reassert the power of the autocracy. By 1881, therefore, Russia's administrative structure remained confused: the principle of self-government had been accepted at the local level, but it had not succeeded in being implemented centrally. This arrangement helped to create tensions between the St Petersburg government and the zemstva, especially over the jurisdiction and revenue-raising authority of the local bodies. This reflected the basic inconsistency which the introduction of zemstva represented, since the establishment of organisations with independent authority was not accompanied by a recognition on the part of the state that its power was correspondingly reduced.

The zemstva were not, however, the only independent institutions which the regime established, for in 1864 a major reform of the Russian judicial system was instituted. Legal reform posed the same problems for the autocracy as did the introduction of local self-government. It too threatened to limit the sphere of action of the monarch and his advisers by instituting a means by which the actions of all members of the Russian state – rulers as well as ruled – could be tested against a body of law and which would not allow the government to interfere in the process. Pressure for reform came from two main sources: the first half of the nineteenth century had seen a significant growth in legal education in Russia, so that the central bureaucracy was increasingly staffed by men who had, in Wortman's phrase, 'a legal consciousness' and wanted to see the inefficient and arbitrary system of Russian justice replaced by something which corresponded more to the concepts of law which they had studied. Secondly, the emancipation of the serfs made legal reform imperative. The peasants were now individuals with legal status and they needed to be provided with the means to obtain legal redress for grievances, whilst the nobility needed legal protection now that they were deprived of the crutch of serfdom. During 1862 the basic principles for judicial reform were set out inside the government by a group of reforming bureaucrats led by S. I. Zarudnyy: an independent court system was to be established with easy access for the public to its institutions, juries were to be introduced and proceedings in courts were to be oral and conducted according to adversarial procedure. This was to be the system for dealing with important criminal and civil cases, and Russia was divided into a set of judicial regions; for more minor matters, however, Justices of the Peace were to be elected by the zemstvo, although most cases involving only peasants were to continue to be dealt with by the elected peasant courts which had been established as part of the emancipation statute.

These were the main features of the judicial statutes which were implemented in November 1864 [I.6]: it removed an important section of Russian life from the purview of the regime and made it difficult for the government to interfere in judicial matters. The foundations of the *Rechtsstaat*, the rule of law, were being laid. Judges were appointed for life and were paid a substantial salary, thus obviating any temptation to take bribes, whilst the structure of the new courts meant that a legal profession came into being for the first time in Russia, a group of trained professional lawyers who were ready to defend the new system vigorously. The new circuit courts were able to attract highly educated and experienced personnel as judges and prosecutors, but there was difficulty in attracting candidates of a similar calibre to act as JPs. Whilst the new legal system was initially greeted with approval, there is evidence to suggest that it became less popular during the 1870s: at the local level, delays continued to be experienced in using the courts and there were suspicions as to the relationship between the JP and his electors in the zemstvo. The government too found aspects of the reformed courts not to be to its taste: public courts provided a platform for those opposed to the government to make statements, whilst the jury system sometimes resulted in verdicts which the government felt to be wrong – the most celebrated case was that of Vera Zasulich, who in 1878 attempted to assassinate the St Petersburg chief of police, but was acquitted by a jury. The regime increasingly tried to find ways of transferring 'political' offences to the jurisdiction of non-jury courts and to claw back some of the concessions which it had granted in the reform of 1864.

The regime acted unsurely during the 1870s; the reforms of the 1860s had not served to quell discontent and the government was unable to decide upon any concerted set of actions to deal with a situation which was increasingly threatening. Whilst some ministers wanted to widen the base of support for the regime, others, with the support of the Tsar for all but the last year of his reign, wanted to deal firmly with opposition. For at the same time as reform was taking place in the administrative and legal spheres, the means by which the regime exerted control over the empire's population were also undergoing change. The weakness of the army had been all too clearly demonstrated during the Crimean War, the local police were generally recognised as incompetent and insufficient in number and the censorship provoked anger amongst those who were affected by it, without appearing to contain the spread of opinions distasteful to the government. If the autocracy was to be able to deal effectively with opposition and discontent, reform was needed in these areas too.

Army reform was a slow process since it involved dealing with very large numbers of men and a substantial proportion of the state's budget: D. A. Milyutin, the Minister of War, moved to try to create a cheaper and more effective army by improving military education, rationalising the administrative structure of the Ministry of War and introducing a system of conscription which would apply right across the Empire [2.1]. Instead of military service falling largely on the peasantry and being effectively for life, Milyutin intended that it should apply to all classes and should last for fifteen years, only seven of which would be spent on active service, with the remainder in the reserves. This move, implemented in 1874, was aimed at producing a better-trained army with a reserve which could be easily mobilised in time of need. Milyutin's reform laid the basis for a modern army in Russia able to cope better both abroad, as it did during the Balkan War of 1877-78, and at home, where the army and its institutions became increasingly used by the government to maintain control. The emergency powers statute of August 1881 which gave greater scope to military legal institutions and allowed provincial officials to use the army more easily to deal with disturbances was only the most extreme example of this trend.

Increasing reliance on the army was, in part, an admission that the ordinary police forces of the Empire were unable to cope with maintaining order in Russia [2.2]. The number of ordinary police was very small: the province of Yaroslavl, for example, which covered 22 400 square kilometres and had a population of almost one million, had only 244 police officers. Nearly 200 of these were located in urban centres, so that the countryside was effectively almost unpoliced. The situation was made even worse by the duties which were imposed on the police, with nearly half their time being taken up by acting as local agents for central government in such matters as tax-collection and the gathering of statistics. This executive police force was only one part of the apparatus of policing which the regime possessed, for a separate security police – the Corps of Gendarmes under the control of the Third Section (of the Tsar's chancellery) – also existed. The basic duty of the gendarmes who were stationed in every province of Russia, and in European cities abroad [2.2], was 'surveillance', but they often acted without any consultation with either the local executive police or the provincial administrative authorities and this impaired their efficiency.

Two main areas were identified where reform was necessary: the number of ordinary police needed to be considerably increased and coordination between the two branches of the police force required improvement. Although proposals were made by Valuev in the mid-1860s to increase the number of rural police, it was only in 1878 that the Tsar approved the creation of a new force of 5000 mounted police for the provinces: the quality of these men turned out to be no better than the existing police and they continued to be regarded by contemporaries as the 'dregs of society'. When Loris-Melikov was entrusted with the task of combatting terrorism, he included the police in his examination of how institutional structures might be amended to give the regime greater authority. 'Unity of command is the only sure way to attain success against sedition', Loris-Melikov asserted in a report to the Tsar and, in response to this, the Third Section was placed under his control on a temporary basis; the situation was made permanent in November 1880 when both arms of the police force were combined under the command of the Ministry of Internal Affairs. This gave the Ministry an additional staff of nearly 7000 gendarmes, but the total number of policemen in the Empire still remained inadequate.

The third means of control which the regime possessed was the censorship of publications. Under Nicholas I, censorship had been rigidly imposed and a system of pre-publication examination of all works had been utilised to try to ensure that nothing objectionable to the government appeared in print, whilst from time to time blanket restrictions had been placed on mentioning certain subjects, such as serfdom, in print. This system was disliked both by writers and by the censors themselves since it placed huge obstacles in the way of works appearing in print, whilst it was the censor who was held responsible if he omitted to prohibit a work which was later recognised as unsuitable. Censorship also presented a problem to the regime since it came under the control of the Ministry of Education and successive censors and ministers found that their duty to prohibit works which appeared dangerous to the regime was in conflict with their responsibility to promote education and literature in Russia [2.4]. The Ministry of Internal Affairs was as eager to acquire responsibility for censorship as the Ministry of Education was to lose it; Valuev's department was granted control of the procedure in January 1863 and continued the review of the whole question which had already begun. The results of this work were enacted in 1865: large volumes were exempted from censorship altogether and the system of censorship before publication for other works was replaced by censorship after printing, but before they were distributed. This put the responsibility for allowing a work to appear on the author and publisher, rather than the censor and transgressions were to be dealt with in the courts, although periodicals could be subjected to administrative penalties imposed by decision of the Minister of Internal Affairs.

Censorship did not, however, succeed in preventing the growth of opposition to the regime which was manifest during the 1870s, nor was the government able to prevent the flow of *émigré* publications across the Russian border and the press itself was seen by the government as actively hostile to its intentions [2.4]. This was a situation which the regime wanted to change and at the end of the 1870s it moved to allow the press more freedom, in the hope that this would lead it to assist in the task of bringing the government and Russian educated society closer together. Loris-Melikov declared to a group of editors in September 1880 that he intended to allow them much more latitude to discuss government policies, so long as they did not insist on the need for some sort of public participation in the work of legislating [2.4]. A significant number of liberal publications began to appear and during late 1880 and early 1881 censorship was much less severe than it had been over the preceding decade.

The fundamental problem which the autocracy faced in dealing with administrative reform and with the coercive forces at its disposal was to find the most effective means of strengthening its own position and gathering support around itself. Reform was the method chosen during the early 1860s and the introduction of the zemstvo, of a new legal system and of a relaxation in censorship were intended to demonstrate that the autocracy was prepared to listen to its subjects and that it was able to tolerate the existence of independent institutions. The concessions which Alexander II had made served not to quell discontent, but to stimulate calls for futher change: the regime adopted a schizophrenic policy during the 1870s of both considering proposals for further reform which would have drawn the Russian gentry firmly into the work of legislating, whilst at the same time trying to clamp down on demonstrations of opposition. Loris-Melikov attempted to draw these two strands together by recognising that the creation of a consultative legislative assembly by itself would not be sufficient to deal with opposition; the whole administrative structure of the Empire needed overhauling, contradictory elements inside it needed to be eliminated and the means of control would have to be managed so as to deal severely with those elements of Russian society which were opposed to the regime root and branch but also to allow conservative and moderate opinion to be freed from unnecessary restrictions. The experiment of 1880–81 was intended to give Russian educated society a new confidence in the regime; Alexander II's assassination meant that it had hardly a chance to work for his successor, Alexander III, moved quickly to institute a policy of unmitigated repression.

THE RURAL SCENE

These political questions were, however, only adjuncts to the central problem which the Russian autocracy faced, that of the rural economy. Of the Russian population 90 per cent lived in the countryside and it was on their fate that the fate of the state itself ultimately rested. The peasanty presented a permanent latent challenge to the government, for memories of the great rural revolt led by Pugachev in the 1770s still moved men and the regime was well aware of the problems which a rebellion on a similar scale would pose. Whilst the peasant, therefore, had to be kept quiescent through a mixture of force and judicious concession, the landowners too had to have their position protected. The regime could not hope to prosper if it alienated the groups which stood as intermediary between it and the peasants; in dealing with rural matters it therefore had to tread a fine line between these two sets of interests, whilst keeping its own needs firmly in mind all the while.

The problem which Russian agriculture presented was one of extremely low yields. Whilst the output of agriculture had steadily increased during the century before emancipation, this was solely as a result of new areas being brought under cultivation. There was a substantial increase in the quantity of land under the plough both in the highly fertile black earth regions of central Russia and in the frontier districts in the south and east during the first half of the nineteenth century; it is estimated that in four provinces along the middle and lower Volga it grew by 450 per cent in this period. Agricultural output per unit, however, remained static and Russia remained firmly at the bottom of the table of European countries in terms of agricultural yields per unit. Russia could produce only six hectolitres per acre of cereals whilst Britain and Holland achieved fourteen hectolitres, France and Prussia over nine, and Spain and Greece just over six. Agricultural methods and techniques remained antiquated: the three-field system was still practised across most of Russia, although in the thinly populated regions in the south and east it was common to find that fields were tilled continuously for a number of years and then left fallow for as long as seven years. Crop rotation was hardly used as a means of regenerating the soil and even the extent of manuring was hardly adequate: there were insufficient animals to cope with the quantity of arable land. The equipment which Russian farmers used was primitive and had hardly changed for centuries. The basic implement was the plough, made almost entirely from wood and pulled by a single horse; because it was so light it was inadequate to deal with heavy soil and could only produce a shallow furrow. Other equipment was similarly basic, with sickles and scythes being used for harvesting and flails for threshing. Farm machinery and improved techniques of cultivation had hardly made their mark on Russia before 1860; although the first factory producing such equipment was opened in 1831, between 1833 and 1846 it produced only 1600 ploughs and 6060 winnowing machines. The evidence of Russia's agricultural backwardness was clear, but for contemporaries it could be blamed on the existence of the social structure which reigned in the Russian countryside – serfdom.

In 1855 the system of serfdom was deeply entrenched in European Russia proper – it had been abolished in the early part of the nineteenth century in Poland and the Baltic provinces – and nearly half of all Russian peasants were enserfed. Besides the private landowners the imperial family also owned many serfs. The adult population of the Empire in 1860 included 22.8 million private serfs and 27.3 million state and crown peasants. The state peasants existed in conditions which were generally rather better than those which private landlords' serfs suffered, since reforms undertaken by Kiselev during the 1840s had resulted in considerable improvements to the material situation of the state peasants. The relationship between lord and peasant was one where the law hardly interfered; it only declared that the peasant 'must not suffer ruin' as a result of the impositions of the landlord and that he must be allowed adequate time to carry on his own farming. The demands which the landowner put upon his serfs fell into two areas: labour service (*barshchina*) and quitrent – payments in cash or in kind (*obrok*). Most peasants who had to work directly for their lord did so for three days a week but there was no consistency between different areas of the country, or indeed between different villages in the same area. Labour service placed the serf at the direct disposal of the lord in a way which direct payment did not, and the serfs were well aware that it was preferable to make such payments than to have to work for the lord. The quitrent system meant that the serf could often leave his village to take up a job, especially during the winter when agricultural work in the harsh Russian climate was nigh on impossible. Whilst these were the two main burdens which were imposed on the private landlords' serfs, other obligations could also be levied, the most common of which was the requirement for the serf to use his own horse and cart to transport his master's goods either to market or to the lord's home in the town. The landlord was also responsible for the collection of taxes from his serfs and their transmission to the government. The obligations which the serf had to perform could be varied by the lord at his will and when this happened the serf had no means of redress or complaint to any other authority, for he did not exist as a person with legal rights which could be upheld through the courts.

The state peasants lived in somewhat better conditions than did private serfs, especially after the reforms in their situation carried through under Nicholas I in the 1830s and 1840s by Kiselev, the Minister of State Domains. Even before these reforms the state peasants were recognised as being quite different to private serfs, for they had an individual legal status and were defined in law as 'free rural dwellers' with civil and political rights. Whilst the state had traditionally overridden many of these provisions, the condition of the state peasant had never deteriorated to the level of the private serf since most of them paid quitrent rather than perform labour service, which was the lot of 70 per cent of private serfs. Further improvement came through the work of Kiselev: he established a separate Ministry of State Domains to deal with the affairs of the state peasants, undertook an extensive land survey to ensure that the state peasants had adequate holdings, simplified the tax system as it applied to the state peasant and attempted to provide better advice for the peasants on agricultural matters as well as to improve their standard of living through the provision of improved medical services. These changes to the administrative and agricultural structure of the state peasantry helped to bring about a higher level in their prosperity, but Kiselev's reforms had a much wider impact. The

Ministry of State Domains acted as a training-ground for many of the bureaucrats who were to deal with the emancipation legislation during the late 1850s, and the principles which Kiselev adopted in relation to the state peasantry influenced the wider problems of emancipating the entire serf population.

By the 1850s it was generally recognised that serfdom needed abolition [3.1]; even Nicholas I stated that 'there is no question that serfdom . . . is an evil' but he rejected any idea of abolishing it lock, stock and barrel, adding that 'It is not necessary to give freedom, but it is necessary to work out a way to a transitional state. . . .' The moral arguments against serfdom were supplemented with economic reasons for its abolition, relating especially to the supposed disadvantages of using serf labour. It was believed that serfdom prevented the emergence of a free and mobile labour force and thus restrained economic development, whilst since serf-owners extracted as much as possible from their serfs this prevented the creation of a prosperous peasantry able to exercise a demand for industrial products. Lastly, the use of serf labour was *per se* unproductive since it was forced. These arguments were extended to cover the impact of serfdom on many other aspects of Russian life, and the defeat in the Crimea was partly laid at the door of serfdom; a serf, it was argued, had less incentive to fight well than a free man. Serfdom was thus perceived by liberal theorists, and increasingly by the government as well, as the root cause of Russian backwardness both in the economic and in the social and military aspects.

There were, however, much more fundamental reasons for Russia's backwardness which suggest that, as Olga Crisp has written, 'Russia was not backward because serf relations dominated her economy; it was her backwardness which made serf relations persist.' Serfdom had been formally institutionalised during the seventeenth century for political reasons as much as economic considerations. It was a means of ensuring that the thinly scattered population of the vast lands of Russia could be controlled by the state, through the intermediary of the gentry. Collective responsibility for payments of tax and provision of men for military service was imposed on all communities, thus tying the population closely to the land, whilst the gentry were given the task of ensuring that these financial and military obligations were carried out, in return for the state allowing them the use of serf labour and providing help in dealing with peasant disturbances. The geographical and political causes which gave rise to serfdom also help to explain Russia's continued backwardness: Russia covered a huge expanse of territory with an extreme climate and communications were therefore very difficult. It was difficult for both people and goods to move inside the country, whilst Russia's position on the edge of Europe made external links time-consuming and expensive as well. The second set of circumstances which contributed to backwardness resulted from the need to ensure the security of the Russian state. Without easily defendable borders and with a history of foreign invasion, most seriously from the East, the state's primary concern was to use all its resources to defend itself and to gradually win back areas which had been lost to foreign powers, later moving to find frontiers which were more easily defendable and new ports which would provide better access to European markets and resources. To be able to mobilise Russia's resources for these purposes, the state itself had to take a much greater part in the economic and social life of the country; complete control over the population was vital if the state was to be able to pursue its aims and preserve itself. Serfdom was thus a symptom of Russia's backwardness and expectations that its abolition would of itself produce an improvement in Russia's fortunes, both economic and political, were thus doomed to disappointment. The emancipation of the serfs was however crucial for the future development of Russia, since the very existence of the institution created strains inside Russian society which needed to be dissipated for other changes to be successful [3.2].

This was not, however, the contemporary perception of the position of serfdom in Russian society. The existence of serfdom appeared to pose a threat to the stability of the regime itself, for instances of peasant disturbances were on the increase during Nicholas I's reign. Between 1826 and 1854 there were an average of twenty three cases a year which were sufficiently serious to be noted by the Ministry of Internal Affairs, but in the late 1850s this figure rose substantially. In 1858 there were eighty six occasions when peasant unrest needed action by 'higher government authorities', rising to ninety in 1859 and one hundred and eight in 1860. Whilst some Soviet historians have argued that a 'revolutionary situation' existed in Russia during the 1850s, this does not seem plausible, given the very small number of uprisings in relation to the total expanse of the Empire. Although the secret police reported in 1858 that 'Not one disorder has taken on significant proportions . . . in the vast Empire they are scarcely noticeable . . .', the attitude which the regime continued to hold was that expressed by Alexander II in his famous speech to the Moscow nobility in March 1856 that 'it is better to abolish serfdom from above than to await the day when it will begin to abolish itself from below'. The regime believed that it had to treat the peasantry with extreme caution and was deeply concerned about undertaking any measures which would affect the peasants as a whole. The government recognised that serfdom had to come to an end but was unsure of the reception which this move would have among the peasants themselves and it made elaborate arrangements for soldiers and police to deal with any instances of trouble following the announcement of the government's decision.

After Alexander's speech in March 1856 the Ministry of the Interior was entrusted with the early work of preparing for emancipation and in January 1857 it set up the Secret Committee on Peasant Affairs to act as a forum for discussion of the serf problem. The government recognised at an early stage that it could not hope to enact this major piece of legislation – which would have a profound effect on the gentry – without obtaining the gentry's views and agreement to such a change. In November 1857 the government issued the first regulation which allowed the provincial gentry to establish committees to prepare proposals for emancipation. This Nazimov rescript, named after the Governor-General of the three Lithuanian provinces to whom it was addressed, formed the model for subsequent announcements addressed to the gentry of the other provinces. Each province was to be allowed to establish a small committee made up of two representatives elected by the gentry, together with two 'experienced landowners' appointed by the provincial governor. The principles which the government set out for emancipation, and within which provincial discussion had to remain, were still vague in places, but the regime had made some fundamental decisions about the course which reform should take. The most important of these concerned land and the way in which it was to be dealt with after emancipation: there was no question of all gentry land being expropriated and handed over to the peasants. This was a politically unacceptable course of action, since the government required the active cooperation of the gentry in implementing emancipation, cooperation which would not be forthcoming if the gentry were to lose their land. On the other hand, however, the serfs could not be emancipated without their being granted some land. The Baltic peasants had been freed without land in the early part of the nineteenth century, leading to substantial poverty, and the government was determined to avoid such a situation arising across the rest of the Empire. It was fearful of the consequences of a landless peasantry, believing that this could easily lead to rebellion since the primary means by which the regime had maintained its control over the serfs – making it difficult for them to leave the land – would be destroyed. If the peasants were freed without land it would be difficult both to prevent disturbances and to extract from the peasantry the taxes upon which the financial well-being of the regime depended. The serfs therefore had to be freed with some land, but the exact quantity remained a matter for discussion.

The second area where the government limited the area of discussion concerned the financing of emancipation. The Crimean War had imposed very heavy burdens on the Russian treasury and the government was unwilling to see its own resources committed on a large scale to finance the acquisition of land by the peasantry. The initial resolve of the Ministry of Internal Affairs was to press for emancipation on limited terms: the peasant should only receive personal freedom and the right to the communal ownership of their homes and their immediate surroundings, without any agricultural land, a procedure which would not involve any major financial commitment by the government. The regime also envisaged that there would be a long transitional period for the new arrangements to be implemented at the local level and during this time the peasants would remain obligated to the landlord.

If the government had expected to find rapid agreement from the provincial gentry as to the course emancipation should take, it was disappointed. Whilst the gentry on the whole accepted that emancipation was now going to take place, the precise terms for its implementation were the subject of fierce discussion. The government attempted to forestall wide-ranging criticism of its plans by limiting the extent of the discussion which could take place in gentry committees. In April 1858 it stipulated that for the first six months the committees could only deal with proposals for the transitional period and were allowed to move to look at ideas for the final form which emancipation should take only at a later date. This did not, however, prevent the gentry from expressing their views and the government was attacked from all parts of the political spectrum over its plans. Liberal members of the gentry proved vociferous in their calls for the serfs to be freed with farmland and for this to be financed by a statebacked redemption scheme. This view had been put forward earlier in the 1850s by men such as K. D. Kavelin but was now adopted by gentry committees across Russia; especially prominent were the Tver gentry who put forward a plan for emancipation which proved to be the most radical to come from any provincial committee. This encompassed Kavelin's ideas but also provided that the obligations which the peasant owed to the landlord should be much reduced in return for a generous allotment of land, that the landlord should lose all his personal control over the peasants and that the peasants should be granted full civil rights, including a say in local administration. They further proposed that emancipation should be implemented quickly without any transitional period intervening. These views were expressed by a minority of the gentry committees, with land-redemption being favoured by only fourteen out of a total of forty eight bodies, but it has not proved possible to classify successfully in terms of regional or agricultural variations. Liberal ideas as to how emancipation should be carried out came from gentry who had widely differing economic and social positions but were united by a common intellectual outlook fostered through university education, contact with foreign ideas and literatures and a belief that, in the words of a contemporary, 'all our failures in the last two years of the reign of Emperor Nicholas were the result of our internal disorder, and that the root of this failure lies in serfdom'.

Most of the gentry, however, wanted to see emancipation carried out on terms which would protect the interests of the landowners by giving the peasants very little or no land – in those areas where the landlord relied heavily on agricultural income for his livelihood – or in regions where the landlord obtained large sums from serfs' quitrent, the gentry wanted to see high redemption payments to cover the loss of this source of income. The majority of gentry committees wanted to see the size of land-holding which the peasant would receive reduced in comparison with the area which they worked under serfdom, and only eleven committees declared themselves in favour of an increase. Although almost every committee wanted to see a reduction in the obligation which the peasant would owe to the landlord, there were only two which recommended a complete end to labour services or the payment of quitrent. Quite clearly, the Russian gentry had no intention of submitting meekly to the government's plans to emancipate the serfs if this meant a reduction in gentry prosperity and power.

During 1858 the government received the proposals which the provincial gentry committees had made and these were passed to Editing Commissions which were to draft the eventual emancipation statute. The two Editing Commissions were formed on the initiative of a trusted servant of the autocracy General Ya. I. Rostovtsev who, during 1858, addressed a series of letters to the Tsar which were to prove important in determining the final course which emancipation was to take. Rostovtsev had become a convinced supporter of emancipation and he suggested that the government should move towards seeing the peasants redeem their allotments of land, whilst the landlord should lose all his personal power over the serfs. These two provisions became part of the programme which was presented by the government to the Editing Commissions which were appointed to draw up the detailed proposals for emancipation. Recommendations were also made that any transitional period should be as short as possible and would be best avoided altogether, that labour service should be abolished within three years, unless the peasants themselves desired its retention and that the peasantry should be granted communal autonomy. Although half the members of the Editing Commissions were themselves landowners, with the remainder being government officials, the membership was firmly weighted in favour of emancipation and only about one quarter of the members were opposed to emancipation or else in favour of conservative schemes for its implementation. The Commissions made very little use of the work of the provincial committees, since the majority of these bodies had been opposed to the sort of programme which the government now favoured and the Commissions also succeeded in seeing the Tsar's original declaration that the provincial nobility could participate in the final decisions on the reform reduced so that the nobility could give their views on it, but without any power to vote on the measure. It took over eighteen months for the Commissions to complete the drafting of the law and it was October 1860 before it was submitted to the Main Committee which, in its turn, passed the draft to the State Council at the beginning of 1861. The statute on emancipation was finally promulgated on 19 February 1861 although its formal announcement was only made to the population two weeks later, on 5 March [3.4], in a separate manifesto, written by Metropolitan Filaret, the chief prelate of the Orthodox Church, and couched in arcane language.

The law itself was an immensely detailed document which ran to almost 400 pages. It dealt with the general principles which were to be applied right across the Empire, as well as with the regulations for their implementation which differed from region to region. It stated that the peasants were emancipated, but a transitional period of two years was to operate during which time land surveys were to be carried out and the other necessary arrangements made. During this period, however, the peasants were to continue to have to provide the same payments and services to their landlords as under serfdom. When each property had been surveyed at the end of this two year period, the process of emancipation proper was to begin. The peasants were to continue to work the holdings they had been accustomed to, unless this meant that the landlord would be left with less than one half of his property, in which case the peasants' holdings would be reduced. Even then, however, the peasants did not become full owners of their holdings, since they had to redeem them from the landlord over a period of forty nine years; initially redemption was optional and depended on the landlord's agreement – if he chose not to consent, the peasant had to continue to pay rent to him – but in 1881 it was declared compulsory for all holdings. Redemption payments were not to go directly from peasant to landlord, for the state acted as intermediary in the process. The government was immediately to pay the landowner 75 or 80 per cent of the amount owed in government bonds, and the peasant was to pay the remainder directly to the landlord, assuming that redemption was being carried out on mutual agreement – if it was being performed at the landlord's request the peasant was excused this payment. In both cases, however, repayments were then to be made by the peasant to the government over the next forty nine years.

In terms of the actual quantity of land which the peasants were to receive, there was great variation among different regions in the Empire depending on the precise economic and agricultural conditions present. A provision did exist, however, for a peasant to take a holding of one quarter of the size of that which was laid down as being the maximum for a particular area, and not to have to make any payment for it: these became known as 'beggar holdings'. In making apportionments of land the landlord was not to include the forest areas which were so vital for the peasants to collect wood, nor did he have to give them land needed for transport and communication between different holdings. Land was not to be divided among peasants by the landlord, but by the peasant commune, which was to play a major role in both the economic and social life of its members [3.7]. The commune was to have the continuing power to redistribute land amongst its members at intervals, and thus property of the land allotted to the former serfs was vested not in the individual peasants, but in the commune. It held further sway over its members through having collective responsibility for the various obligations which were laid upon the emancipated peasantry; taxation, redemption payments and performing the duties owing to the landowner during the transitional period. At the same time, the elders of the commune were responsible for policing their own community, and the emancipation statute gave peasant courts, with judges elected by the members of the commune, the power to deal with minor criminal offences and almost all civil disputes which concerned peasants alone. The commune thus became the central institution in rural life and it exercised a powerful hold over the peasants who belonged to it; communal responsibility for taxation meant that it was very difficult for peasants to leave the commune, since all its members were needed to pay their share. The combination of this economic power with the responsibility for policing gave the commune unparalleled influence over the lives of the peasantry in post-Emancipation Russia.

The immediate consequences of the proclamation of the emancipation legislation across Russia was an increase in peasant disturbances [3.4]. Whilst 1860 had only seen 108 cases of discontent which required action by the government, the first five months of 1861 – and especially March, April and May – witnessed more than 1300 outbreaks of trouble and over 700 of these needed to be put down by troops. Very few of these involved violence by the peasantry and mostly comprised peasants refusing to carry out labour service obligations, seizing landowners' property and resisting orders given by the authorities and this reflects the opinions which the peasants held about the emancipation provisions. The most notable example occurred at Bezdna in Kazan province, where an attempt by the authorities to arrest a peasant who had convinced his fellow villagers that they need no longer listen to the landlords resulted in over 100 peasants being killed. There was a widespread belief amongst the peasantry that the land which they worked really belonged to them and in the climate of rumours which grew up in the period before emancipation was formally proclaimed, many serfs came to believe that they would at last be given the land which they saw as their own. There was therefore substantial disappointment when the emancipation itself included no such provision, and disillusion was intensified when it was realised that freedom was not to come immediately. The fact that the peasants still had to perform their obligations to the landowners for another two years especially rankled; the first reaction of many peasants was that the emancipation manifesto had not been fully explained to them and this later gave way to a belief that the real provisions of the legislation were being concealed by the landowners and bureaucrats [3.4]. It was only with the arrival of the peace arbitrators in the villages in the early summer of 1861 that the legislation was properly explained to the peasants [3.5] and the number of disturbances dropped, so that just over 500 were recorded during the second half of the year. This did not mean, however, that the peasants were satisfied with the provisions of the statute, since nearly half of the charters setting out the arrangements for land settlement and obligations after the end of the two-year transitional period were imposed without the agreement of the peasant communities to their provisions. In the short term, therefore, emancipation did not live up to the expectations which had developed amongst the peasantry; its long term impact was to be even less satisfactory and it became a focal point of dissent and gave rise to political programmes to overcome the perceived inequities of the settlement.

Peasant well-being entered upon a gradual decline in the years after 1861 [3.8]. Firstly, there was a steady increase in the population of the

Russian Empire, growing from some 70 million in 1863 to over 94 million (on an equivalent area) by 1885. The peasantry, comprising almost 90 per cent of the population, therefore had to produce enough food to keep one-third as many again alive. Secondly, emancipation brought increased financial burdens to bear on the peasant household: redemption payments had to be made, taxation paid to the village, the local zemstva and to the state, whilst on top of this the amount of revenue which the government was raising from indirect taxation on such items as vodka and sugar grew substantially. The imposition on the Russian peasant therefore increased enormously in the years after 1861; not only did they have to feed more people but they also had to find cash – either by selling surplus produce or by earning a wage – in order to make the various payments demanded of them. That the peasantry was unable or unwilling to meet these demands is clearly demonstrated by the rising level of arrears; by the early 1880s they had reached an average of 22 per cent of the sums due and there was no region of the Empire in which the peasants' payments were up to date [3.8]. It seems clear that the first priority of the peasantry was not, unnaturally, to feed themselves and their growing families; payments to outside bodies took second place. When additional cash did become available it was spent on renting more land rather than on redemption or other payments.

The problems of the peasant after emancipation were intensified by the difficulties of obtaining extra land to cultivate to keep up with the pace of population increase. The quantity of land allocated to each household after emancipation varied from region to region, depending on local economic conditions, and in overall terms the peasantry ended up with only very slightly less land to cultivate after 1861 than they had worked as serfs. This, however, conceals regional variations whereby areas which had particularly poor land, such as the extreme north, tended to see an actual increase in the size of peasant allotments, whilst the most fertile agricultural areas suffered a substantial decrease. What was even more important than the precise quantity of land received by each household was its quality and many difficulties were experienced here. Peasants often found that the holdings they were granted after emancipation were difficult of access, contained the poorest quality land from the landlord's estate or were scattered across a substantial area. As well as this, forest land was not included in the land settlement, thereby depriving the peasants of access to timber for fuel, nor was the pastureland which was vital for the well-being of the peasants' animals. Even before trying to cope with the increase in population, the peasant was faced with an uphill struggle simply to maintain his standard of living at its pre-emancipation level: landlords now rented out access-land, woods and meadows, thus placing a further burden on the already frail peasant economy. When the increase in population began to show itself, the peasants began to look for ways to increase their land-holdings either by renting or by purchase. The heavy demand for additional land which was manifested during the later part of the nineteenth century resulted in substantial increases in rents and prices for land which offset the benefit gained from the extra cultivated area.

The situation of the peasants who had received a full allotment of land after emancipation was, therefore, increasingly difficult. A substantial number of peasants were, however, very much worse off; no land was allotted to household serfs, serfs from some estate factories and various others, so that it is estimated that about 2.6 million male peasants found themselves landless after emancipation [3.6]. The numbers electing to take the 'beggar-holding' were also substantial and amounted to over 400 000 households; the increases in land rents and prices after emancipation made it difficult for these peasants to augment their holdings as many of them wished to.

The fundamental problem of Russian agriculture, that of low yields, remained largely untouched by emancipation [3.8]. The act of itself did nothing to improve methods of cultivation and the precarious financial situation in which many peasants found themselves reduced any incentive they may have had to experiment with new techniques; the risk was simply seen as too great since a peasant household's entire livelihood would depend on the outcome of the experiment. The extra influence which the commune gained after emancipation also served to discourage agricultural improvements by individual peasant households, since a uniform crop-rotation was usually forced upon individual households by the fact that their strips of land were mixed with those belonging to others in the commune. The commune's power to repartition the land which it held at regular intervals also reduced any incentive for a peasant household to improve the land which it held from the commune, as it could easily be redistributed to another household at the next repartition. Emancipation, therefore, avoided facing the most important difficulty which Russian agriculture presented; although the average size of a peasant allotment in European Russia was nearly five times as large as that in France in the late 1870s, productivity remained at only about two-thirds the French level.

Emancipation both failed to meet peasant expectations and to deal with the most basic problem of the empire's agriculture: the Russian government was unable to see beyond the removal of the institution of serfdom to the wider horizons of rural backwardness. It succeeded in 1861 in removing the symbol of Russia's backwardness but was unwilling to face the prospect that deeper structural changes were necessary to deal with its causes. In particular, the state was loath to proceed with a reform which would reduce the level of control which it could exert over the rural population; its commitment to economic development was severely moderated by its concern with internal security and stability. Freeing the peasants from the supervision and tutelage of the commune would have meant that the government would have had to increase substantially the share of its own resources which it allocated to policing and the like; using the peasant commune to maintain discipline was both effective and cheap. The 'peasant problem' was of more than just economic significance and its political dimensions served to narrow the government's field of vision in preparing any reform.

Whilst emancipation did nothing to improve the standard of living or productivity of the peasantry, it did serve to reduce the prosperity and significance of the landowning nobility. The implementation of the act immediately deprived the gentry of up to half the land they had previously used to make their living, whilst at the same time they lost the use of serf labour to work their land, or else the payments made in lieu of such labour. It was, of course, intended that the landowners would be compensated for these losses, but the government's difficult financial position meant that the system of compensation which was adopted also contributed to the decline of the Russian gentry. The state was unable to advance the gentry the value of the redemption payments in cash, and so it resorted to issuing government bonds which immediately depreciated by some 20 per cent of their nominal value. Furthermore, the government took the step of deducting debts owed by the gentry to the Treasury from the total value of the bonds which were issued, a move which reduced the total sum advanced by nearly half in the first ten years after emancipation. The gentry therefore found themselves in straitened circumstances after 1861 and many had to resort to selling further portions of land in order to make ends meet. Between 1862 and 1877 noble landholding in Russia fell from 87.1 million desyatinas to 77.0 million – a drop of 12 per cent. In the last quarter of the nineteenth century the process accelerated so that by 1905 the gentry owned only 51.2 million desyatinas, a reduction of 41 per cent on the 1861 total.

This rapid decline in the economic fortunes of the gentry was accompanied by a fall in their political and social significance. The landowning nobility felt themselves abandoned by the government, for they had been accustomed to filling the most senior posts in the administration on the empire and had been the mainstay on which the government relied to keep order in the countryside. The gradual development of an independent bureaucracy and the influence which it had succeeded in acquiring only fully came home to the gentry when they saw the government prefer the advice proffered by its bureaucrats to the wishes of the gentry over the provisions of the emancipation statute. There was no longer an automatic guarantee that the gentry could gain the ear of the Tsar; thus the landowning nobility began to look for other ways of exerting political influence. They found their attempts stymied at every turn, however, since the government firmly rejected calls made from noble assemblies for some form of national assembly – and the government's own plan to institute such a body came to an end with Alexander II's assassination. At the local level too, the gentry found their attempts to widen the competence of the newly instituted zemstvo treated with deep suspicion and sometimes direct opposition by central government and its agencies in the provinces. For the landed nobility too, therefore, the much-heralded rural reform of 1861 was a disappointment. The great majority saw a sharp and relentless decline in their fortunes and status.

URBAN GROWTH

The Russian government had viewed emancipation as a means of promoting economic growth and the development of industry. Whilst Russian industry had not remained stagnant during the first half of the nineteenth century, its rate of growth still lagged far behind that of the economies of Western Europe. In 1860 Russia's industrial production was less than one quarter of that of Great Britain and was below the average level of production for the whole world. Industrial development did begin to pick up from the 1830s; internal trade and foreign commerce expanded, although Russia's share of world trade remained constant during the first half of the nineteenth century. Manufacturing industry also experienced growth; a number of enterprises grew from 2400 in 1804 to 5306 in 1830 and 15 338 in 1860. This was accompanied by an increase in the labour force from some 95 000 at the beginning of the century to 252 000 in 1830 and 565 000 in 1860. The most significant place in manufacturing industry was occupied by textile concerns, but metal industries were beginning to make felt their place at the base of an industrial economy. Perhaps the most important development which took place in industrial terms during the first part of the century, however, was the huge improvement in communications which came with the opening of the first railways in Russia and the development of water transport. In 1837 the first short length of railway track was opened between St Petersburg and Tsarskoe Selo, but construction was quickly begun on lines to link the capital with Moscow and the important industrial centre of Warsaw. By 1861 Russia had nearly 1500 km of railway, but this was still only a small proportion of the amount of track in the much smaller countries of Western Europe. The Russian industrial economy was, therefore, beginning to grow by the middle of the nineteenth century, and whilst it seems an exaggeration to see the 1830s and 1840s as marking an industrial revolution, as some Soviet historians have done, by 1860 the basis for an industrial economy was well on the way to being laid.

An important reason for the relatively slow growth of industry during the first part of the century was the attitude which the state itself adopted to the problem. The Russian state had traditionally, and especially during the country's first concerted phase of industrial growth under Peter the Great, acted as the initiator of economic development and had played the leading role in stimulating what industry did exist in the country. Under Nicholas I, however, the government viewed the prospect of industrial expansion on a West European scale with deep suspicion, for the leading officials involved in financial and economic matters believed that social disruption would follow as a consequence of such expansion. This fitted in well with the Tsar's own concern to maintain order inside the Empire and not to embark on any project which might conflict with this overriding policy. The main industrial sector which prospered before emancipation was that which supplied consumers: this did not require the large investment which only the Russian state could provide and it depended especially on agricultural prosperity to provide a peasant market for its products. The expansion of the cultivated area during the first part of the century, together with high tariffs on imported goods and Russia's ability to benefit from Western technical advances, all helped stimulate consumer-goods and especially textile industries.

There were still, however, important sectors of Russian industry which remained backward; the coal and iron-producing industries were only beginning to develop whilst the banking sector was almost non-existent. The deficiencies of Russian industry were clearly revealed during the Crimean War when the country's transport system proved incapable of supplying the army and the industrial base was insufficiently large to be able to provide high-quality equipment for the troops within a reasonable period of time. In the industrial sphere, as in all others of Russian life, the country's defeat in the Crimea proved to be the catalyst for a wide-ranging examination of the reasons for Russia's backwardness. Serfdom was identified by many contemporaries as the prime retarding factor on Russian industrial growth, for it was argued that its existence prevented the creation of an industrial labour force through its restriction of peasant mobility, whilst it encouraged the gentry to continue investing in land, rather than using their savings to help in the process of capital formation needed to develop industry. The tentacles of serfdom were also believed to penetrate more deeply into Russia's industrial malaise by restricting the income available to the peasantry and hence the purchasing-power which could be utilised to stimulate industrial production. It was believed that the removal of the shackles of serfdom would provide a cure for these ills and would transform Russian industry so that it would be able to develop to a state commensurate with Russia's desired status as a Great Power. The government regarded industrial expansion in the 1860s and 1870s as an essential pre-condition if Russia was to regain her military and political status and to replenish a treasury which had been severely depleted by the strains of war.

In the industrial, as in the agricultural sphere, emancipation aroused enormous expectations. How far were these satisfied during the ensuing twenty years? It is undeniable that the 1860s and 1870s did see continuing growth in Russian industry: the quantity of railways inside the Russian Empire grew from less than 1500 km in 1861 to nearly 20 000 km by 1881 [4.1] whilst coal production also increased nearly ten-fold during the same period. There was also an increase in the quantity of iron and steel produced and the Russian oil industry began to develop during this period [4.1]. The immediate aftermath of emancipation, however, was marked by substantial problems for Russian industry: production in certain areas actually fell during the 1860s. One of the main reasons for this was that some industries had relied heavily on serf-labour for their workforce and the implementation of the emancipation act meant that these serfs were now free to go elsewhere without fear of punishment. This particularly affected the mining and metal industries located in the Urals and enterprises situated on estates across Russia: sugar production, for example, almost halved during the first half of the 1860s, and many industries experienced a sharp reduction in their workforce through the departure of former serfs. A second difficulty which affected the textile industry was the unavailability of raw cotton from the United States during the American Civil War. The cotton industry collapsed during the years immediately after 1860, and this reverberated through the rest of the Russian economy: it is difficult, therefore, to disentangle the effects of this phenomenon from those of the emancipation act. The economy had largely recovered, however, from both these setbacks by the end of the decade and growth resumed at a pace which was still modest compared with that in Western Europe.

Emancipation did not result in an industrial 'take-off' in Russia and its hoped-for effects did not materialise. Peasant purchasing power was not dramatically increased after 1861, for although grain prices rose substantially during Alexander II's reign, so the burdens upon the peasant household also grew heavier. Furthermore, many peasants preferred to use any disposable income which they had to acquire more land, either through purchase or renting, so that money was continuing to be put into agricultural development rather than into areas which could directly affect the levels of industrial production. The labour supply too did not experience a sudden and huge growth after emancipation; the idea that serfdom was a severe restriction on the mobility of the peasant population was misconceived, since during the first half of the nineteenth century the factory labour force had grown more than five-fold. Whilst there were aspects of the emancipation settlement which released large numbers of peasants for work elsewhere, such as the freeing of household serfs without land, other of its provisions, and especially the communal authority which could be exercised over individual peasants, served to prevent the emergence of a large landless free peasantry. The character of the labour force and its availability was determined more by features relating to the patterns of agricultural work and the need to earn more to maintain a growing population. In terms of the capital made available for investment, most landlords of medium and small estates found that their redemption bonds, minus the debts which they owed, hardly provided sufficient cash for their everyday expenses let alone for modernising their estates or investing in industry. It was only the large serfowners who had sufficient residue from their redemption bonds to be able to afford to put money into railway companies and banking enterprises. It is not surprising that emancipation did not produce results to satisfy expectations in the industrial sphere since it was a measure which had its origins in political affairs. Economic development was a hoped-for result of emancipation, but the measure was not primarily constructed with this in mind and Russian industrial development in the 1860s and 1870s proceeded at a modest pace.

Even so, however, the cities of the Empire expanded substantially during this period; although the proportion of town-dwellers in Russia remained constant at about 10 per cent of the population, the increase in population of 30 per cent over the twenty years from 1861 meant that the cities of Russia also expanded by a third. This does not indicate an absolute break between the rural and urban environments for the expanding workforce and population, since an important feature of the Russian working class was that it retained very close links with its rural origins [4.2]. This was largely a result of the fact that the agricultural season over most of the cultivated area of Russia was short and lasted for only five months, so that for the majority of the year the peasants were available for other work. Employers recognised this phenomenon and wages were lowest during the winter, whilst factory-owners also concentrated their most labour intensive work during these months. When employers were organising their enterprises they had to be aware that this seasonal pattern of employment was likely to disrupt their production. As well as this, the workers who came to the cities to settle and work for the whole year were overwhelmingly rural in origin. Over 30 per cent of the population of St Petersburg in the 1869 census was of peasant origin and during the following decade this proportion increased dramatically so that by 1881 over 70 per cent of the city's population had been born outside it. The same was true of Moscow. There was thus during this period little differentiation between the urban and rural populations of Russia; the constant contact between the two sectors meant that a Russian city was really only a large village and that a worker would continue to be aware of the concerns and pressures felt by his family in the countryside.

This was made all the more pronounced by the fact that a very large number of workers came to the city alone and their families remained at home in their native village. In St Petersburg as a whole in 1869 there was an imbalance between the sexes of 830 women for every thousand men, a proportion which drops substantially when only peasants are included in the sample to only 454 women for each thousand men. The 1882 Moscow census recorded that amongst industrial workers there were only 160 women to a thousand men. The conditions of life for the urban worker contributed to his reluctance to settle in the city with his family as many workers had to live in cramped and unsalubrious accommodation. Although some enterprises did provide some form of accommodation for a worker's family, this was the exception rather than the rule. The wages which were paid during the 1860s and 1870s declined in real terms and this was a further incentive for a worker to live by himself in the city where the cost of living was high, whilst the remainder of his family stayed in the countryside where expenses were not so substantial and where casual employment might be available. Factory owners tried to counteract these centrifugal tendencies amongst their labour forces by imposing strict labour discipline [4.3]. They hoped to keep their workers tied to the factory through devices such as paying wages very infrequently and imposing heavy financial penalties for any breaches of factory rules. Such conditions of work added to the difficulties of the Russian industrial worker, difficulties which the government did little to ease.

Although the state wanted to see the industrial base of the country strengthened and recognised this as vital for Russia's prestige and power abroad, the government was not prepared to take actions to improve the living and working conditions of the people who were employed in the industrial sector. Factory inspectors only had jurisdiction over enterprises which employed more than sixteen workers so that very many employees had no protection from the system of inspection. Furthermore, the scale of abuses which was revealed by factory inspectors meant that it was difficult for them to take action to remedy them all. Urban life in general was not pleasant for the majority of the inhabitants of Russian cities, as the very rapid growth in the urban population resulted in overcrowded cities without proper facilities being provided for the increased population [4.4]. St Petersburg, for example, did not possess a proper sewage system until well into the twentieth century and the water supply was a constant source of disease.

The state did make some effort to improve the administration of the towns and cities of the Empire by introducing elected municipal councils in 1870 [4.4]. This legislation paralleled the introduction of zemstva into the rural areas of Russia and was based on the same principles as the earlier reform; the right to vote was restricted, so that on average only 5.6 per cent of the urban population were enfranchised, the powers of the new urban councils were limited and any sort of contact between councils was prohibited. Conflict between the local institutions and central government became commonplace. The Russian government was prepared to promote economic development inside the Empire, but it was very reluctant to make provision for the social and political consequences of this policy. The state still wished to exercise as close control as possible over its population, but the growth of cities presented it with a problem. There appeared to be little realisation within the government that by its inactivity it was serving to promote discontent and so make the state's task of maintaining control even more difficult.

An important area in which the cities did have an advantage over the Russian countryside was in their literacy rates [4.4]. Whilst the average literacy of the rural population at the beginning of the 1880s was slightly over 10 per cent, more than one third of the urban population could read and write, and in the largest cities the proportion was significantly higher, reaching 55 per cent in St Petersburg. This difference can hardly be attributed to improved schooling in the cities, but in the factory environment it was easy for groups of workers to study together and to acquire the rudiments of literacy reasonably rapidly and easily. The higher rates of literacy in the urban environment also helped to facilitate the growth of groups opposed to the Tsarist regime much more effectively than in the countryside, for political literature could be more easily circulated in the cramped setting of the city and its availability served as a further incentive for discontented workers to improve their standard of literacy.

The urban problem which was to confront the Tsarist authorities at the end of the nineteenth century did not reach its full force under Alexander II, but all the ingredients were in place by the time of his assassination. The rapidly growing urban workforce which was providing the muscle power for the expanding Russian industrial sector was also to prove to be the nucleus of mass opposition movements. By its neglect of conditions in the cities, the government was, even before 1881, sowing the seeds for the discontent which was to come to fruition when Russian industry entered on its period of greatest expansion at the end of the nineteenth century.

SOCIETY AND THE REGIME

Whilst the government paid little attention to ways of preventing the emergence of discontent amongst the growing working class, it did expend much energy on curbing expressions of disagreement with the regime from the educated sections of Russian society. Issues of the control and content of education, especially at its higher levels, were seen both by the government and its opponents as being of the highest importance and much legislation and discussion was devoted to them. It was recognised by the government that the universities were the source of the majority of the opposition which was displayed to them – almost all the members of groups analysed by the secret police during the 1840s and 1850s had received a higher education – and steps were taken to try to remove some of the immediate causes of discontent among students.

A new university statute was enacted in 1863 to try to remove some of the most restrictive of Nicholas I's regulations on higher education: more independence was granted to the university authorities themselves to deal with cases of student indiscipline, and the academic affairs of the institution were now to be dealt with by a self-governing professorial council [7.3]. This measure did help to put an end to the severe disorders which had characterised St Petersburg university in 1861 and 1862 [7.3]. The government also hoped to reduce the role of the universities in stimulating and spreading opposition through ensuring that the students who entered them were more carefully selected. A reform of secondary education made in 1864 placed greater stress on the learning of classical languages and made it difficult for students who did not have such an education to gain access to higher education. At the same time, provision was made for the introduction of secondary schools which gave only a four-year course, as opposed to the seven years of the grammar schools proper. These pro-grammar schools were to concentrate on more 'modern' subjects, such as the natural sciences, but this additional component to the secondary system did not succeed in reducing demand for higher education. A 20 per cent drop in the number of university students between 1861 and 1865 was made good in the following five years and by 1870 student numbers stood at over 6500, more than a thousand more than in 1861.

A new Minister of Education, Count D. A. Tolstoy had been appointed in 1866 and he saw the secondary school system as the key to the whole educational structure; during 1870 he proposed further changes to strengthen the classical emphasis of the grammar schools and to ensure that the Ministry of Education in St Petersburg could exercise greater control over what was taught in them [7.4]. These alterations to the secondary school system, implemented during 1871, paralleled the attempts being made by the government to reduce the impact of its local government and legal reforms. The attempt to assassinate the Tsar in 1866 and the appearance in power of more conservative ministers pushed the central administration in the direction of trying to reassert its own authority against what were seen as the independent institutions which had grown up in the administrative, legal and educational fields [5.5]. The fact that a significant portion of those opposed to the Russian autocratic regime came largely from within the ranks of those who might have been considered to be its most reliable supporters – the nobility – made the government's task more difficult in the educational sphere. The groups surveyed by the secret police during the 1840s and 1850s had shown over three quarters of their adherents to come from noble families, so that the government, by restricting access to education, was unlikely to be able to reduce the flood of opposition to any great extent. In 1880 the social composition of university students still revealed domination by the nobility – over 46 per cent of students were classed as noble, the next largest group being 24 per cent from the clergy. The end of the 1870s also witnessed a renewed rise in student discontent and in overt revolutionary activity; the debate inside the government about the best way to combat this – concessions or repression – was also renewed [7.5]. Two ministers, D. A. Milyutin and A. A. Saburov, proposed further relaxation in university discipline [7.3], a course of action which the remainder of the government, discussing the measures at the end of 1880, found unpalatable. The changes in emphasis in policy under Alexander II were nowhere more evident than in the educational field, for student disturbances demanded immediate action by the regime and the lack of success which the authorities had in putting a lasting end to the troubles forced them to rethink their policy at frequent intervals.

The severe restrictions placed upon educational institutions in terms of their curriculum, as well as the limitations which the censorship imposed on discussion of political and social issues in print meant that art and imaginative literature came to occupy an extremely important place in Russian society. Since the Russian public was prevented from making statements about its political and social views in an open manner, it was forced to adopt a less direct approach and to present its ideas under the camouflage of art and, especially, literature. This phenomenon had been noticeable from the very beginning of the great flowering of Russian literature in the first part of the nineteenth century, when Nicholas I himself had insisted upon acting as a censor for the works of the great poet Pushkin, and by the 1850s literature and literary criticism were well established as a forum in which the great issues which faced Russian society could be debated, albeit in an oblique manner. Turgenev, in his *Sportsman's Sketches* (1847–52), laid bare the iniquities of serfdom, Goncharov's *Oblomov* (1859) depicted the malaise of the gentry, whilst Dostoyevsky attacked the rationalism of the early 1860s in his *Notes from the Underground* (1864). Literature in Russia in the nineteenth century was *engagé*, its authors determined to deal with the problems which Russia possessed [7.8].

In this situation the position of the writer and the artist was viewed with particular importance. Art, in all its forms, was a serious matter and those who were responsible for creating it were expected to maintain the high standards of their predecessors and to continue to fulfil the duty which fell to them of exposing and discussing the evils which beset Russia. Russian educated society looked down on art which was produced solely for art's sake, dismissing it as trivial and demeaning of the profession of artist [7.9]. Art was intended to be tendentious [7.9], to reflect the specific conditions of Russia; some artists took this to mean that they should take sides and provide solutions to the difficulties confronting Russia. N. G. Chernyshevsky, a social theorist and literary critic, produced his novel *What is to be Done?* (1863) as a means of advocating the formation of cooperatives and communal groups as the answer to Russia's problems: unsuccessful as a novel, it proved nevertheless to be the inspiration for a whole generation of Russian young people.

The greatest literature written during the 1860s and 1870s adhered to the 'tendentious' approach and provided a realistic description of different facets of Russian life. The great novels of F. M. Dostoyevsky, *Crime and Punishment* (1866), *The Idiot* (1868) and *The Brothers Karamazov* (1879–80) and of L. N. Tolstoy, *War and Peace* (1869) and *Anna Karenina* (1875–77) all appeared during these twenty years, as did I. S. Turgenev's *Fathers and Sons* (1862) and a host of lesser works. These novels, combining discussion of the specific social and political issues of the day with topics of universal relevance, were accompanied by a remarkable new school of realist painting. The *Itinerants*, so called from their commitment to circulating exhibitions of their work around the chief cities of Russia, emerged in opposition to the rigid traditions of the Imperial Academy of Arts and deliberately set out to provide an art which was specifically Russian in its context [7.10]. The realist paintings produced by members of the *Itinerants* such as Kramskoy, Repin and Levitan dealt with topics such as the problems brought by urbanisation and the position of the peasantry after emancipation, whilst portraiture and landscapes also featured large. Critics, especially V. V. Stasov, were important in publicising and explaining the new artistic movement and their influence was also felt in supporting new musical trends. A tradition of strongly national music which had been begun by M. I. Glinka during the first half of the nineteenth century was developed and strengthened by a group of five composers known as the *Mighty Handful* – M. A. Balakirev, M. P. Musorgsky, A. P. Borodin, N. A. Rimsky-Korsakov and C. A. Cui. The use of folk song and the introduction of eastern elements into their music was characteristic and intended to draw music, and art in general, closer to the life of the Russian people as a whole [7.12]. In literature, painting and music the 1860s and 1870s witnessed parallel trends: the life of the people was reflected to a much greater extent in all forms of art and social issues became central to the activity of artists. The absence of any other forum for public discussion of such questions left Russian art as the sole outlet for them; the outstanding quality of the work produced is perhaps a result of the pressure placed upon the artistic community.

The fact that themes related to the nature and needs of the Russian people were a major part of art during the reign of Alexander II reflects the importance which the people, and especially the peasantry, played in the social and political thought of the time. Although the government tried hard to stem the development of any sort of grouping which expressed opposition to Tsarism or any of its policies, it found it increasingly difficult to do so. The institution of zemstva in 1864 and of municipal councils six years later provided an institutional channel through which ideas could be channelled to the government, despite the express prohibition on such actions. The fate of members of the Tver noble assembly in 1862 was intended by the government to act as a deterrent to other groups who contemplated expressing a view on matters outside their jurisdiction, but it proved unsuccessful. The St Petersburg zemstvo was closed by the government in 1867 when it declared, in relation to a dispute over the taxing powers of the zemstvo, that there needed to be protection for the rights of both central government and the zemstvo. Three years later, the newly constituted Moscow municipal council submitted an address to the Tsar in which they called for greater freedom of the press and of religious toleration, together with a veiled suggestion that a national assembly would be a useful way of promoting the unity of the state [5.7]. The government reacted angrily to the presentation of the address [5.7]: it forbade its publication in the newspapers, the Moscow mayor was forced to resign and members of the council who held government posts had to reaffirm their loyalty to the state.

The way in which the government approached all these incidents is revealing of its sensitivities, for despite the heartfelt protestations of loyalty with which all these three declarations were accompanied, the government treated them as expressions of outright opposition and dealt with them severely. It made no attempt to conciliate these influential and moderate representatives of the landed nobility and urban property-holders. Whilst the state hoped that these groups would continue to offer it support and that fewer of them would take the path of outright opposition, it rebuffed their attempts to make constructive and moderate suggestions on government policy. The autocratic regime did not want to admit the public in any form into the machinery of government but it expected to maintain their confidence and support: at a time when Russian educated society was becoming increasingly politically and socially conscious that was an unrealistic approach. The reforms which the regime itself had introduced served to stimulate public expectation of greater participation in national affairs, and when this did not occur and attempts to promote it by people outside the government were snubbed, disorder, both active and latent, grew.

Russia under Nicholas I had been a state in which all possible sources of opposition had been rigorously investigated and eliminated. The accession of the new monarch in 1855, however, provoked expectations that less severe standards would be applied and that some degree of discussion would be allowed without the fear of severe reprisals from the state. The part which Alexander II allowed the provincial nobility in the preparation for emancipation raised these expectations still higher, but the method in which the provisions of the reform were eventually determined and implemented disillusioned many Russians, both members of the nobility and other educated people. The regime was seen as having betrayed its early promise and supposed commitment to genuine reform, and from the early 1860s opposition to Alexander II's government began to manifest itself seriously and consistently. This was not a new phenomenon in Russia, for there had, even in the dark days of the Nicholaen regime, existed small and isolated groups who discussed methods and ideas to bring about the betterment of Russia. The government's effective countering of groups such as the Petrashevtsy in 1849 had prevented any of them mounting an effective challenge to the regime, and it was only under Alexander II that they began to mature into fully fledged revolutionary movements. An important part of this maturing process was for the groups themselves to change in character; instead of being largely devoted to discussing general political ideas and how they might be applied to Russia, they moved to consider the methods which they could use to bring about such changes.

The earlier part of the century had seen a sharp division between Slavophil and Westernist trends of thought: the former insisting that Russia follow her own historical traditions in her future development whilst Westernist sympathisers believed that Russia could only advance by learning from the West and using European models of development. An important and vociferous supporter of the Westernist trend during the 1840s had been Alexander Herzen: imprisoned and exiled under Nicholas I, he emigrated in 1847 and the 1848 revolutions which he witnessed at first hand had a profound impact on his thought. Political liberalism had failed Europe, and Russia would have to rely on her own resources if she was to make a socialist revolution [5.2]. Herzen linked this to ideas which he had earlier expressed about the possible role of the peasant commune as the basis for a future agrarian socialism which could develop in Russia, but he also stressed that this was unlikely to arise spontaneously amongst the peasantry and that Russia needed to produce a cohort of revolutionaries who would devote themselves to bringing about the revolution which was latent in the Russian people by maintaining close and continuous contact with the people. Herzen's influence from his exile continued to be strong inside Russia itself, largely through the medium of a journal, *Kolokol* (The Bell) which he published from 1857 and which reached Russia in substantial quantities until its decline in the mid-1860s. The essentially moderate road which Herzen propounded proved to be of immense influence during the heyday of the Populist movement during the 1870s, but the immediate aftermath of the emancipation of Alexander II saw others turn towards more direct and violent forms of revolution.

The summer of 1861 saw the appearance of an appeal entitled *To The Young Generation*, aimed at the students of St Petersburg, which openly declared that the monarchy in Russia had outlived its time and its usefulness and should be replaced by a system of elected leadership. The period following emancipation was witness to a number of other secret proclamations, of which the most significant was signed *Young Russia* and put forward a plan for a federal-republican Russia, based on the peasant communes [5.3]. To bring this about, *Young Russia*'s author, Zaichnevsky, looked to the young people of Russia who would provide the revolutionary party which would move against the imperial regime and destroy it. This concept of a revolutionary dictatorship seizing power, usefully defined by Venturi as 'Russian Jacobinism', was also to have a lasting impact on the growth of theories of opposition to Tsarism. More organised groups also came into existence, especially one known as *Zemlya i Volya* (Land and Liberty) made up mainly of students in St Petersburg, but with contacts in other cities of the Empire, particularly Moscow. Led by N. A. Serno-Soloveich, *Zemlya i Volya* took up the call for a genuine peasant reform, but it was the group's support for the Polish revolt in January 1863 which brought about its demise. Pamphlets were produced in various centres in support of the Poles, but the authorities acted ruthlessly to seek out their originators, and by the end of the year the different groups had ceased to exist.

At the same time as these practical measures were being proposed, the revolutionary movement was developing in intellectual terms. N. G. Chernyshevsky considered in detail the works of Western socialists and published lengthy articles in his journal, *Sovremennik* (The Contemporary), which although frequently interfered with by the censorship did succeed in providing an outlet for his views. His theoretical analysis of the Utilitarians and the early socialists led Chernyshevsky to argue that the greatest equality and efficiency could be provided through an economic structure of agricultural and industrial cooperatives which the state would protect and take eventual responsibility for. The peasant commune had an important part to play here, but Chernyshevsky believed that it could only operate effectively within the environment of a state which would treat it with sympathy. He saw such change as only occurring in the long term, however, because the existing Russian social and political system was defended by powerful interests which could not be easily overcome. The emancipation and its aftermath served to persuade Chernyshevsky that popular revolts were possible, but the secret police were not to allow him to develop and publicise his theories any longer. In the spring of 1862, Chernyshevsky was arrested and sentenced to exile in Siberia where he remained until 1883.

The failure of reform to bring about any fundamental changes in Russia, the unsuccessful Polish rebellion and the ease with which groups and individuals had been suppressed by the authorities brought about a new trend in the attitudes espoused by revolutionary-minded thinkers and activists. The mid- and late-1860s was a period when hopes that the state could be persuaded to reform itself disappeared and were replaced by faith in the results which could be obtained by small numbers of men acting against the existing institutions. The views put forward by D. I. Pisarev which he called 'realism', but were labelled by others as nihilism, also rejected any role for the mass of the Russian people in bringing about change [5.4]. Nihilism as defined by the conservative publicist, M. N. Katkov, was a lack of belief in anything, a desire to criticise without making any concrete constructive suggestions and this concept has stuck. Whilst Pisarev did see the central task of the 'critically thinking intelligentsia' as being to criticise the trends and theories which had failed to bring change to Russia, the Nihilists whose views were represented in the journal *Russkoe Slovo* had definite and positive opinions. They saw the future of Russia as dependent on the formation of a class of independent thinkers and the main positive work of those 'realists' who already existed should be to try to expand the scientific knowledge available to the population. Such actions would result in individuals being emancipated from the restricting social environment in which they found themselves and in the creation of a class able to dispense with the romanticism which had coloured their predecessors.

This trend in Russian thought helped to feed Bakunin's anarchism through its stress on individual revolt [5.6], as well as to add further to the Jacobin concept of a revolutionary élite which was to prove important during the 1870s.

This emphasis on the role of a small group in promoting change inside Russia was taken to greater extremes by S. G. Nechaev and P. N. Tkachev. The failure of Karakozov's assassination attempt on Alexander II in 1866 led many to turn away from the Jacobin tradition [5.5], but in a series of pamphlets produced at the end of the 1860s Nechaev, in conjunction with M. A. Bakunin, propounded the idea of the small number of dedicated revolutionaries which existed in Russia being able to provoke popular revolution through terrorism and alliance with any group opposed to the regime. Nechaev's attempt to create such a band of committed revolutionaries in 1870 were far from successful and was notable mainly for its murder of one of its own members, ostensibly because he was believed to be an informer, but another reason was to make everyone an accessory after the fact. It was for this murder that Nechaev was arrested in Switzerland in 1872. Tkachev, writing during the 1870s, addressed himself to the revolutionary minority in Russia and stressed the need for an organisation to unite all those who were opposed to the regime. The task of this united and small force would be firstly, to carry out a revolution to seize power, using whatever violence was necessary, and the revolutionary state would then move to make a social revolution inside Russia along communal and socialist lines.

This concentration on the part which small committed groups of revolutionaries could play in opposing the regime was only one trend in the Populist movement which dominated Russian revolutionary thinking and action during the 1870s. Populism was not a united party, but encompassed a wide variety of individual opinions and small groups which sprang from certain common assumptions. The basic philosophical position which Populists adopted was that man was inherently good and inherently perfectible. It was the apparatus of the autocratic state which had repressed these qualities and when the state was destroyed man's natural goodness would bring about the establishment of an order which was just and beneficial to all. Crucial to all Populist thinking therefore was the Russian peasantry, for it would be for them that any revolution would occur. The peasants were the downtrodden masses which bore the brunt of the oppression which the regime practised and it was from them that the genesis of a new order would emerge. Peasant society already contained the foundation for this new structure in the shape of the commune, and the Populists believed that this structure could be extended to transform Russia into a federal state arranged around these socialised and self-governing units. Russia was, therefore, destined to undergo an agrarian socialist revolution and the Populists saw this as the way by which the country could avoid the horrors of large-scale industrialisation. They did not accept that it was inevitable that Russia would have to enter on the capitalist stage of development, for they believed that capitalism was fundamentally evil and that the Russian peasant could escape its effects. The essence of Populism was agrarian socialism, and it was recognised that for this to be achieved the Russian autocratic state would have to disappear.

It is at this point that the common assumptions of the Populists splinter into a myriad of differing ideas as to the precise means which should be adopted to bring about these ends. The Jacobin tradition of Nechaev and Tkachev wanted to see political revolution carried out from above by a small number of disciplined and highly organised revolutionaries. This would then lead to social change promoted by the new revolutionary state. For many other Populists, however, this approach was deeply suspect since it could easily result in an elite simply imposing its views on a populace which was unready and unwilling to receive them. Instead, during the first half of the 1870s a movement known as 'Going to the People' emerged and concentrated on propaganda work in the villages of Russia. Followers of P. L. Lavrov aimed at creating a much larger village intelligentsia which would be able to promote Populist teaching to greater effect, but many of the students who left the cities and went out into the countryside in the summers of 1873 and 1874 simply wanted to spread their ideas amongst the people for whom they were supposed to be working. They hoped that their preaching and persuasion would help bring about a peasant revolution, a revolution from below which would reflect the aspirations of the people themselves rather than the wishes of an educated elite. As Venturi points out, however, the exodus from the cities by students during these two years was also motivated by more elemental considerations. A desire to repay the debt which they believed they owed to the people who had provided them with the opportunity of education, and a wish to enjoy liberty outside the atmosphere of the university and the cities also prompted several thousand young people to spend time in the villages.

The reception which they received disappointed many of them [5.8]. Although some worked as labourers or took up more skilled trades whilst others used their knowledge as teachers, they found that a gulf existed between themselves and the peasants with whom they intended

Introduction 47

to work. Peasant perceptions and attitudes turned out not to be so simple as the students had imagined and in some cases the peasantry even reported the activities of the Populists to the authorities. Over 770 people were arrested during the summer of 1874, but despite the fact that this was the first occasion on which any sort of mass movement had developed against the government, there was little success which the Populists could point to. The attempt to create a movement which encompassed the rural population failed: Populism remained firmly a movement which found its support amongst the Russian social élite and had given insufficient consideration to the question of how to widen its social base. The idealistic aspirations of the urban-centred students proved at odds with the peasants' own concerns and this provided a severe jolt to Populist consciousness.

Revolutionary thought and activity during the second half of the 1870s retreated from the attempt to give Populism a truly mass base and again concentrated on the use of small-scale conspiracy to bring about revolution inside Russia. *Zemlya i Volya* (Land and Liberty) formed the centre of the opposition at the end of the 1870s [5.9]; its first programme was produced in 1876 and reiterated demands for a new order to be based on the commune, a change which could only be brought about by violent revolution. This was to be promoted in two ways: through agitation to organise those in favour of revolution and through 'disorganisation' of the apparatus of the state which they were trying to destroy. The process of agitation involved attempts again to draw the peasantry into the struggle and members of *Zemlya i Volya* tried to settle in areas which they hoped would be particularly receptive. The lands along the Volga were the centre of the new movement, which reached its height in 1877, whilst communities of Old Believers – a religious minority which had suffered much persecution – were also identified as potential sources of support. The government, however, acted to break up any groups which did appear in the countryside and hoped that it could destroy the tacit support which it recognised the revolutionaries had amongst public opinion by staging a series of large trials at which the violent methods of *Zemlya i Volya* were to be well publicised. The government was 'convinced that these delirious ravings of a fanatical imagination cannot meet with any support' but the large trials staged during 1877 and 1878 did not bring about the change in public opinion which the state desired. Harsh sentences were imposed on many of the defendants – out of 110 people tried by the autumn of 1877, only 39 were acquitted and the remainder exiled or imprisoned – and these aroused some sympathy among the public, whilst the defendants seized the opportunity which the trials provided to make speeches in defence of their actions. The government's tactics were far from successful and the trials brought far greater and more favourable publicity to the revolutionaries than the state desired.

The effectiveness with which the authorities had been able to prevent the establishment of rural cells of revolutionaries helped to increase the emphasis which *Zemlya i Volya* placed on 'disorganisation' rather than agitation. 1878 was called 'the year of attempted assassinations' by one revolutionary, a year which opened with Vera Zasulich shooting at the governor of St Petersburg and continued with attempts on the lives of a Kiev prosecutor and the murder of the head of the Secret Police, Mezentsov [5.9]. Terrorism became the most visible activity of the group and although the government made strenuous efforts to apprehend the perpetrators of terrorist attacks, they proved unable to halt their momentum. 1879 witnessed further assassinations, including an attempt on the life of the Tsar in April. This action both galvanised the authorities into taking more radical steps to counter the terrorists and provoked *Zemlya i Volya* to rethink its ideas and ultimately to split. Even in the aftermath of the 1879 assassination attempt on Alexander there was a significant amount of support in the group, not for terrorist activities directed against the institutions and individuals of government, but instead for the old tactic of organising peasant protest. Men such as A. A. Kvyatovsky and A. I. Zhelyabov formed a group within the main groups and tried to win over others to the task of terrorism and, especially, assassination. By the summer of 1879 this group had been formalised as *Norodnaya Volya* (The People's Will) and its aim was clear: the assassination of the Tsar [5.11]. This approach offered a definite programme of action to a revolutionary movement which had suffered a series of setbacks and which appeared to have expended large numbers of its adherents for no discernible gain. There still remained a number of *Zemlya i Volya* who wanted to continue work amongst the peasantry and they took the name *Chernyy Peredel* (Black Repartition) to symbolise their demand for the equal distribution of all land. The leading lights in this faction were G. V. Plekhanov and Vera Zasulich and they stressed the need to prepare for the social revolution and to return to the original Populist ideas of a federal Russia based on the commune [5.10]. *Chernyy Peredel* fared badly, however, with the seizure of its printing press by the police and the subsequent emigration of its leaders.

It was *Narodnaya Volya* which made the running at the end of the 1870s with its concentration on bringing about the murder of the Tsar.

The war against the state would not end with the assassination of its leader, for the revolutionary groups must prevent power simply being transferred from one privileged group to another – the bourgeoisie. Power must instead pass to the people; *Narodnaya Volya* expected that this would occur with the summoning of a Zemsky Sobor – a constituent assembly representing the entire population – either by the new revolutionary state or else by the old state under the pressure which the direct action of the revolutionaries was putting upon it. The efforts of the group were devoted towards carrying out the sentence of death which they had pronounced on the Tsar: attempts were made to blow up the train on which he travelled, to place a bomb inside the Winter Palace in St Petersburg and to kill Alexander whilst he was making his way through the streets of the capital. It was this last method which eventually met with success on 1 March 1881 [5.11], but the death of the Tsar was not the signal for wider revolution inside Russia. There was no great outburst of popular rejoicing at the removal of the Tsar, nor did the government decide that this was the signal for it to concede and grant a constituent assembly. On the contrary, the new Tsar, Alexander III, was a man of much more conservative opinions than his father and with the support of conservative ministers he put an end to Loris-Melikov's plan for a consultative national assembly and moved to deal severely with any form of opposition. A month after the killing of Alexander II the five ringleaders in the conspiracy were executed.

Attempts to bring about revolution in Russia during the 1860s and 1870s failed to grasp the nettle of acquiring mass support. The step from conspiratorial group to mass movement proved too difficult for the small groups which arose during these two decades. The social background of the revolutionaries made it difficult for them to achieve a rapport with the peasants, whilst the efforts of the government to root out revolutionary groups in the countryside prevented the Populists ever being able to establish lasting settlements in the villages. Populism was faced with the problem that it was operating in an environment which had no tradition of experience of politics; anybody in Russia who tried to present political views to the people had first to accustom them to dealing with any sort of political issues, and could only then move to present his own specific ideas. The government had a monopoly on political activity and attempts to provide a basic political education in an environment where the authorities were firmly devoted to preventing such a process taking place stood little chance of success.

Whilst revolutionary opinion has absorbed most attention from historians, the ideas which the autocracy and its conservative adherents espoused had as great an impact on the population of the empire. The regime's lasting aim of maintaining and strengthening its own position was perceived by such publicists as M. N. Katkov as only being possible by the use of traditional methods. The idea of indulging in any form of consultation with the population was rejected as contradictory to the tenets of autocracy itself. The Tsar was the personification of Russia and his views, untainted by any influence from particular interest groups, were therefore what should govern the country. Advocates of a revived autocracy pointed out that Russia's greatest triumphs had taken place under strong and ruthless monarchs such as Peter the Great, and they mistrusted reform which appeared to place any limitation on the power of the state and the authority of the monarch. Conservatives saw the upsurge in revolutionary activity after the reforms of the 1860s and 1870s as the result of these reforms and the men who acted as Alexander III's advisers in the first months of his reign, such as K. P. Pobedonostsev, believed that concessions to public opinion would only serve to increase discontent. For them the only method of strengthening the autocracy was the suppression of all opposition and a resurgence of traditional conservative policies.

Whilst conservative opinion was more tolerated in print and public debate by the authorities, the expression of all forms of political and social ideas were hedged with difficulties. The lack of any recognised forum for the discussion of the problems which faced Russia pushed debate into oblique forms and unusual arenas, such as literature. 'About the most important things we are not allowed to talk' wrote F. M. Dostoyevsky; the restrictions placed on the expression of opinion did not mean that Russian society was bereft of opinions, but rather that those views which were heard tended to be extreme. Moderate opinion found no outlet, and it was those who were prepared to go to extreme lengths to be heard who attracted most attention.

FOREIGN POLICY

The attempts by the Russian state to improve its domestic situation during the 1860s and 1870s were paralleled by its efforts to regain its international prestige in the wake of the disaster of the Crimean War. Russia needed both to restore her situation in the Black Sea and to find some way of ending her isolation in Europe; these two themes were to be interwoven throughout Alexander II's reign. The first years of the new reign saw reconciliation between France and Russia, based on a mutual hositility to Austria, but this came to an end as a result of Russian suppression of the Polish revolt in 1863. A hint of Russia's future international orientation was given by the convention between Russia and Prussia of 1863 aimed at preventing the spread of the rebellion in Poland [6.2], and the emergence of a united Germany in 1871 underlined the greater advantage that alliance with a fellow conservative monarchy could bring for Russia. French defeat in the Franco–Prussian war also provided the opportunity for Russia to declare herself free from the restrictions which had been placed upon her activities in the Black Sea by the Treaty of Paris which had concluded the Crimean War in 1856. The circular issued by the Russian Foreign Minister, A. M. Gorchakov, in 1870 was a unilateral repudiation of the clauses of the treaty which demilitarised the Black Sea, a move which the other European powers somewhat grudgingly agreed to [6.3].

Fifteen years after the end of the Crimean War, Russia's international position in Europe was much improved and she now began to again be accepted as an equal by the other Great Powers. Her concern now was to establish alliances which would guarantee her position, and much of Russian dipolmacy during the 1870s was concentrated on improving and cementing her relations with the other two great conservative monarchies of Europe, Germany and Austria–Hungary. Agreements were signed with both of them during 1873 – although Bismarck refused to endorse the Russo-German convention – and the personal contact between the three monarchs was presented as the establishment of a League of the Three Emperors [6.4]. Much suspicion remained, however, between Russia and Austria over each other's intentions of the Balkans and Russia was well aware of the fragility of the system. The crisis in the Near East in the second half of the 1870s underlined this fact, for Bismarck refused to give Russia any guarantee of support. This again provoked heart-searching on the part of Russia's diplomats as to the best way of providing security for their country and the question of resurrecting an alliance with France was again discussed. The pro-German argument, however, prevailed and P.A. Saburov, ambassador to Berlin from 1880, pressed for the full-blown restoration of the League of the Three Emperors [6.4]. After Austrian hesitation, the agreement was signed in June 1881, settling the orientation of Russia's foreign policy of nearly a decade.

The cockpit around which European diplomacy revolved during the 1860s and 1870s was the Balkan peninsula. Three imperial powers came into conflict here: the declining Ottoman Empire, Austria – Hungary and Russia. Russia's ambitions in the area were long-standing and the waning power of the Turks appeared to offer her an opportunity to fulfil them: all-important for Russian military and diplomatic strategy was the acquisition of control over the Straits which gave entry to the Black Sea, whilst control of Constantinople itself would guarantee Russia's security in the Black Sea. Further incentive for Russia to play a part in Balkan affairs was provided by the multinational nature of the Turkish possessions in the region, for these included peoples who were Slav in origin and Orthodox by religion. The Bulgars and Serbs were especially prominent, and when evidence arose of their ill-treatment by their Turkish and Muslim rulers this provided an excuse for direct intervention by Russia.

There was also an ideological justification for Russia's interest in the area. Arising out of the Slavophil movement of the middle of the century, Panslav publicists and theorists preached that indissoluble links existed between Russia and her Slav brethren and that Russia, as the largest and most powerful Slav state, should act to protect the weaker members of the community. For Russian Panslavs, such as N. Y. Danilevsky and R. A. Fadeev, Russian leadership of the Slav movement was self-evident and this trait in their thought, indistinguishable from Russian nationalism, opened the way to Russian expansion into the Balkans [6.5].

During 1875 and 1876 examples increased of Turkish ill-treatment of the Serbs and Bulgars and enthusiasm inside Russia for the Slav cause was clearly demonstrated. The other European powers were, however, unwilling to see Russian influence extended in the Balkans and made attempts to restrict her growth of influence. Alexander II declared that he was willing to act independently to secure protection for the Balkan Slavs [6.6], and despite efforts by other powers to settle matters amicably, Russia declared war on Turkey in April 1877. Although she suffered early reverses, the Russian forces defeated the Turks by January 1878 and the resulting peace of San Stefano, negotiated largely by N. P. Ignatev, a convinced Panslavist, established a large independent Bulgarian state and gave no concession to Austrian ambitions in Bosnia and Hercegovina [6.6]. The European powers objected strongly to these provisions and insisted on the summoning of the Congress of Berlin in the summer of 1878 to formulate an agreed settlement in the Balkans [6.6]. The treaty which resulted from the congress proved a grave disappointment to Russia: the Bulgarian state was much reduced in size whilst Austria's claims to Bosnia and Hercegovina were recognised by giving her the administration of these areas. Russian expansionism in the Balkans had been checked by the rest of Europe.

The Russian Empire enjoyed far more success in expanding her frontiers during these two decades in Asia. In the Far East a series of treaties was signed with Japan in the late 1850s which established full diplomatic relations between the two countries and allowed for the expansion of trade, whilst ownership of the islands between the Russian mainland and Japan was settled by agreements reached during the 1870s. The late 1850s also witnessed concessions by the Chinese to Russian ambitions and the Treaty of Peking of 1860 gave Russia the Pacific coastline where Vladivostok is now situated. The early years of Alexander's reign was also the period when Russian conquest of the Caucasus was completed. Between 1857 and 1859 the mountain tribes of the region were finally brought under Russian control and imperial troops then moved to deal with the inhabitants of the region close to the Black Sea coast. The process of conquest was over here by 1864 and gave the empire security in the region to the east of the Black Sea.

The most important area of Russian expansion under Alexander was, however, in Central Asia. Both political and economic considerations motivated Russia to extend her authority in this region: Central Asia could act as an important source of raw cotton for the large textile industry of the empire, whilst its population would also provide a new and substantial market for manufactured goods. In political terms, Russian influence in Central Asia would pre-empt any designs which England had on the region and would serve to demonstrate that Britain was not the only European power with interests in Asia. Public justification for Russia's expansion was that it was essentially a defensive move and similar to the policies adopted by all other Western powers in dealing with less civilised nations [6.7]. By the summer of 1864 Russian forces were moving into Turkestan and took Tashkent in the following year. This city became the centre of Russian administration of the newly conquered regions and it was from there that further expeditions were mounted to consolidate Russia's hold over the entire Central Asian area. Bukhara and Samarkand were brought under Russian control, along with the khanates of Khiva and Kokand so that by the end of the 1870s the empire was in full control of Turkestan and the area to its west which bordered on the Caspian Sea [6.7].

NATIONALITIES

The absorption of these Central Asian regions into the empire accentuated the existing multinational character of the state. Whilst Russians constituted the majority of the population, the empire also contained large numbers of other Slavs in the Ukraine and Belorussia as well as in Poland. The western provinces of the empire were also the location of a sizeable Jewish population, whilst the Baltic littoral was populated by Estonians and Latvians who spoke languages unrelated to the Slav group. The acquisition of Finland by Russia in 1809 resulted in two other linguistically and culturally different groups – the Finns and the Swedes – being attached to the empire, whilst Russia's continuing expansion into Asia intensified this process. Not only was the empire racially and linguistically diverse, but it was also religiously heterogeneous. The Orthodox Church had the allegiance of most native Russians and Ukrainians, but related faiths such as the Old Believers also had a substantial number of adherents. Poland and the western provinces of Russia, including Lithuania, were dominated by Roman Catholicism whilst Finland and the regions on the southern shore of the Baltic were largely Lutheran. Russia's new possessions in Central Asia added a large number of Muslim believers to this already complex religious structure. The potential for national conflict was evident inside the Russian empire, for the developed and discrete national and religious groups in the western regions of the state had no desire to allow Russian culture and traditions to dominate them, whilst the nationalities in the regions which the empire was acquiring were fearful of the impact of Russian customs on their ancient cultures.

On the other hand, the autocracy's aim of strengthening its own position and authority implied precisely that extension of Russian influence which the non-Russian nationalities of the empire feared. The first intimations of national discontent arose in Poland, for although Alexander II on his accession showed more sensitivity to the separate identity of Poland than his father had done, he marked his first visit to the country in 1856 by warning the population that there should be 'No daydreaming, gentlemen'. The very limited concessions made by the new ruler, such as permitting the return from their exile in Siberia of those Poles who had been involved in the 1830 rising, however acted as the signal for the Poles to reassert themselves. During the late 1850s and early 1860s Polish society burst into life: political discussion became common, patriotic sentiment was displayed and religious and national demonstrations took place. The Tsar was determined to maintain order in Poland and in 1862 appointed his brother, Grand Duke Konstantin Nikolaevich, as Viceroy with discipline as his watchword [8.1]. It was clear to the Viceroy and Marquess Wielopolski, the head of the civil administration, that a rising was being prepared; to pre-empt this they planned to implement forced conscription to catch most of its potential leaders. This was timed for the beginning of January 1863 and it proved to be the opening shot in sixteen months of hostilities inside Poland [8.1]. The rebels were well organised and financed and were able to fight an effective guerrilla campaign against Russian forces. By early 1864, however, Russian superiority was telling and the revolt was at an end by the spring. In the aftermath of the rebellion the Russian authorities attempted to ameliorate the conditions of the Polish peasantry through land and local government reforms; whilst this was aimed at establishing a peasant class which would be loyal to Russian rule, it failed and Polish society united in continued opposition to Russian rule.

This was provoked by the policy of Russification which was imposed after the revolt. Poland's former separate administration was abolished and Polish affairs were to be dealt with by the appropriate department in St Petersburg; law was to be administered uniformly in Poland and the remainder of the Empire; the Roman Catholic Church had many of its monasteries closed and all its property confiscated [8.2] and education was to be conducted on the same basis as elsewhere in the empire, including the proviso that teaching at Warsaw University was to be in Russian. The reasoning that uniformity of things Russian right across the state would act to damp down separatist tendencies and increase the coherence of the empire was applied in other regions where non-Russian nationalism reared its head. In the Ukraine greater attention was being paid to its native language and history, despite the assertion of conservatives that it had no separate traditions from those of Russia [8.5], and a Ukrainian national consciousness was beginning to appear. To try to nip these tendencies in the bud, the government took action in 1876 to prohibit the use of the Ukrainian language and to make it difficult for Ukrainian teachers to teach in their native areas [8.5].

A very different approach was adopted by the imperial government in its dealings with Finland, for the Finns had shown no separatist tendencies and the empire had inherited a system of administration in Finland which gave much more autonomy to the local authorities. Alexander II did nothing to restrict this autonomy and, on the contrary, acted to extend it. In 1863 he summoned the Finnish Diet [8.4] and the following years saw important steps to widen the areas in which the Finnish and Swedish languages were to be used in administration, whilst education in Finnish was also extended. The Tsar appeared deliberately to use Finland as an example that autocracy was not incompatible with constitutional forms of government; whilst the Finns remained peaceful the policy worked.

Two other important national groups were the Jews and the Germans (largely Baltic Germans). Most of the Jewish population was concentrated in Poland and the western provinces of the empire and the Baltic Germans had their roots in Estonia and Latvia. Attitudes towards the Jews were ambivalent and whilst Alexander II and his government took some steps to improve slightly their position, local officials and popular prejudice often acted against them. Some relaxation on residence restrictions for limited classes of Jews was introduced, but the nature of Jewish occupations made the Jews easy targets for harassment by minor bureaucrats [8.6]. The Baltic Germans, on the other hand, aroused hostility among some sections of Russian opinion because of the very success which they enjoyed in trade and in obtaining privileges for themselves [8.3]. Attacks on the Baltic Germans came from Slavophil sympathisers who protested that Russians were discriminated against in the Baltic regions, but the government did not share their opinions and continued to act tolerantly towards the Baltic Germans.

The varied nature of the national minorities inside the Russian empire meant that the regime could not apply a uniform policy towards them. Whilst the government was prepared to allow national and religious groups to continue to follow their own traditions, should this develop into any sort of agitation for separatism then the authorities would clamp down severely on them. Alexander II certainly did not practise the policy of wholesale Russification that his son was to, despite encouragement to do so from some sections of public opinion: as ruler of an expanding empire, he tried to minimise pretexts for discontent amongst newly conquered peoples, believing that force was hardly an effective way of promoting sympathy for things Russian amongst other nationalities [8.7].

CONCLUSION

An elaborate and sizeable memorial to Alexander II erected inside the Moscow Kremlin in 1898 was demolished after 1917, and no monuments to him stand today in the Soviet Union. He is remembered in statue form only in three cities elsewhere: Helsinki, Sofia and Belgrade, but whilst the Finns, the Bulgars and the Serbs have good cause to remember his reign, the twenty five years he ruled over the Russian Empire were of extreme significance for the remainder of the imperial regime.

His achievement was substantial; by 1881 Russia's international position had been restored so that she again ranked as one of the European Great Powers, whilst at home Alexander had implemented a series of reforms unparalleled in their scope and impact since the time of Peter the Great. Yet the Tsar was assassinated in 1881, not by some isolated lunatic, but by a member of a group which, after careful consideration and much theorising, had come to the conclusion that his murder was a precondition for Russia to progress. This is the paradox of Alexander II's quarter century on the throne; he had ruled Russia in a manner quite different from that of his much-disliked father but opposition to him had been manifested in a way that Nicholas I had not seen. It was the inability of the autocratic regime to bring about a stable and coherent society in Russia, and indeed its success in achieving the exact opposite, which forms the hallmark of the modern Russian state.

Alexander II's destruction of his father's static society in the first years of the new reign was not, however, welcomed right across the empire especially by some noble landowners. Nevertheless reform was recognised as vital by many and the willingness of the new ruler to undertake it was acknowledged. The aims which the regime set itself in enacting reform inside Russia also met with a wide measure of approval: to take steps to remove the stigma of backwardness which clung to Russia, to provide a more effective and less arbitrary government for the empire and thus to enable Russia to reclaim her rightful place amongst the European powers. It was, however, the means which were adopted to bring about these aims which caused controversy and aroused discontent. The autocratic regime had no intention of seeing its own authority weakened as a result of reform, and instead saw reform as a way of enhancing its power. The regime hoped that the successful implementation of reform would provide it with new and durable sources of support and that opposition would disappear as the autocracy demonstrated that it was capable of transforming Russia into a modern state.

Although the reforms of the 1860s and 1870s had a clear aim from the government's point of view, their actual impact was far from being coherent and they failed signally to enhance the authority of the regime or to deal with the real causes of Russia's backwardness. Instead the reforms introduced a series of unresolved problems and were seen as being incomplete. Confusion was engendered by the varying emphasis placed on the authority of the state and of institutions established independently from it, as well as by the tensions between collective authority and individual rights. Reform served to stimulate the appetite of Russian society at all levels for yet more changes and the belief that the changes were incomplete was largely brought about by the disappointed expectations of society and the clearly apparent inconsistencies in the package of reforms. The problem arose from the way in which the reforms had been prepared and indeed from the nature of

Russian government itself, since each piece of legislation was prepared independently of all the others and there was no coordinating body able to oversee the whole process and consider the problems which might arise from the introduction of the entire body of reforms.

Alexander II's reforms were the last major set of changes to be introduced into imperial Russia and they set the pattern for the last two generations of the regime's existence. The state wanted to strengthen its base of support, but the measures which it took served to disillusion much of Russian society. The opinion of the gentry was asked whilst the emancipation was being prepared, but the views of the majority were then ignored in the reform as it was enacted. The introduction of new systems of local government and justice provided forums for public opinion to be heard, but the state took measures to limit its expression as much as possible. The autocrat insisted on remaining an autocrat, despite having enacted measures which clearly limited his powers, and it was this inability to recognise that the traditional means of maintaining control were incompatible with the reforms of the 1860s and 1870s that was most responsible for the upsurge in public discontent which Alexander II's reign witnessed.

Whilst the Russian social élite became polarised and open rebellion developed amongst those people whom the regime wished to recruit as its chief supporters, the mass of the Russian population felt themselves cheated by reform. Emancipation was a severe disappointment to the peasants and they saw their standard of living slowly decline in the decades after 1861, whilst those people who sought work in the cities of the empire were forced to exist in miserable and degrading conditions. By the end of the 1870s the regime appeared bemused by the result of its changes of the previous decade since reform had provoked precisely the opposite reaction to that which was intended. The state was divided internally about the best way to combat the deepening divisions in Russian society and to provide the coherence and stability which it desired. Loris-Melikov's plans to make a concerted effort to placate the Russian gentry and at least to begin the process of investigating the problems in the countryside were a possible solution, but one which was never given a chance to develop. The accession of Alexander III in 1881 marked a reversion to the conservative policies of Nicholas I: the new Tsar and his advisers failed to recognise that the pressures unleashed by Alexander II's reforms could not simply be contained, but needed to be released. The modern Russian state tried to cope with social and economic modernisation by using antiquated political techniques: this contradiction was to be its eventual undoing.

Documents

1 Government Structure and Personnel

1.1 THE IMPACT OF AUTOCRACY

Contemporaries recognised that the impact of autocracy permeated every level of government. Here Boris Chicherin, professor of Law at Moscow University during the 1860s, discusses the functioning of the Russian autocratic system.

* * *

Under a constitutional system there exists an opposition which vigorously voices its criticisms and provides an alternative view on each problem; in an autocracy, where society is silent, there need to be individuals amongst those men who are charged with the conduct of affairs who will bring different points of view to the attention of the monarch. Consequently, the government is made up of conflicting elements who carry on a muffled struggle amongst themselves, and the supreme authority itself supports them in this, and sees in it the guarantee of its own independence. But this struggle is a futile waste of energy, people lose faith in their work and get into the habit of taking actions which are unprincipled, a secret and sly, and worrying less and less about it. The autocratic monarch is accustomed to looking at people simply as pieces which can be moved at his will and which can be pushed to one side at the first sign of the spectre of independence. . . . In these conditions, where, due to the system, a deep contempt of people becomes established, strength of character and honesty of conviction become, of course, less and less valued. Everybody adopts fawning attitudes; everybody considers it his duty simply to carry out orders, even though they run counter to his whole way of thinking. . . . Such a policy plays into the hands of scoundrels; and ordinary people are either got rid of or else, seeing the fruitlessness of their work, retire voluntarily.

(B. N. Chicherin, *Vospominaniya. Moskovskyy Universitet* (Moscow, 1929) pp. 112–13)

1.2 PROVINCIAL ADMINISTRATION

Provincial administration was expensive and inefficient. Calls for reform such as that made by Kaznacheev, a provincial governor during the late 1860s and early 1870s, continued, however, to go unheeded by central government.

* * *

The provincial administration is like a factory which produces a multitude of papers and I had to expend much time examining them, since only attentive inspection can protect the population from the dispiriting and wicked activities of this institution. . . . In 1870 I wrote the following in a report to Petersburg. . . .

The new conditions of public life, produced by the reconstruction which has been made, demonstrate daily the shortcomings of our administration and demand its reconstruction to make its methods more convenient for the population. Further, the provincial administration costs about 30,000 rubles a year and it is filled with eighty civil servants who deal with up to 1,500 matters a year. I have counted fourteen steps through which each document in the general provincial office has to pass, and have noted the low level of literacy, ability and honour of the instruments of this complex machine. The advisers give no advice, they do not read documents from other departments but sign them unread. Understandably, I have concluded that the provincial administration stifles life, that it has outlived its time and that it only exasperates by its fruitless, antiquated babble. Administrative matters which need collegiate discussion should be dealt with in a council, under the chairmanship of the governor, consisting of the marshal of nobility, the chairman of the Zemstvo executive board, the chairmen of the financial and auditing departments, procurator, the military commander and other specialist advisers, depending on the exact measures to be discussed. . . .

(A. G. Kaznacheev, 'Mezhdu strokami odnogo formulyarnogo spiska', *Russkaya Starina*, vol. 32 (1881) pp. 861–2)

1.3 THE MARSHAL OF THE NOBILITY

Administration in the district was very much a personal matter, since the Marshal of the Nobility had no institutional authority. This extract from the memoirs of a district marshal in the province of Tver describes the differing responses the new marshal met on his appointment. The volost was the smallest unit of administration in Russia, comprising two or three peasant villages.

* * *

I took up my duties (as District Marshal of the Nobility) about a week before the meeting of the Zemstvo assembly, so that I could somehow acquaint myself with my duties. It fell to me to preside *ex officio* in the Zemstvo and up to then I had not only never taken part in, but had never even attended a meeting of a similar institution – and all I knew about parliamentary law came from poor quality books. The marshal's jurisdiction included the gentry board of guardians, the conference of peace arbitrators, the conscription board, the prison committee – I had to learn about the business of all these bodies, with their members, secretaries and officers, all of which were dependent on the marshal. The most important of these was, of course, the conference of peace arbitrators, and I there immediately met very definite and very open opposition. The district had not really had a marshal for several years, since [the previous marshal] had come to the area once or, at the most, twice a year, and all the bodies which he chaired had managed to organise themselves so that they could completely ignore the marshal. The arbitrators did not want to know me – they unanimously decided amongst themselves to oppose any attempt on my part to interfere in any way in the affairs of the conference. Its secretary was a hardened bureaucrat of the good old days and after the first meeting of the conference I felt the complete falsity of my position.. . . . One of the members was my uncle, an old and sick man . . . an arbitrator only for the money. . . . The other two members were middle-aged men who had tasted of the tree of serfdom and believed with all their heart in the fist and stick. They were sergeant-major types to the teeth, acting as gods to the volost administrators and vigorously extracting arrears, flogging peasants by the dozen on this account. Up to then, this was all that their work amounted to, and they had not thought it necessary to take any interest in the activity of the volost administration or volost courts. They had installed their favourites as volost elders and secretaries, and allowed them to lord it over the volost without any form of supervision. A more formalistic, superficial and careless attitude to work I have never encountered anywhere, before or since. The secretary of the conference galloped through his reports, with decisions already written out, and the meeting approved them one after the other, without any discussion or comment. Enquiries into complaints about the decisions of volost courts were invariably entrusted to the volost administration, and the decisions of the conference were based exclusively on their findings and reports. Because however in the overwhelming majority of cases the volost court was run completely by the volost secretary, it thereby turned out that they ruled on complaints against themselves. The number of decisions of the conference on these matters which were rejected, following complaints to the provincial board on peasant affairs, surprised me straight away.... In the educational council which I attended out of curiosity, I had a completely different reception; its members were the acting chairman of the council, the ubiquitous police chief, a priest from one of the town's churches and the inspector of the district school. These last two were very respectable men, loving education and having a lively and sympathetic interest in it. They did not indulge in long theoretical wrangles, but kept up sensibly and attentively with educational needs and with the teachers. They frequently travelled around the district and clearly had a good knowledge of their business. The prison committee, it was reported to me, never met – the necessary papers and lists were signed by the members individually in their homes, when the secretary required this.

(P. A. Dementev, 'Vospominaniya starogo zemtsa' in *Vestnik Evropy*, vol. 223 (1903) pp. 159–62).

1.4 LOCAL SELF-GOVERNMENT

The Zemstvo Statute, 1 January 1864

1. Provincial and district zemstva are set up to manage affairs relating to local economic welfare and the needs of each province and district ...
2. The jurisdiction of the zemstva in the provinces and districts they cover includes:
   (i) the management of the property, capital and financial levies of the zemstva;
   (ii) the upkeep of buildings and other equipment belonging to the zemstva, as well as roads maintained at the zemstva's expense;
   (iii) measures to assure food supply for the population;

(iv) the management of zemstva charitable institutions and other measures to alleviate poverty; looking after the building of churches;
(v) the administration of matters concerning zemstva mutual property insurance;
(vi) looking after the development of local trade and industry;
(vii) participation, primarily in an economic capacity and within the limits defined by the law, in looking after public education, public health and prisons;
(viii) cooperation in preventing cattle disease and also in protecting crops from destruction . . . by harmful animals and insects;
(ix) the execution of the obligations placed upon the zemstva by the military and civil administrations, and participation in matters dealing with postal obligations . . . ;
(xi) the fixing, allocation, collection and expenditure, on the basis of the zemstvo statute, of local taxes to satisfy the needs of the provincial or district zemstva;
(xii) the presentation, through the provincial authorities, to central government, of information and opinions on subjects relating to the local economic welfare and needs of the province or district, and the presentation of petitions on these subjects . . . ; the furnishing of information relating to the economy of the zemstva on the demand of the central organs of government and provincial governors;
(xiii) the holding of elections for membership and other positions in zemstva institutions, and the allocation of funds for the maintenance of such institutions . . .
6. Zemstva institutions operate independently within the sphere of activity entrusted to them . . .
9. The provincial governor has the right to prevent the implementation of any decision of the zemstva institutions that is contrary to the law or to the general welfare of the state . . .
11. Zemstva institutions may complain to the Senate about measures taken by the provincial governor and the central administrative authorities which concern them . . .
13. The district zemstva institutions are: the district zemstvo assembly and the district zemstvo executive board.
14. The district zemstvo assembly is composed of zemstvo members elected: (a) by the district landowners; (b) by the urban communities; and (c) by the rural communities . . .

38. Members are elected for a period of three years . . .
39. Service in the zemstva gives no special advantages to members, nor do they receive any payment . . .
43. The district zemstvo assembly is chaired by the district marshal of the nobility . . .
46. The district zemstvo executive board is made up of a chairman and two members, elected for a period of three years by the district zemstvo assembly from among its own members. The zemstvo assembly may, if necessary, increase the size of the elected executive board to six members . . .
48. The chairman of the district executive board . . . is confirmed in office by the provincial governor . . .
50. The provincial zemstva institutions are the provincial zemstvo assembly and the provincial zemstvo executive board.
51. The provincial zemstvo assembly is composed of members elected by the district zemstvo assemblies for a period of three years . . .
53. The provincial zemstvo assembly is chaired by the provincial marshal of the nobility . . .
56. The provincial zemstvo executive board is made up of a chairman and six members, elected for a period of three years by the provincial zemstvo assembly from among its own members. . . . The chairman of the provincial executive board. . . . is confirmed in office by the Minister of Internal Affairs.

(*Polnoe Sobranie Zakonov Rossiiskoi Imperii*, 2nd Series, vol. 39, pt. 1, no. 40457

The Zemstva and the Administration

The introduction of local councils into the Russian countryside following the 1864 Zemstvo law and into the larger Russian cities after 1870 provided wide scope for friction between the new institutions and central government. Here the chairman of the Chernigov provincial Zemstvo for thirty years, V. M. Khizhnyakov, complains about the way his council was treated by the administration.

* * *

When the Zemstvo opened both central government institutions and the local administration openly displayed their animosity to its activity and

Government Structure and Personnel 67

tried to hinder it in every way possible. Over the past half century there stretches an interminable martyrology of various petitions, representations and complaints from the Zemstvo which have received a negative answer, or in most cases no answer at all. Addresses to the government sent by our Zemstvo which have suffered a similar sad fate are numbered in hundreds. The government gave a negative reply in many cases because it did not regard the request in the petition as pressing, since other Zemstva had not yet made petitions about it. But at the same time attempts to establish contact between provincial Zemstva were invariably prohibited . . .

In one of the first Zemstvo meetings which included representatives of large landowners and peasant delegates the extreme injustice of imposing taxes in kind solely on the rural population was vigorously demonstrated and the provincial executive board was instructed to investigate the conversion of these dues into money taxes, and their levying on all classes. To the shame of our Zemstvo, I have to say that even half a century later, most of these taxes in kind are levied, as before, exclusively on the Cossacks and peasants.

The Zemstvo rapidly took complete responsibility for the upkeep of post and military roads. The repair of country roads remained the responsibility of the rural population. But the police did not take any notice of the law and in special cases they rounded people up to work on roads whose repair was no longer their responsibility. Such special cases occurred when some senior official was expected to travel along the road in question. . . .

And such senseless compulsory road maintenance goes on, without any technical supervision, everywhere. Tens of thousands of working days are lost each year in the province on such muddles – and country dwellers have to tolerate such treatment. Any objection or disobedience results in detention, cruel beatings and even political prosecution for going against the all-powerful and completely unregulated village police.

At the beginning of the 1865 Zemstvo meeting the then important question of the progress of the provincial land survey was raised . . .

The first provincial Zemstvo meeting pointed to various defects and abuses in the work of surveying and resolved to present a range of petitions to improve it . . . and in general to request that surveying be transferred to the jurisdiction of the Zemstvo.

All these petitions were completely ignored by central government. . . .

The meeting also raised the question of establishing a Zemstvo bank and passed a resolution petitioning for this to be allowed. For four years there was no answer. Enquiries and reminders were made, and finally it was given up as a bad job.

There were many debates in the meeting about primary education in the villages and, to begin with, about the training of teachers. On the first occasion it was decided to ask for the establishment of a temporary teacher-training school attached to the local grammer school, and 2800 rubles was assigned for this. The head of the local educational administration refused this request, since there was no law which permitted outside bodies to open institutions of this kind.

Attempts to organise teacher-training schools were repeated by the Zemstvo in the following years.

(V. M. Khizhnyakov, *Vospominaniya zemskogo deyatelya* (Petrograd, 1916) pp. 120–31)

Two Opposing Views

This first opportunity for the local population, and especially for the local gentry, to play a continuing role in the administration of their own regions produced extreme reactions. The first extract, by a provincial governor, depicts his local Zemstvo as a group of feckless men concerned firstly with protecting their own interests and having little regard for the well-being of their province. Chicherin's reminiscences of his service on a Zemstvo in the province of Tambov, on the other hand, are from the point of view of a convinced supporter of local self-government. He acknowledges the limited role which the peasantry played in the work of the Zemstvo, but insists that the council as a whole was concerned with the wider interests of the region.

* * *

The newly-introduced Zemstvo only affected the peasantry by significantly increasing taxation and by the new burden of electing the requisite number of representatives to sit in the Zemstvo. They then had the duty of attending the Zemstvo meetings, where their opinions were rarely asked and where they had little comprehension of the speeches that were made. . . .

I gained my first impressions of the Zemstvo during its initial phase. These impressions were not wholly favourable. The Zemstvo members were recent civil servants, or men of the same ideas and habits, brought up under the influence of our . . . regime, and they most valued in their work their independence from the administration, which could not dismiss them, transfer them, threaten them with legal or disciplinary proceedings or issue orders to them. The Zemstvo members were careless in the execution of their duties; each considered himself at liberty to perform his duty or not. This led to delays in repairing bridges, ferries and roads, there was no supervision of grain stocks and the Zemstvo did not even know the quantity of available reserves. It collected about 350 000 rubles a year in taxation. Of this 59 000 was spent on the upkeep of the administration; 48 000 on peasant institutions; 17 000 on medical provision and only 19 000 on education. Medical provision was lost in the expanse of the province, and showed its presence in only a few places: remote areas and the vast majority of the population had no access to it. Altogether there were 36 doctors in the province and 19 vets. . . .

After some observation, I was surprised . . . at an important defect in the organisation of the Zemstvo: a small number of representatives located in the district are, first of all, distributors of the more sought-after-jobs – and half of those go to the favourites of the Zemstvo members themselves. This distribution of jobs was the Zemstvo members' first task after which all their remaining work appeared uninteresting and was fulfilled any old how. It was a powerful weapon with which to influence electors and absorbed the most important interests of the Zemstvo. Thus, the Zemstvo seems to have been created for the personal benefit of its members and not for the population of the district.

(A. G. Kaznacheev, 'Mezhdu strokami odnogo formulyarnogo spiska', *Russkaya Starina*, vol. 32 (1881) pp. 857–9)

* * *

Participation in Zemstvo affairs over many years has left me with very good memories. . . . There is hardly another environment in Russia where the feelings and needs of the ordinary man are present to such an extent. This is not an assembly of civil servants, who always bear in mind what the administration is thinking or saying; this is not a conference of people concerned solely with their own personal interests; this is not an academic meeting . . . ; it is not an urban society, where extremely uneducated elements often come forward; and lastly, this is not a noble assembly which because of its composition and its means of procedure seems like some sort of incoherent chaos. The Zemstvo is the flower of the gentry, planted in the most favourable conditions for rational discussion of social questions; this is an assembly of independent men, who have a close knowledge of the matters at hand and deliberate on the sacrifices which they are prepared to make for the general good. Of course no family is without its black sheep. Especially where there are few educated gentry living in the countryside, the Zemstvo members can be men of very low quality. But if there are some honourable and ordinary men ready to act harmoniously in a district, the Zemstvo will always progress well. Over my more than twenty years as a member of the Zemstvo, I have seen a lack of effort, carelessness, levity, sometimes minor disagreements, but I have not seen anything outrageous, or foul intrigues. A feeling of decency and moral distinction has always ruled in the meetings. . . .

We treated the peasant deputies as equals, and extended our hand to them, but for the most part they remained silent spectators. We got the most business-like to join commissions, questioned them and asked their opinions on matters which they knew intimately and which closely concerned their vital interests; but it was rare that one of them would get up by himself to speak. Their main significance was that they were witnesses to what went on in the meeting and could vote for those whom they trusted. They could report to the population that affairs in the Zemstvo were conducted with complete justice, not only without prejudice to the peasants, but with careful attention to their needs and interests. The taxes in kind which lay on them were removed and replaced by monetary payments levied on everybody. . . . Schools began to appear; medical provision – so important for the peasant – was improved, since up to then it had hardly existed. And this was done rationally and gradually. . . . The district flourished and the future appeared in the most favourable light. Speeches at the meetings were almost extremely friendly. After the meeting we all had a noisy and jolly dinner together. Then the commissions went to work, usually lasting into the night: the remainder spent the evening in the club. The three or four days when the meetings took place were landmarks in the life of the district.

(B. N. Chicherin, *Vospominaniya. Zemstvo i Moskovskaya Duma* (Moscow 1934) pp. 20–3)

1.5 AUTOCRACY AND POPULAR REPRESENTATION

A Zemskaya Duma

The logical consequence of popular involvement in local government was believed by many to be a form of national representative assembly.

For some this meant returning to the concept of a consultative body which had been summoned by the tsars in the sixteenth and seventeenth centuries. Here Koshelev, a Slavophile who believed that Russia should develop by building on her historical roots and traditions, advocates the summoning of such a body in order to unite the autocracy with the Russian people.

* * *

We have voted for autocracy:

Firstly, because we know that, out of 100 Russians, 99 are in favour of it, and to foist on the people something which only a few want and demand is foolish and quite impossible. Ask the people both of Russia and of all the countries united with her, including the Baltic and Polish provinces, and an enormous majority will reply 'the Tsar should be an autocrat'; for the people suffer incomparably more from the nobility, from merchants, clergy and especially from bureaucrats, than they do from the autocratic power of the Tsar, whom they consider to be their defender, their guardian and the only just punisher of wrongdoing....

Secondly, because autocracy is far from meaning the limitless, irrational and arbitrary rule of one man acting on his own whims and opinions. Even less does it mean the pride and arbitrariness of ministers, provincial governors, police officers and the like, who give orders in the name of the supreme authority and consider themselves, and appear to others, to be some sort of mini-Tsar. Autocracy, as it is understood by the people and our pre-Petrine history, is the power of a sole sovereign, total power unrestricted by the limits of the law . . . illuminated by the advice and knowledge of the people's delegates. Thus such an autocracy is not a despotism, is not a bureaucracy, it is far from being hostile to popular desires, but is enlivened and strengthened by them.

... Our present position is such that the autocracy by itself is not in a position to lead us out of the crisis in which we find ourselves, nor would a national representative body with a limited monarchy be able to do so. What is necessary is the combination of knowledge which can be achieved only by representatives of the people, and the authority which is entirely present only in an autocracy. . . .

The summoning of a Zemskaya Duma is, it seems to us, the only way out of the critical and unbearable position in which we now find ourselves. The Duma should be summoned by means of a manifesto in which the Tsar . . . declares to all that from this time hence there is no authority higher than, or outside of, the law; and all laws will now be given a preliminary examination in a Zemskaya Duma; . . . no law will be promulgated without discussion there; nobody will be subjected to any form of punishment or penalty without trial; the budget will be presented annually to the Duma in good time; and the people's representatives will have the right to submit for the Duma's discussion the views of their provincial assemblies and to send petitions from the Duma to the sovereign.

(A. Ya. Koshelev, *Konstitutsiya, samoderzhavie i zemskaya duma* (Leipzig 1862) pp. 18–21; 22–3; *Kakoy iskhod dlya Rossii iz nyneyshnego ee polozheniya?* (Leipzig, 1862) pp. 38–9)

Constitutional Reform – Proposals by Grand Duke Konstantin Nikolaevich

There was pressure from the highest levels of Russian government for greater involvement by selected groups of the population in the work of government in St Petersburg. Grand Duke Konstantin Nikolaevich, Alexander II's brother, proposed the establishment of a consultative assembly in 1866; this extract is from his slightly revised version of 1880, and includes the Grand Duke's response to some of the criticisms of his proposals.

* * *

. . . Leaving aside the senseless dreams of extremists, who contemplate a complete revolution in our state structure or at least a limitation of Autocracy, . . . I believe we should concentrate on the opinions of the majority of thinking people who, although they disapprove of many of our existing procedures, are at the same time in general moderate and devoted to the Government. Whilst they have many different viewpoints, in essence one thread stands out from them all: 'The truth is not reaching the SOVEREIGN; the administration and bureaucracy have taken possession of us; the civil service stands as an uncrossable wall between the SOVEREIGN and His Russia; the SOVEREIGN is surrounded by guards'...

This complaint, it seems to me, contains a deeply serious desire which can and should be satisfied...

In my opinion it is necessary to stick to the fundamental view that the careful application and further development of the good principles which already exist in our legislation should undoubtedly be preferred to ideas borrowed from abroad which do not always correspond to our needs. This path will enable us to achieve the desired aim without the slightest infringement of the sacred rights of Autocracy....

I propose ... the summoning, as a matter of necessity, of a consultative assembly, attached to the State Council, made up of experts or councillors elected by the provincial Zemstvo, and the larger town councils. I would propose to entrust this meeting ... with preliminary examination of legislative proposals which require local needs to be taken into consideration, and also with preliminary discussion of petitions from Zemstva, town councils and noble assemblies.

... I ... do not at all share the ... fear ... that the summoning of a consultative assembly could create great problems for the government.

Such a fear would, in my view, only have substance if the assembly was extremely large, if the representatives were chosen indiscriminately, if the assembly were in continuous session and also public, and finally if the assembly were left to its own devices, without any supervision on the part of the Government....

... I propose the election of one representative from each province where Zemstva exist (35) and one from each of the eleven largest towns.
...

... if experience shows it to be necessary, the assembly can be subdivided into sections, entrusting each with the discussion of different matters. Thus any developing opposition can immediately be split up and weakened....

Furthermore, the assembly will not be in continuous session and it will not in general examine all matters, but it will meet for periods precisely defined by the Government and the items to be discussed will be stipulated. The members will not have the right to raise new topics or to depart from the limits of the subjects laid down for discussion. The chair at meetings of the assembly will be taken by members of the State Council. Ministers will attend its sessions. Finally, the sessions will not be public....

Legislative proposals should be subjected to as wide a discussion as possible. Not only, that is, from the point of view of high state or theoretical considerations, but also from the view of the possibility and ease of their application in this or that province. In this respect officials in the central government, who live permanently in the capital and are burdened down with a mass of current paper work, do not always have sufficient information. For this reason, proposals from ministries, although sometimes excellent from the theoretical point of view, often do not coincide with the needs of real life and do not bring about the results which the government desires. . . .

My proposed law . . . will not restrict the Government in any way, since the Government will be able to summon any number of representatives for any period of time to discuss various matters or just a single measure and . . . it can refrain from summoning the consultative assembly for a period. In a word, the Government is not imposing any duty on itself, but, when it feels it would be useful and necessary, it would be able to consult with people who know the real needs of the population.

(K. L. Bermansky, ' "Konstitutsionnye" proekty tsarstvovaniya Aleksandra II', *Vestnik Prava*, vol. 35 (1905), pp. 271–81)

Loris-Melikov's Plan for a Consultative Assembly

By 1881 Alexander II was ready to accede to proposals for a consultative assembly with the aim of strengthening the social base of support for the autocracy. Loris-Melikov, the Minister of the Interior, proposed a three-tier system of assemblies and his proposals were accepted by the Tsar. Before they could become law, however, Alexander II was assassinated.

* * *

It is unthinkable that Russia should have any form of popular representation borrowed from the West; these forms are not only alien to the Russian people, but they could even . . . introduce total discord. . . . Equally, a suggestion made by some supporters of the ancient forms of the Russian state about the benefit of creating a Zemskaya Duma seems to me far from timely. Our era is so far from the period of these ancient forms of representation . . . that the simple re-creation of ancient representative forms would be difficult to accomplish and, in any case, a dangerous experiment in returning to the past. . . .

It would seem to me that we should concentrate on the establishment in St Petersburg of temporary preparatory commissions, similar to the 1858 editorial commissions, with the addition that representatives from Zemstvo and some significant towns should participate in dealing with the work of these commissions.

The composition of these commissions should come . . . from representatives of central government ministries and invited . . . informed and reliable persons both in government service and outside it, known for their special scientific work or their experience in some branch of administration or national life.

The chairmen of the commissions should come from high government officials. . . .

The number of commissions should, at first, be limited to two . . . administrative-economic and financial. . . .

The work of the administrative-economic commission can include the following subjects. . . .

a. The reorganisation of the local provincial administration, with the aim of defining its rights and duties and bringing the administrative institutions into conformity with legal and social organisations and the needs of the administration;
b. Additions . . . to the law of 19 February 1861 . . . in accordance with the expressed needs of the peasant population;
c. Finding methods (1) to end quickly the number of former serfs still owing duties to their landlords and (2) to ease redemption payments by peasants in those areas where experience has shown them to be an extreme burden;
d. Reviewing Zemstvo and town council legislation. . . .

Legislation proposed by the commissions would then be passed, for preliminary examination, to a general commission under the chairmanship of an individual specially nominated by the crown, with members from the preparatory commission, representatives from the provinces where Zemstva exist, and also from some important towns – two from each province and one from each town. To attract the most useful and knowledgeable people, provincial Zemstva and municipal Dumas should be given the right to elect not just their own members, but also others resident in the province or town. . . .

Legislation which has been examined and approved by the general commission will then be submitted to the State Council, along with the comments of the relevant ministries. To facilitate the State Council's discussions Your Imperial Majesty may summon between ten and fifteen representatives from social organisations, who display special knowledge, experience and outstanding ability to attend its sessions as voting members.

The work of both the preparatory and general commissions should be exclusively consultative and should introduce no changes into the existing system by which legislative questions are raised and discussed in the State Council.

The establishment of this . . . system of preliminary discussion of the most important subjects which touch on the interests of national life has nothing in common with western constitutional forms. The supreme authority retains intact its exclusive rights of initiating legislation at a time and within limits which it sets out itself.

('Konstitutsiya grafa Loris-Melikova', *Byloe* (1918) nos 4–5, pp. 163–5)

1.6 THE LAW AND LEGAL REFORM

The Judicial Reform, 20 November 1864

. . . we find these bills are in complete accordance with our desire to establish courts in Russia which are swift, equitable, merciful and equal for all our subjects, to elevate legal authority, to give it appropriate authority and in general to strengthen among our people that respect for the law without which public welfare is impossible and which should be a constant guide for the actions of one and all, from the most exalted to the lowliest.

The Establishment of Judicial Institutions
1. Judicial authority belongs to:
    Justices of the Peace
    Conferences of Justices of the Peace
    Circuit Courts
    Judicial Tribunals
    The Senate, acting as a supreme court of appeal.
2. The judicial authority of these extends to persons of all classes and to all cases, both civil and criminal.
    Note: The judicial authority of ecclesiastical, military, commercial, peasant and native tribe courts is set out in special regulations.
3. The Justice of the Peace is an individual authority; conferences of

Government Structure and Personnel

Justices of the Peace, circuit courts, judicial tribunals and the Senate are collegiate institutions....

6. Examining magistrates are appointed to conduct investigations in criminal cases.
7. In instances designated in the statute on criminal procedure jurors are to be added to the composition of the court to determine the guilt or innocence of the accused in criminal cases.
8. Chief prosecutors, prosecutors and their assistants are appointed to supervise prosecutions....
17. Assemblies of both honorary and district Justices of the Peace of each judicial circuit constitute a court of higher instance, entitled the conference of Justices of the Peace. These conferences are under the chairmanship of one of the Justices, elected by their own number....
19. Local residents may be elected to the post of Justice of the Peace if first, they are aged at least twenty five; second, they have received a higher or secondary education . . . or have served for not less than three years in a post which could enable them to acquire a practical knowledge of judicial procedure; and third, in addition they themselves, their parents or wives own . . . land worth at least fifteen thousand rubles, or property in towns valued at not less than six thousand rubles in Moscow and St Petersburg or not less than three thousand rubles in other towns....
23. Honorary and district Justices of the Peace are both elected for a period of three years.
24. Elections of Justices of the Peace are held at district zemstvo assemblies....
40. In St Petersburg and Moscow Justices of the Peace are elected by the municipal councils....
81. Jurors are elected from among all classes of local inhabitants who are Russian subjects . . . are aged between twenty five and seventy . . . and have lived in the district where the election takes place for not less than two years....
202. The posts of chairmen, assistant chairmen and other members of the judiciary, including the examining magistrates, and likewise of prosecuting officials, chief secretaries, secretaries and their assistants may be filled only by persons who have completed a course in jurisprudence in a university or other institution of higher education....
212. Chairmen, assistant chairmen and members of circuit courts,

including the examining magistrate and likewise senior chairmen, chairmen, of departments and members of judicial tribunals are appointed by supreme authority upon the recommendation of the Minister of Justice. . . .
216. Senators . . . are appointed by sovereign decree, at the discretion of His Imperial Majesty. . . .
243. Chairmen, assistant chairmen and members of the judiciary may neither be discharged except at their own request . . . nor transferred from one locality to another without their consent. . . . They may be relieved of their duties only in the event of their being brought to trial, and they are subject to final dismissal or suspension from duty only by decision of a criminal court.

(*PSZ*, 2nd series, vol. 39, pt. 2, nos 41473, 41475)

The 1864 Legal Reforms

The legal reforms of 1864 provoked the same wide spectrum of reaction as did the introduction of Zemstva. In the first two extracts A. F. Koni, a distinguished member of the Russian legal profession, explains why he was an enthusiastic supporter of the reform but he also shows an appreciation of the reasons why the new system of justice was unpopular with many members of the administration.

* * *

The new legal statutes were one of the best links in the chain of Alexander II's reforms. The old system of courts which had gained universal disapproval was completely and irreversibly abolished. The 1850s had seen protests against it not just by . . . writers . . . but also by the growing sense for justice which the public possessed. This could not be reconciled with the organised summary justice, decaying and armed with bureaucratic chicanery, with the silence, the mercenary red-tape and the means of getting to a more dubious truth which were contrary to common sense and justice and were typical of the old court. Therefore the proclamation of the legal reform was greeted with unanimous sympathy. Old officials and clerks of all ranks who harboured bitterness in their soul humbly submitted to the new officials who served the reform enthusiastically, trusted in the spiritual strengths of their people and had a proud faith in the soundness of their work. But the new courts' honeymoon period did not last long. Vigorous public interest in the novelty of an open court, its oral proceedings, its direct way of considering proofs and legal arguments, and also its adversarial basis cooled as the court became an everyday phenomenon and part of the flesh and blood of justice. Little by little it was replaced by just an unhealthy curiosity of the masses in the sensational details of trials. Along with this, those whom we might describe as having suffered from the new courts began to show their faces – people unhappy with the equal rights everyone had before the court and with the application of the new law without respect of persons. Thus people who observed the oaths of the Legal Statutes and gave their entire effort to the legal reform found themselves . . . to be in a difficult and often completely defenceless position against malicious and one-sided insinuations and printed attacks, which were often based on ignorance. . . .

The jury courts, as they were actually implemented, focused all the general concepts which the legal reforms had introduced into the conduct of criminal justice. Specifically they brought together the independence of judges, . . . a definite verdict as to guilt or innocence which could not be overturned or reviewed, . . . the rule of the spoken word in place of the colourless monotone of written documents . . . and, finally, the participation of the public itself in the conduct of justice. . . .

From the start the jury court was greeted with general sympathy even from those who were to be its insistent and bitter enemies in the future, and for a short time it was able to boast of an attitude of peace and goodwill towards it. When this interest in its novelty had passed and a number of verdicts had been brought in which did not have the approval of the government, or did not satisfy prejudiced public opinion, and which also appeared to the readers of the superficial and one-sided press reports as baseless, at first isolated and then systematic attacks on the jury court began. People who were not themselves present at sittings of the court . . . began to consider themselves justified in attacking the representatives of the public conscience. . . . They called their decisions disgraceful and said that the jury court itself was 'a street court'. All this created an atmosphere of ill-will and at best indifference around the court and there was extreme delay in dealing with defects in its organisation and the rules of procedure. Nothing was done for many years to improve compilation of the lists of jurors, to put an end to the . . . prohibition on telling jurors of the sentences which would result from their verdicts, or to stop superfluous ceremony . . . The officials of the Ministry of Justice recognised these defects and took no part in attacks on the jury courts for a long time. They understood what a help it was to justice and saw from personal experience that the jurors, by their daily bringing in of verdicts on a mass of cases, were performing and were aware of their official duty and moral responsibility to society.... Under pressure from influential discontented parties there were continuous meetings... on the need to make changes to the court in some way or other.... These attempts took shape, finally, in the bill to stop juries taking part in cases about crimes committed by officials and against the administration, and were implemented in the law of 1878. This followed the famous trial [of Vera Zasulich] where the verdict, instead of teaching an instructive lesson, was seen only as a means to reduce the jurisdiction of the jury court.

(A. F. Koni, 'Na sluzhbe Sudebnym Ustavam', *Golos Minuvshego* (1914) no. 11, pp. 5–32)

The Reform and the Administration

During the first ten years of the implementation of the judicial reform the relations between the prosecutor and the top levels of local administration were a most significant question in the operation of the public prosecutor's system. The judicial statues were a wedge pushed into the antiquated structure of provincial organisations which were fossilised in the state they had been in the time of Catherine II.... This state of affairs was facilitated by the commonplace lack of consistency between our laws which made it possible to look at any social queston from points of view which were completely contradictory, but in formal terms equally legal. Here was wide scope for all kinds of misunderstandings and conflicts. This was particularly evident during the initial period of the introduction of the judicial reform into the provincial towns. The governor was, in most cases, accustomed to seeing himself not just as the highest representative of local administrative authority, but also as head of the province in all respects, a man before whom local society bowed with civility, with the exception – and even not always – of the provincial marshal of nobility and the archbishop. The governor frequently became angry and puzzled when authority began to develop close at hand, but with local agents who were independent of him and from whom he could not demand or expect obedience, but only courtesy and superficial respect, since real respect still had to be earned.... Most governors did not stint in writing to Petersburg about the threat to authority posed by the judicial officers, and in personal conversations in the capital they put significant emphasis on each unevenness, something so characteristic of an innovation, and elevated every individual awkwardness from the level of anecdote to that of scandal. On the other hand, they dressed up their own individual petty tyranny in the shape of innocent anecdotes which appeared as pure amusement. . . . People who benefitted from the new courts have no opportunity or possibility to express their debt to them, but dissatisfied voices quickly created an atmosphere of latent malevolence and suspicious distrust of the legal institutions. . . . Civil servants from various institutions were unhappy with the special rights and privileges of the judges, as well as with the fact that the judges received a far larger salary than other civil servants of the same level, with the exception of the excise department. . . . Envy, clothed in various forms, did not want – and perhaps was unable – to understand that there was a huge difference in moral responsibility between the work of a thinking and feeling judge and of bureaucrats of various levels.

(A. F. Koni, *Na zhiznennom puti*, vol.1 (Moscow, 1913) pp. 201–4)

Justices of the Peace: Conflicting Views

Whilst the courts preside over by Justices of the Peace were praised for being 'quick, correct and merciful' by P. M. Maykov, himself a St Petersburg Justice during the first years of their establishment, there was criticism, especially in the countryside, of the calibre of men elected to the post of Justice.

* * *

JPs conducted civil and criminal trials according to the judicial statutes, of course, but in differing ways. One judge, for example, would call the plaintiff the defendant to his table and ask the *plaintiff* 'You are demanding so much from the defendant. What proof do you have?' The plaintiff submitted the documents he possessed to the judge, who passed them to the defendant to examine and then offer his objects to the charge laid. The judge would then announce his decision. It often happened, however, that the plaintiff had no written proof of his charge or else the documents which he produced did not prove the charge. . . . In such cases some judges did not show these documents to the defendant and simply asked him 'What do you wish to say?' or 'Do you consider the charge justified or not?'. To this the defendant usually replied straight away that he did not accept the charge and the judge, according to the law, would reject it. Other judges, believing that it was not worth anybody's while to bring a charge with no foundation, and that in all probability the charge was correct etc., began by thoroughly questioning the defendant as to how he could prove his objections. . . .

None of these differences or nuances in the JPs' conduct of business was permanent; for many reasons they changed little by little and with time became smoothed over . . . and were no obstacle to the fact that the JPs in the capital city very soon acquired huge responsibilities and most important – the trust of the inhabitants of the capital. . . . The legal statutes of 1864 were to provide Russia with courts which were 'quick, correct and merciful'. In comparison with the operation of the previous legal system they fulfilled this task without any question. But besides this . . . the JPs, provided society with a court which was *free*, this is, taking a case through the JP's court did not require any expenditure on the part of the litigants. They simply had to address themselves to the court and then everything took place free of charge, according to the law. Russian society quickly grasped this and, evidently, valued it.

(P. M. Maykov, 'Vospominaniya', in *Petrogradskiy mirovoy sud za pyatdesyat let 1866–1916*, vol. II (Petrograd, 1916) pp. 1356–61)

*   *   *

The JPs were unsatisfactory as a result of a shortage of people from whom they could be selected. The nobility of the province included rich landowners with famous names, but these men neither stood for election nor voted in them. Some districts, because of the absence of nobles, had to be attached to other districts for gentry elections. The Zemstvo assemblies sometimes could not take place because of the lack of a quorum. Sometimes they had to agree to the unanimous election as JPs of men without the necessary property or educational qualifications. The distribution of districts amongst JPs was an inconvenience and the majority of peasants have no opportunity to turn to the JPs.

(A. G. Kaznacheev, 'Mezhdu strokami odnogo formulyarnogo spiska', *Russkaya Starina*, vol. 32 (1881) pp. 862–3)

2 Mechanisms of Control

2.1 THE ARMY

Military Reform

Army reform was recognised as much-needed in the aftermath of the Crimean War. D. A. Milyutin, Minister of War between 1861 and 1881, wrote this report in 1862 but it was twelve years before his proposals for universal military service were implemented in the reform of 1874.

* * *

The most significant difficulty and the first area of concern at the Ministry of War is the size of the military budget. . . . The main reason for the size of the budget is the number of troops. Therefore I must firstly examine to what extent it is possible to reduce the number of soldiers, bearing in mind the present position of Russia and the existing organisation of the army itself. . . . Whilst each of [the European powers] has a very substantial standing army . . . Russia can only maintain a similar political significance by means of corresponding military strength. . . .

Together with appropriate support for Russia's political position, the size of our army is also determined by: the continuing fighting in the Caucasus, the need to maintain the distant borders of the empire in the Orenburg region and in Siberia, the strain of our forces to maintain order and calm in Poland and the western provinces and, finally, the need to ensure the proper and peaceful establishment of new class relations across the entire Russian empire. . . .

Thus the present state of affairs does not permit consideration of a significant reduction in the size of the army at the moment. . . . It is clear that a reduction in the expenditure on the army can be hoped for only over a number of years, by means of certain changes urgently needed in our military system itself.

We have the following number of regular forces: in peacetime 798 194, . . . in wartime 1 410 027 . . . the difference between the two being 611 000 men. To make up this difference we have only 242 000 reserve troops ready; and therefore the remaining 369 000 must be drawn from the population as fresh and unprepared recruits. . . .

The enlargement of the army in time of war by this mass of recruits leads in reality to a weakening in military strength; but as well it exhausts the state to a large degree. . . . The sudden disruption of work in hundreds of thousand of households, completely unprepared for it, the sudden increase in demand for all the materials needed to supply the army leads to an enormous rise in prices, all depress the economy of the state in a single blow and makes entry into a war a very difficult matter. . . .

It is now necessary to find the measures to prepare gradually the military forces of the empire – both men and material – for mobilisation which is as orderly and as cheap as possible and thus to pave the way for rational savings in annual military expenditure. . . . To do this the following main tasks must be accomplished:

1. the reduction, as far as possible, of the non-combatant element in the army. . . .
2. The gradual formation of a reserve of prepared men who are really able to make up the difference between the peacetime and wartime strengths of the army. . . .

When, at the moment we need to bring our troops into military preparedness, the 369 000 recruits must be drawn from the population, that is thirteen to fifteen young men from each thousand of population. Such extraordinary levies have a very poor effect on the physical strength of the population and on the economy. On the other hand, such an enormous number of new recruits cannot be prepared rapidly and properly for their task. To eliminate both these deficiencies I consider the best solution is to make the number of permanent and temporary reserve troops equal to the figure which will represent, in the new organisation of the army, the difference between the peacetime and the wartime strengths of the army. This can be achieved easily and gradually, without aggravating the population; it requires only to set the normal number of annual recruits at a level which exceeds the annual decrease in strength of the army. Insofar as the number of recruits exceeds this annual reduction, so long-serving soldiers can be released into the reserve. . . .

But to make the selection of recruits equitable we need to change the existing system of conscription by zones. This means has never achieved its aim and has only been the source of all the unjustness in the distribution of liability for conscription. . . . Instead of recruitment by zones it is necessary to introduce an annual rational and proper selection of recruits from the whole empire.

And so an annual *general* levy on the whole empire *four men per thousand*, giving a permanent body of 100 000 recruits, is an essential condition for protecting the economic life of the population and providing a ready source of men, without which our existing system will not endure. . . .

(*Stoletie voennogo ministerstva*, vol. 1, *Prilozheniya* (St Petersburg, 1902) pp. 71–83)

The Statute on Universal Military Service, 1 January 1874

1. The defence of the throne and the fatherland is the sacred duty of every Russian subject. all males, irrespective of class, are subject to military service. . . .
5. The armed forces of the state consist of a standing army and a militia. The latter is only utilised during the extreme circumstances of wartime. . . .
10. Conscription into the service is determined by lot, which is drawn once in a man's life. Those who draw a number exempting them from conscription into the standing army are enrolled in the militia.
11. Each year only one age group of the population is called upon to draw lots: namely, young men who have reached the age of twenty by January 1 of the year in which the levy is held. . . .
17. The total term of service in the army for those conscripted by lot is fixed at fifteen years, of which six years are spent on active service and nine years in the reserve. . . .
18. The total term of service in the navy is fixed at ten years, of which seven years are on active service and three years in the reserve. . . .
36. The state militia is composed of all male inhabitants between conscription age and the age of forty who are not enrolled in the standing army but are capable of bearing arms.

(*PSZ*, 2nd series, vol. 49, pt. 1, no. 52982)

Reception of the Reform

This description of the reception of the 1874 reform by the Russian population is by a soldier who was part of the first levy of conscripts after the new law had been implemented.

* * *

Six months after finishing my university course the statute on the introduction of the universal military service was issued. It reverberated like thunder across Russia. Everyone was expecting it and talking about it, but when expectations turned into reality, society was terribly alarmed. Everyone began to talk, to explain, to argue; everybody had a son, a brother, a cousin who was going; even those who because of their age were no longer liable to be called up were afraid. . . . Various charters and documents with tempting titles such as 'complete', 'detailed', etc. were rapidly concocted from newspaper articles by crafty speculators and appeared with exceptional speed. In Kharkov over two to three days one bookshop sold three hundred copies of this sort of thing and had to telegraph to Petersburg for more to be sent. However, despite the extreme desire of the population to find out quickly about the new law, there were a huge number of misunderstandings. Many, in particular, were confused by the term 'universal military service'. 'How can this be, that they'll take everybody' a merchant told me 'no, that isn't the way; take the gentry, they have a warlike nature, but don't touch the merchant, the merchant is needed for trade. The merchants provide bread for the army, again, cloth and leather both come through the merchant. No that isn't the way.' . . . The peasants gave the new law an even wider interpretation: in their opinion, it would apply to girls as well as boys. I myself heard similar ideas on a couple of occasions. . . .

('Iz zapisok ryadovogo pervogo prizyva', *Vestnik Evropy*, vol. 55 (1875) pp. 269–70).

Army life

Life for the ordinary soldier was tedious and provided little scope for recreation. The education provided for the ordinary soldier was almost non-existent and it is not surprising that many turned to drink.

* * *

The company to which we were assigned was quartered on the lower floor of an old stone building, painted in some faded pink colour. The dirty, old staircase (senior officers used another, cleaner one) led into a wide corridor with rooms on both sides which accommodated about 120 men all told. Since, however, four rooms were taken up by the sergeant-majors, NCOs, the office and tailors' workshop, each of the five remaining rooms had 15 to 20 men in them, and it was so cramped that the soldiers pushed two beds together and then three of them would sleep there. An unpainted floor, so dirty as if it had never been mopped, air which was dense and foul, despite the ventilation and permanently open flues, dusty walls with shelves on which lay brightly-cleaned copper helmets, a long row of piled up weapons – this was the overall look of the new stage on which we were to be the actors. . . .

In some regiments, according to the newspapers, a type of club has been organised for the lower ranks, where for a small charge they can get tea and bread, can pass the time playing draughts and chess and where, eventually, newspapers were available. Nobody can doubt the immense moral benefit of such institutions. Unfortunately in the Guards, as far as I know, there was nothing like this and the soldiers were deprived of any sort of recreation for their whole period of service. This isolation had a bad effect on the health and the morals of the lower ranks. They lived for six years far from their families and homes, repeating, with machine-like regularity, the same drills, which would bore even the most patient. And so in order to relax somehow flagons and bottles of vodka were brought into the barracks at any opportune moment. Neither repressive measures nor strict supervision helped in the struggle with soldiers' drinking and it can be said with certainty that as long as the lawful demands of human nature – which include a need for relaxation – are not met in any other way, vodka will, as before, serve as the only amusement for each soldier. . . .

We can only expect an improvement in educational and moral spheres if serious attention is paid to schools, libraries and soldiers' activities during their leisure time. Unfortunately these questions are only of interest to a small number or else are put on the back burner. . . . With the exception of a few lucky men (no more than five or six per company) who are posted to the regimental educational unit, where NCOs are trained and where some serious attention is paid to the intellectual department of the trainees (I am speaking, or course, only of the Guards), all the rest of the soldiers go in succession to company schools during their first winter in the army. Sentry duty, inspections, mounting guard etc. are how the remaining years of service are filled, and so there is no time to think about school work. In view of this the store of knowledge which the ordinary soldier acquired in the first two or three months remains the basic fund to which he is, by necessity, limited. But even in this short period of time the soldier is taught less than might be expected at first sight. Of the thirty hours of lessons for the literate soldier, at least twenty were devoted to Chetkov's soldier's manual and only ten to writing, reading and arithmetic. The position of the illiterate was even worse; they had only eight lessons. All the remaining time was spent on military training, on dismantling and assembling weapons whose construction recruits spent a long period trying to understand, and, of course, everyone will agree that even by the oral method little can be achieved in eigh hours. . . .

(Ibid., pp. 276–87)

2.2 POLICING

The Local Police

The ordinary police of the Russian Empire were despised by every section of the community. Nazarev, a Simbirsk landowner, makes a number of suggestions to improve the quality of the local police force, whilst Kaznacheev, a provincial governor, provides a wider view of the Russian bureaucratic mentality.

* * *

The vacant position [of local police superintendent] was occupied by one of those unfortunate people who indulge in periodic bouts of drunkenness. This resulted, firstly, in unimaginable chaos and then the pace of administration slowed down and came to a prolonged halt. The arm of the local law which had been so sincerely extended at first, weakened noticeably and was then withdrawn. It soon completely disappeared and left only the volost administrators at the service of the population. They somehow or other continued to assist the judges, until the 'unfortunate' was replaced by a new officer, this time a respectable and reliable man.

The same story was repeated in other areas and towns. Justified comments were heard everywhere about the lack of ability and apathy of the police. . . .

It is immediately obvious that the present composition of the police gives little cause for comfort, although one does meet able and honourable individuals who are policemen. In most cases the police do not help matters but hinder them. It is clear that the effort which the police expand in using their fists and in unending cursing – alongside the courts which adopt a completely different tone – is not only inappropriate, but undermines the work of the police once and for all and harms it in the eyes of society. . . .

I refuse to believe that it is impossible to achieve anything better. I am firmly conviced that the police need to recruit men of a different mentality, peaceable rather than bellicose, efficient and dependable rather than fussy, men capable of instilling trust and respect who do not just maintain the centuries-old feeling of insurmountable fear and apprehension for the inviolability of their person, men able to preserve their human dignity both during and outside the performance of their duties. Finally, they must recruit volost elders and their assistants for police duties as well as capable local inhabitants as village policemen, with proper payment and incentives for the conscientious fulfilment of their duties. All this, together with some effort from the people at the head of the police, would quickly advance the local police, and give them a proper opportunity to really work hand in hand with the local courts.

As far as our village police are concerned . . . the same can be said for them as for our country roads. It is possible to use the road only when it is dry; the first rain makes travel difficult and after prolonged bad weather it is absolutely impossible to travel, so that all communication ceases. Anyone who lives deep in the countryside knows that there are no real country roads, but only places marked where they should be, places in the guise of roads and nothing more. Our village police are just like this; they only see and know anything when the horizon is clear and bright; at the first sign of a storm they are at a loss and then completely disappear. Everyone is convinced that the village police do not exist at all, or else are there only to have jolly conversations with.

(V. N. Nazarev, 'Sovremennaya glush', *Vestnik Evropy*, vol. 34 (1872) pp. 167–8).

* * *

The abilities, policy and methods of action of the police all display an incomprehension of reality which is a burden on it. The police are inadequately paid by comparison with the new institutions, they are overloaded with files, with correspondence and most of all with the maintenance of formalities which nobody else observes. Their primary care is for them, as the best way of avoiding responsibility. The demands of real life have no significance for them, and when it makes persistent reminders of its presence, the police take such a reminder as an intrusion into their peace, as something which is obstructing civil servants from their real duties (*read* dealing with papers). . . . Beneath all this the life of the population is forgotten. . . . The police have lost the ability to distinguish the important from the insignificant in the mass of matters which, because of their enormous number, it is impossible to deal with in good time. Important matters are defined as those for which the officers could be held responsible. . . . There is always an attempt to please one's superiors, influential and necessary people. For the benefit of the latter, formalities which are insurmountable for anybody else can be dispensed with. I am not talking about what is common everywhere – bribe-taking, embezzlement of public funds, careerism. . . . Nobody cares about work, duty or the public good. These words are uttered in certain situations, as full dress uniform is worn at certain times. I soon had to defend two or three of those whom I succeeded in persuading to take up the position of police chief from attacks and reproaches by the nobility, merchants, the Zemstva and from the nagging of the provincial administration.

(A. G. Kaznacheev, 'Mezhdu strokami odnogo formulyarnogo spiska', *Russkaya Starina*, vol. 32 (1881) pp. 859–60).

The Secret Police – the Arrest of Nechaev

The secret police, the gendarmes, operated abroad as well as inside the confines of Russia. This report to P. A. Shuvalov, the head of the secret police, by one of his staff, describes the arrest of S. G. Nechaev, a noted revolutionary, in Zürich in 1872. The arrest involved the use of Stempkovsky, a Polish *émigré* and acquaintance of Nechaev, to identify the revolutionary.

* * *

I went to see the head of the Zürich Cantonal police and to my surprise, I suddenly saw Stempkovsky in his office. The police chief asked me to wait and when he then received me, Stempkovsky had gone. He had left by a secret door. I introduced myself as Konevich and the chief of police immediately told me that he had been informed of the reasons for my visit. I then had to tell him my real name and showed him my passport, where my position as adjutant to the chief of gendarmes was written in. In reply to my question as to whether I could count on the cooperation of the Cantonal police, the chief of police assured me of his willingness to help, but added that Nechaev was no longer in the city, and had fled two weeks ago, as a result of careless searches by French agents. I then repeated my question as to whether he would cooperate – yes of no – in the arrest of this murderer. The chief of police agreed, and I undertook to point out Nechaev to him. We arranged that on the right day he would be with me, together with a major of gendarmes. After this I returned home where, at my invitation Stempkovsky visited me. I there succeeded in finally persuading him and won him over to making the arrest on the next day. Stempkovsky told me that Nechaev would be in the Café Müller in Seefeld at 1 pm the next day. The chief of police and the major of gendarmes then arrived. I was able to get rid of Stempkovsky, but I supposed that the chief of police noticed him. I again ensured that the chief of police was willing to cooperate with me, and asked him to arrange for eight gendarmes in plain clothes to be stationed at the points I would indicate. . . .

At 12.00 noon on the 14th of August, Major Netzli arrived. Arrangements were made in good time for five gendarmes to wait inside the café and three on the road leading to where Nechaev lived. They all knew Stempkovsky by sight and would arrest the man with whom he walked along the road or sat in the café. Nechaev's description was given to them. If there were several men, they were all to be arrested together. At 1.15 pm the major and I were in position and paced up and down a side street. The gendarmes remained where they were stationed. Before 2 pm Stempkovsky was sitting in the café drinking coffee with two members of the International, Greilach and Remi.

At two o'clock Nechaev himself went in. Stempkovsky left his table and sat down with Nechaev, who asked for a glass of beer. The table was near the doors. A few minutes later a senior sergeant, who was sitting opposite, went over to Nechaev and asked him to come outside for a couple of minutes so that he could pass a message on to him. As soon as Nechaev was outside the door the remaining gendarmes threw themselves at him and the sergeant got handcuffs on him. . . .

In his pockets were found an excellent large six chambered revolver (fully loaded), two old notebooks in which were written many names of senior officials of the Russian empire, two letters – one in French, the other in Russian (Nechaev asked for the reply to the latter to be sent to the editorial staff of the newspaper *Birzhevnye Vedomosti*), five copies of the new revolutionary programme in Polish and four addressed envelopes. . . . Three of the addressees were Serbs and all the addresses were in Zürich. Besides this a number of notes were found, including one to Mlle Herzen in Paris, and finally, an old leather purse with 1 franc and 40 cents and an old medium-length penknife. The gendarmes took Nechaev, without any opposition on his part, to the city's chief prison.

(R. M. Kantor, *V pogone za Nechaevym. K kharakteristike sekretnoy agenturoy III otdeleniya na rubezhe 70-kh godov* (Leningrad–Moscow 1925) pp. 131–4).

2.3. THE EXILE SYSTEM

Internal exile was a common punishment for those accused of political crimes. N. F. Vishnevetsky was arrested in 1876 for distributing illegal literature: here he describes his journey to Eniseisk, some 2000 miles east of Moscow, and his subsequent exile there.

* * *

As soon as the Volga was open after the winter we were despatched by rail in a prisoners' wagon. There were fourteen of us under the escort of twenty eight gendarmes, an NCO and a captain. In Nizhniy Novgorod we were transferred to a barge towed by a steamship. We left one prisoner in Perm and the remaining thirteen of us were transferred to troikas with one 'criminal' to two gendarmes. . . . The journey to Tyumen only took about three days. . . . We went on to Krasnoyarsk as previously, each with two gendarmes, and there I found out that . . . I was going to Eniseisk.

On arrival in Eniseisk in October 1878 the gendarmes handed me over to the police. From there, under the escort of a Cossack, I was taken to the police superintendent who asked a number of questions to check that I was the same person as recorded in his papers. He told me that I did not have the right to send or receive letters without his inspection; I did not have the right to give lessons, to have any contact with the teachers and pupils of the grammar school or district school, and could not write articles for newspapers. . . . Finally, he sent me to a different officer who ordered me to report to him daily, since I did not have the right to leave the town. . . . I then asked him where I was to live . . . 'How do I know? Now go.' . . .

I went outside. I was free!

The street was almost empty. I looked back – there was nobody there. What if I was to run off? And I ran twenty paces or so, looked back – nobody. . . .

I knew that there were two of the Karakozov group in Eniseisk: M. O. Marks and Maevsky.

I soon found Marks. . . .

'What can I do for you?' asked Marks.

'I am a so-called traitor . . .'

I was unable to get out more than a word. The old man seized me by the hand:

'Forgive me, we will look after you as one of our children. Sit down! What's your name?' . . .

With the help of Marks' wife I found a flat within two days for 17 rubles a month, including board, tea and laundry. All I had in my pocket was 20 rubles, so that I had to find some work.

A month went by before I was able to find a job, or more accurately to fall in with a group. I was taken on in a workshop.... I got a bed in the corner of the workshop and board: tea twice a day, lunch and dinner. My laundry was done along with the household's. The first month I worked without wages on probation. Work began as soon as we got up – the boss woke us. On Sundays there was no work, but otherwise we worked a fifteen-hour day, with breaks for lunch and tea of no more than an hour. We were not allowed to light candles when work was over, even if they were our own. The boss was afraid of fire....

My health, broken in prison, weakened all the time. The month came to an end: and it was Sunday. I asked the boss how he intended to calculate my pay, daily or monthly.

'Why should I pay you', he said, 'I give you all this: lodging, food, do your laundry?'

I silently went for a walk around the town and met Shibkovsky who owned a workshop. He invited me to drink tea . . . and I told him of my life.... Shibkovsky suggested I should immediately come to work for him.

Life was now completely different. The pay was more than adequate. I joined the library of the local liberal, Nikita Skornyakov. The library was small, but all the same had the classics.

M. O. Marks gave private lessons and carried out meteorological observations for the main Physical Observatory in Petersburg. The Eniseisk police ignored this tuition, which political exiles were forbidden to give. This was not, however, surprising. In reality, all power in the town belonged to the merchants and the men who owned the gold industry – and it was easy for them to get rid of an official who was inconvenient for them. The bourgeoisie put their children into the local boys' and girls' grammer schools and needed tutors. . . .

The local police, the superintendent and his sergeant, hardly interfered in my life. However, all the same, there was something missing. Work, real revolutionary work was missing. Where were the people? Mine workers, navvies, face-workers and other forest-dwellers dispersed to their villages when they left the forest. The urban workers, such as metal workers and joiners, were in essence petty-bourgeois in their ways: they had their own workshops, their own machines, in short this was cottage-industry run by small proprietors. They hired workers only rarely and if so it was not for long. The peasants came on market days to buy and sell and imagined nothing better for themselves. . . .

So six months went by and I saw not a single worker like those in European Russia.

All that there remained to do was propaganda work amongst the intelligentsia and students.

(N. F. Vishnevetsky, 'Eniseiskaya ssylka v 1878–1893 godakh', *Katorga i ssylka*, vols. 69–70 (1930) pp. 157–63)

2.4 CENSORSHIP

Government Calls for Reform

The press posed consistent problems for the government. This is an extract from a report written in 1863 by the Minister of Education, A. V. Golovnin, enumerating the difficulties faced by his ministry in imposing censorship and suggesting that the Ministry of the Interior would be a more suitable body to take on this responsibility.

* * *

The Ministry of Education has the duty to act as a patron to literature, to concern itself with its development and with its success. It therefore has closer relations with literature than any other department, and it is completely natural that as a result of its duty as a patron of literature, it cannot act as a severe judge. It has been so under all Ministers of Education. The Ministry of Education takes an interest in all aspects of literary activity and sees not just literature's mistakes and deviations, but also the services which literature renders to education, and this leads all the more towards indulgence in the execution of its censorship duties.

As well, the Ministry of Education must help in the progress of science in all its branches, and for this freedom of analysis is necessary.

Truth only emerges triumphant as a result of free argument, from the clash of different opinions. Censorship, as if mistrustful that truth will triumph, protects what is, at a given moment, regarded as truth and lays out the limits of free discussion. The Ministry of Education, in controlling censorship, is attempting slowly and carefully to extend these limits and to allow literature more and more freedom, restraining it and prohibiting the extremes. In judging what is extreme, of course, the arbitrary judgment of each individual censor in the Ministry of Education operates, subject to general policy, *and this general policy is a*

more indulgent one, aiming to give more scope to the printed word. . . .
In general, the position of the Ministry of Internal Affairs in relation to literature is quite different. It has no duty to protect literature, to aid it and find means for its development. It has a duty only to ensure that the law is not broken and it is more able than the Ministry of Education to estimate the importance of any breach, since it has information from the Police Department about the different ill-intentioned tendencies which appear in the state through different routes and it is therefore in a position to judge whether there is any link between them. The role of the Ministry of Internal Affairs in censorship is clearer, better-defined and simpler and therefore its aim itself is more achievable. . . .

(M. K. Lemke, *Epokha tsenzurnykh reform 1859–1865 godov*, St Petersburg, 1904, pp. 261–3)

The 1865 Reform

The censorship reform of 1865 did not put an end to attacks on the government by the press. Here the annual report of the secret police for 1869 castigates those responsible for administering the censorship for their laxity.

* * *

That the law of 6 April 1865 granted to the press not rights, but only privileges, is proved by the fact that permission to publish magazines and newspapers without preliminary censorship is not given to all publishers. . . . If the 1865 law was intended to grant complete freedom of the press, there would doubtless be no need to have, along with the uncensored press, preliminary censorship.

Unfortunately, authority has refrained somewhat from using the measures which the law gives it. It has . . . treated the press with excessive consideration. . . . Our press becomes more unruly each day, and has turned the privilege granted to it by the law of 6 April 1865 into the right of the freedom of the printed word. . . .

The law of 6 April coincided, as is known, with the beginning of public court proceedings in Russia. Anti-religious ideas, parliamentary propaganda and the plague of rejection (nihilism) which exists here could not but have a moral influence on the pattern of thought of teachers in higher education establishments. The representative form of government found especially vigorous support amongst former teachers in the school of law who, during the first period of the existence of open courts, occupied positions as judges and barristers. The bar especially came to attract figures unhappy with the government. Many judges and barristers belonged, and belong to this day, to the ranks of regular advisers to different publishers and thus there is an underground union between some organs of the press and the open courts which is and has been reflected (i) in judicial decisions on matters with a political content; (ii) in the speeches of defence lawyers and (iii) in the periodical press.

All magazines and newspapers which consciously pursue opposition to the government can be . . . divided into groups according to the programme which they set for the fulfilment of their aims. The first group, with more moral force and material means than the others, has the following programme: (a) to disseminate the works of Western socialists and to show the superiority of the elective, limited system of government by means of articles in the form of scientific criticism; (b) to deny biblical stories through such articles, with the aim of undermining the foundations of Orthodoxy; (c) to demonstrate the powerless condition of our economy and the excessive, in their opinion, expenditure on the court and the military through articles on the state economy and finances; (d) to develop in the people a hatred for non-Russian nationalities and for the establishment, through the unification of all its Slav tribes into one, of a Slav empire, through articles on nationalities and so-called nationalism; (e) to spread revolutionary ideas and show the inadequacy of our administration by means of stenographic reports of speeches by lawyers, belonging to the anti-government party and (f) to supply the publishers of popular works with money, so that . . . hatred of the people for the government can be encouraged. . . .

The second group deals with general social and anti-religious propaganda. . . .

The third group develops hatred of the lower classes of society for their superiors, it depicts the arbitrary nature of our administration and preaches, allegorically, of the need for revolution. . . .

A press which stands up for the principles of its nationality has artificially formed outside these groups as a result of the encouragment . . . of a crusade against the Germans. Such a press would have no reason to exist if the Slavophile party had not disturbed the Baltic provinces. . . .

It is undeniable that those organs of the press which, under the guise of conservatism, patriotism and devotion to the ruling dynasty stir up grumbling and discontent in Russian society are far more dangerous for the government than those which express their opinions directly and thus give the government the opportunity to take appropriate measures against them. . . .

All this makes one wish that the Press Administration would show more energy than it does at the present in its struggle with the evil aims of our press. . . . Instead of restraining the periodical press within its defined limits, instead of dealing with attacks on religion, morality and government power, the Press Administration in most cases takes no action, it takes none of the legal measures allowed it, and emerges from its passivity only in those cases when some article oversteps all bounds in its criminality, and when it attracts even the attention of Your Majesty.

('Literatura 60-kh godov po otchetam II otdeleniya', *Krasnyy Arkhiv*, vol. 8 (1925) pp. 228–31)

The Government and the Press

Part of Loris-Melikov's policy of widening the base of support for the autocracy involved seeing the press transformed into an institution which would restrain from extreme attacks on the government. This report which he wrote in September 1880 is optimistic about the progress of his policy, although a marginal note by Alexander II expressed doubt at Loris-Melikov's assertion that the direction of the press had improved over the last few months.

* * *

Because of articles which have recently appeared in certain periodicals, I found it necessary to invite the editors of the most significant newspapers and magazines for a detailed discussion and to give them a severe reprimand. . . . Careful examination of our press leads me to the conclusion that its direction has improved a little in the last four to five months, although it is still far from reaching the level which a serious and honourable press should occupy. Until quite recently the periodical press was as if ingratiating itself with the opposition section of society and even gave serious consideration to sedition, recognising it as a force. Moreover, it got into the habit of expressing dangerous ideas between the lines, ideas comprehensible to the reader, but in forms which were rarely open to prosecution. Now the press discusses the more interesting social questions more directly and even with some degree of independence. In articles of this type, with very few exceptions, although there is nothing harmful to the government, there is sometimes criticism of institutions and even of the activity of some senior officials. Articles with this type of content aroused displeasure from those they concerned. These people . . . tried to introduce the idea into their own circles that the blame for this rests on the institution responsible for supervising the press. The creation of a press which would express only the need and desires of the rational and sensible section of society and would, at the same time, be a faithful interpreter of the intentions of the government, is a very difficult process and is attainable only over a long period of time. I recognise the full importance of such a press and will energetically strive to attain it. I hope that I shall achieve this aim, although it is impossible that deviations will not occur in individual cases. But, until I succeed in this difficult task, it will be I who appear to those whose interests are harmed as responsible for any such deviation by the press, and sometimes even for justified criticism and I will attract displeasure on myself.

('Gr. Loris-Melikov i imp. Aleksandr II o polozhenii Rossii v sentyabre 1880 g.', *Byloe*, 1917, no. 4, pp. 36–7)

3 The Rural Scene

3 THE NEED FOR REFORM

Except for a significant minority of landlords almost everybody in Russia believed that serfdom was an evil which had to be eradicated. Here Yuriy Samarin, a noted Slavophile writing in autumn 1856, argues that serfdom must be reformed in order to renovate Russia's internal structure and thus enable her to regain external strength.

* * *

We were defeated [in the Crimean War] not by the external forces of the Western alliance but by our own internal weakness. This belief has obviously percolated everywhere and has supplanted the feeling of . . . complacency which until recently clouded our vision and for which we have paid a high price. . . .

We have lived too long and too exclusively for Europe, for external glory and external brilliance and we have paid for our scorn of Russia with the loss of precisely that which we revered – our political and military superiority.

Now, when Europe welcomes the peace and rest desired for so long we must deal with what we have neglected. Now that military exploits are ended, there is wide scope for peaceful work in front of us, but it demands no less courage, persistence and selflessness than did war. We must attend to ourselves, search for the fundamental causes of our weaknesses, listen to the true expression of our internal needs and dedicate all our attention and all our means to their satisfaction. We will regain the place in the assembly of European powers which belongs to us neither in Vienna, nor in Paris nor in London, but only inside Russia. The external strength and the political significance of the state depends not on its family ties with ruling dynasties, nor on the strength of its diplomats, nor on its reserves of gold and silver locked in the state treasury, nor even on the size of its army, but most of all on the unity and strength of its social organism. The stagnation of thought, the depression of productive forces, the rift between government and the people, disunity between social classes and the enslavement of one of them to another – no matter which of these, or similar ailments, the state suffers for they inevitably have an impact on the general trend of military and political matters and they prevent the government having at its disposal all the means subordinate to it and, in case of danger, of being able to count on arousing the strength of the nation.

This truth has, under the hard blows of fate, gradually penetrated the public consciousness. It is more willing to hear the bitter truth at moments like the present than in a time of calm; the social conscience speaks louder, the old neglected illness pains more deeply and, it seems as if the resolve to make any sacrifice for a fundamental recovery grows in proportion.

At the head of the contemporary domestic questions which must be dealt with, the problem of serfdom stands as a threat to the future and an obstacle in the present to significant improvement in any way. Wherever we were to begin our internal reconstruction, we inevitably come up against it. We cannot avoid it and we ought not to put it to one side unsolved, because the moral and material needs of whole classes which arise historically and legally from this situation are subject to the rational direction of governments to a certain extent. These needs can be recognised, considered and the means can be set out for their satisfaction; they can also be stubbornly denied and suppressed. In the first case, a transformation takes place in the public consciousness before it does in practice, and therefore the existing order of things which is gradually falling apart gives way to a newly created phenomenon; in the second, the needs which are being ignored and which are meeting systematic opposition at all points appear to disappear, but this is deceptive: they are only subsumed. Deprived of public manifestation and far from view, they ripen in the silence and the gloom and there turn into dark and irrational passions, like spontaneous forces, but also invincible. Finally, as a result of general poverty, hunger, fires, epidemics, foolish rumours, spread it is not known where or by whom . . . they break out suddenly, by that fatal time developed to such an extent that no human force can hold them back or direct them. There remains only material struggle with them which will shake the foundations of society for a long period, no matter what the outcome is. This is what the example of other peoples and our own historical experience teaches us. . . .

It is completely certain that the question of serfdom has developed to full maturity; that its solution requires not only strong will on the part of the government, but moreover and more importantly, clear recognition and sincere cooperation by that class which is most interested in its solution.

(Yu. F. Samarin, 'O krepostnom sostoyanii i o perekhode iz nego k grazhdanskoy svobode', *Sochineniya*, vol. 2 (Moscow, 1878) pp. 17–20)

3.2 THE IMPACT OF SERFDOM

Kavelin, a university professor and political liberal, here extends Samarin's analysis to demonstrate that serfdom has permeated every aspect of Russian life. The publication of this piece, written in 1856, resulted in Kavelin's dismissal from his post as tutor to the heir to the throne.

* * *

Many people are convinced that Russia is, by virtue of its natural conditions, one of the richest countries in the world, but it is also true that there is hardly another state where public well-being is at such a low level, where there is less capital in circulation and where poverty is so widespread amongst all classes of society. Whilst external peace and political strength blinkered us, we paid little attention to this phenomenon, but now, when an unsuccessful war has made us exert all the forces at our disposal, this lack of material wealth involuntarily stares us in the face and makes it the duty of every Russian to think seriously about the reasons for such a situation and ways of improving it.

The reasons for our poverty are very numerous: an incorrect system of administration; the absence of rigid justice and proper credit; a whole list of restrictive rules for trade and industry, as a result of which neither can develop freely as in other countries; the disastrous basis of our economic resources and our economic administration in general, which has, unfortunately, been so widely applied in our political administration; the deep ignorance of all sections of society, not excluding the upper classes from which most of our civil servants and government officials are drawn.

All these reasons have a more or less disastrous impact. But none of them penetrates so deeply into popular life, not one of them affects the economic activity of the people in embryo, not one of them kills any moral or material success in Russia as does serfdom which ensnares half of the rural population of the empire. . . .

In the economic sphere, serfdom brings the whole state into an abnormal situation and gives rise to artificial phenomena in the national economy which have an unhealthy influence on the whole organism of the state. As abnormal circulation of the blood gives rise to the most varied complaints and illnesses in the body, so serfdom does in the state. . . .

In the moral sphere, the influence of serfdom is just as pernicious, if not more so. The almost unconditional dependence of one person on another in the civil sphere is always and without exception the source of unrestrained arbitrariness and oppression, on one side, and servility, deceit and lying on the other. Violence and guile complement each other and therefore always go hand in hand, supporting and developing each other. . . .

Thus serfdom is an inexhaustible source of violence, immorality, ignorance, idleness, parasitism and all the vices and even crimes which flow from them. All our social and personal relations are infected by the influence of serfdom: our civil servants, since they are mostly drawn from the upper class, have no concept of law and justice; we have no honour in our civil relations, since as a result of serfdom, the two main classes in Russia, landlords and serfs, have from childhood grown used to deceit and do not consider their words and promises to be binding. . . .

Finally, serfdom does not just destroy and corrupt the state but it threatens it with calamities and great dangers in the political sphere. Since serfdom first became established in Russia, the state has, thanks to it, stood on the brink of destruction on several occasions. . . . Now, when things are a little more relaxed and the ways in which serfs are brought up have changed, serfdom still retains its political danger to the state. Any absurd rumour, or improbable excuse would be sufficient basis for the serfs to demonstrate their ancient claims to freedom. An ominous premonition of this has been that semi-peaceful serf risings have gradually assumed a larger and larger scale. . . . All this would persuade even the most short-sighted and blind that the people are much oppressed by serfdom and in unfavourable circumstances these irritations could flare up and make a blaze with consequences which it would be hard to predict.

However, this is only one aspect of the political danger which serfdom threatens us with. There is a second, at first glance less noticeable, but in essence no less real. Serfdom is the stumbling-block to all success and development in Russia. . . . All significant internal changes in Russia are without exception so closely linked to the abolition of serfdom that one is impossible without the other. . . . Thus, for example, the reform of the conscription system is impossible, because it would lead to the abolition of serfdom, it is impossible to change the present tax system because its roots lie in serfdom; for the same reason we cannot introduce a different and more rational passport system; it is impossible to extend education to the lower classes of society, to reform the legal system and civil and criminal proceedings, to reform the police, the administration in general, the existing censorship which is fatal for science and literature – all because these reforms would directly or indirectly lead to the weakening of serfdom, and the landowners do not want this on any account. Russia is condemned to fossilise, to remain in its present position, without making any step forward. And nothing is strong enough to change this position whilst serfdom lies at the foundation of our social and civil life, for this is the Gordian knot which ties together all our afflictions.

(K. D. Kavelin, *Sobrannye sochineniya*, vol. 2 (St Petersburg, 1898) cols 5–34)

3.3 EMANCIPATION AND THE NOBILITY

Reaction amongst the landed nobility to the prospect of emancipation was very varied. In the first extract Semenov-Tyan-Shansky, a noted geographer and statistician and himself a landowner in the province of Voronezh, reviews the differing opinions amongst the nobility at the end of the 1850s. The second extract, taken from a letter by a Tambov landowner written in 1857, shows the strength of opposition to emancipation.

The Situation Reviewed

At that time the gentry was extremely agitated. The majority of them were not just unsympathetic to the idea of emancipating the serfs which had been raised by some of the leading nobility . . . but were firmly opposed to it. To begin with only a small number of the more enlightened noble landowners were in favour of emancipation. But the more the problem was explained, the larger this number became, since every day the gentry realised more and more that, after the initiative which the Nizhniy Novgorod and Moscow gentry had taken, and after the Tsar's rescripts of 25 December 1857 and 17 January 1858, the question of emancipation was already irrevocably settled in their eyes and, even more, in the eyes of the Russian peasantry. It remained only to arrange the conditions for emancipation so that the landowners lost as little as possible. The instruction given by the Tsar to provincial committees to draw up proposals on this question greatly reassured the gentry, for these committees were made up exclusively of provincial gentry. The initial irritation of the gentry was directed towards those whom they understood as the government, but it was then transferred to the so-called 'Petersburg bureaucracy' and then to the liberal minority of the noble class, who were accused by the majority inimical to emancipation of revolutionary aims and were plastered with the label of *reds*.

However, when the gentry themselves came to the conclusion that the emancipation was inevitable, they moved to practical matters and aimed at carrying out the emancipation on the most favourable terms possible for the gentry. Different opinions appeared amongst the gentry themselves, brought about not just by differences in individual viewpoints, but also by different conditions which existed even within a single province. In Ryazan and Tambov provinces two-thirds of the land was in the black-earth region of Russia, with the northern third outside it. This difference had the result that in the northern third of both provinces the landowners hardly farmed and made the peasants pay quitrent, whilst in the southern two-thirds, on the contrary, they derived all their income from their own arable land, worked by the compulsory labour of the peasantry.

It is understandable that the landlords of quitrent estates did not find it especially difficult to dispense with serf labour. Their peasants enjoyed adequate freedom, and arranged their own work, partly in agriculture to meet their own needs, but mostly in cottage industry. This produced an income for themselves and the profit enabled them to make the substantial payments due to their landlords. For these landowners who rarely utilised compulsory labour from their peasants the whole question of the abolition of serfdom boiled down to not losing any of their quitrent income, as well as keeping all the land which the peasants did not farm. To these landowners the most advantageous solution seems to be immediate redemption by the government of the peasants' quitrent, the rapid personal emancipation of the peasants who would keep their farms and arable land and the landlords would get all the remaining land which was not directly farmed by the peasants, especially the valuable water-meadows . . . forests and vacant lands which nobody farmed. Under these conditions the landowners of quitrent estates were ready to see the temporary obligatory duties of the peasants last for a very short period.

Landowners of labour-service estates approached the question of emancipation completely differently. These landlords were used to living on their estates and farmed the land themselves for their own benefit with the help of the peasants' compulsory labour. . . . It is understandable that in these conditions such landowners would find it difficult to dispense voluntarily with this way of doing things which they were used to. It seemed impossible to them all that they could make an income from land granted to them without using compulsory labour. . . .

Therefore the majority of owners of labour-service estates in Tambov

and Ryazan, once they had concluded that the question of emancipation was finally decided, and knowing that it was impossible to break the age-old link between the peasant and the land, adopted the following method of solving the agrarian question:
1. To prolong serf labour by the peasantry for as long as possible and to maintain the disciplinary powers of the landlord whilst it still existed. . . .
2. When compulsory labour came to an end and the peasants were recognised as having complete personal freedom, they were to be given . . . the right to redeem their area of land for a price which would recompense the landowner for the loss of his right to the peasant's serf labour.
3. To recognise the right of the peasants to permanent use of only the small area of arable land from the estate which would be needed for them to feed themselves (a beggar-holding) so that the peasant would be economically dependent on the landlord and could be made to work on the landlord's fields at a price advantageous to the landowner.
4. All the rest of the land on the estate was to be recognised as the complete property of landlords, and they were to be relieved of all the duties which rested on them through customary law. . . .

However, amongst the nobility of the provinces there were a number of educated and generous landowners who were deeply patriotic and at the end of the Crimean War became convinced of the complete bankruptcy of the existing political and social structure and of the extreme necessity of radical reforms. The starting point for these would be the emancipation of the entire Russian people from serfdom, which assumed more and more the character of slavery, and the replacement of burdens on the peasant and the hated compulsory labour by free work, with the absolute condition that they were granted the use of land.

The highly-educated and prosperous landowners who were part of this minority stood firmly for emancipation of the peasants with land and for the most rapid transition to free labour.

(P. P. Semenov-Tyan-Shansky, *Memuary*, vol. 3 (Petrograd, 1915) pp. 39–43)

* * *

A Personal View

You asked me about the plans to abolish serfdom. I have read them with care and with sorrow. If there exists any sort of order amongst the people of Russia, it will be completely destroyed if serfdom is abolished. . . . Our peasants still have traces of their primitive, semi-barbarian life, and are still not sufficiently developed to receive new rights. . . . Before serfdom is abolished, we must reduce drunkenness amongst the people and they must be brought to see reason. The clergy must be educated so that, like the Lutheran clergy, they can have an impact on the conscience of the people and improve their morality. I tell you that along with giving the peasants freedom, the Tsar is signing a death warrant for me and many thousands of landowners. A million troops will not stop the peasantry's fury.

('Na zare krestyanskoy svobody', *Russkaya Starina*, vol. 92 (1897) pp. 237–8)

3.4 EMANCIPATION

The Emancipation of the Serfs, 19 February 1861

1. The serfdom of peasants settled on estate owners' landed properties, and of household serfs, is abolished forever. . . .
2. Peasants and household serfs who have emerged from serfdom are afforded both the personal and property rights accompanying the legal estate of free rural dwellers. . . .
3. Estate owners, retaining the right of ownership of all land belonging to them, afford the peasants, in return for the decreed obligations, the permanent use of their dwellings and in addition, in order to provide for their well being and the fulfilment of their duties to the government and the estate owner, that area of arable and other agricultural land which is calculated according to the principles laid down in the local statutes.
4. In return for the allotment afforded them according to the provisions of the preceding clause, peasants are under obligation to the estate owners to carry out, either in work done or in cash, the duties laid down in the local statutes. . . .
43. Each volost is to contain a minimum population of about three hundred male souls, and a maximum of about two thousand. The distance between the most outlying settlements of the volost and their administrative centres is not to exceed about twelve versts. Note: In those localities where, due to the lack of population, there are less than three hundred peasant souls within the area defined in

this clause, or where, on the contrary, over two thousand souls are concentrated over a large area, deviations from the above rule are permitted, with the consent of the head (*nachalnik*) of the guberniya

CHAPTER II: THE ADMINISTRATION OF THE RURAL COMMUNITY

46. The administration of the rural community consists of;
    i. the rural assembly (*selskii skhod*);
    ii. the village elder (*starosta*)
    In addition, those communities who so desire may have: special tax collectors; supervisors of the granaries, schools, and hospitals; forest and field wardens; rural clerks and so on.
47. The 'rural assembly' consists of peasant householders belonging to the rural community and, as well, all elected rural officials.
51. The rural assembly has jurisdiction over:
    i. the election of rural officials and the nomination of delegates to the volost assembly;
    ii. Decisions involving the expulsion of harmful and depraved members from the community; the temporary exclusion of peasants from involvement in the assemblies, for not more than three years;
    iii. The freeing of members from the community and the confirmation of new ones;
    iv. The appointment of guardians and trustees; the checking of their activities;
    v. The settlement of family (property) disputes;
    vi. Matters relating to the communal use of land belonging to the commune, ie: the redistribution of land, the levying and annulling of taxes (*tyaglo*), the final distribution of communal land into permanent peasant plots, and so on;
    vii. Where the land is in plots or in household use, any communal land which is lying idle or is not in household use will be disposed of by the assembly;
    viii. Consultations and petitions about community needs, the organisation of public services, and the teaching of reading and writing;
    ix. The passing to the appropriate authority of complaints and requests about community affairs, by special delegates;
    x. The setting of levies for communal outlays;
    xi. The assessment of all fiscal taxes, land and communal financial

levies, and also the land and communal obligations in kind imposed on peasants; and the keeping of accounts for these taxes and levies;

xii. The checking of the accounts of officials elected by the rural community, and the fixing of a salary or other reward for their services;

xiii. Matters concerning obligations to provide army recruits, as far as they concern the rural community;

xiv. The levying of obrok (quitrent) and compulsory labour services by means of household taxes (*tyaglo*), souls or in any other customary manner, where the obligations to the estate owner are the joint responsibility of the whole community;

xv. Actions to prevent and recover payments overdue;

xvi. The apportionment of loans from the rural reserve storehouses and of other kinds of aid;

xvii. The confirmation of individuals to represent the community in legal affairs. . . .

54. The consent of not less than two thirds of all peasants having a vote in the (rural) assembly is required in order to decide the following matters:

    i. Transferring land in communal use to plot or household use;
    ii. Allocating communal land as permanent hereditary plots;
    iii. Redistributing communal land;
    iv. Setting up voluntary communal associations and using communal capital;
    v. Expelling dissolute peasants from the community and handing them over to the government. . . .

69. The volost administration consists of:

    i. The volost assembly;
    ii. The volost elder and the volost executive board;
    iii. The volost peasant court. . . .

71. The volost assembly consists of rural and volost officials who have been elected to office . . . and of peasants elected by settlement or hamlet in the volost, one per ten households. . . .

78. The volost assembly is responsible for:

    i. The election of volost officials and volost court judges;
    ii. Decisions about the economic and public affairs of the volost;
    iii. Caring for the poor; the setting up of volost schools; looking after volost reserve storehouses, where they exist;
    iv. Passing on to the relevant office complaints and requests about volost affairs, by special delegates;

The Rural Scene

- v. Assessing and apportioning communal taxes and duties concerning the whole volost;
- vi. Checking (the accounts) of elected volost officials and supervising their activities;
- vii. Confirming recruiting lists and apportioning responsibility to provide recruits;
- viii. Confirming the right to represent the volost in legal affairs. . . .

81. The volost elder is responsible for the maintenance of general order, peace and quiet in the volost. As regards the above rural elders are completely subordinate to him. . . .

93. To form the volost court the volost assembly shall elect annually . . . four to twelve . . . judges. The court is only in session if there are three or more judges present. . . .

95. The volost court hears . . . disputes and litigations between peasants and also minor peasant offences.

96. The volost court decides: all disputes and litigations between peasants each up to one hundred rubles inclusive in value, involving, not only immovable and movable property within the confines of the peasant allotment, but also loans, purchases, sales and other types of transactions and liabilities, and also matters involving compensation for losses and damages caused to peasant property. . . .

102. The volost court may, when dealing with such offences, sentence the guilty: to public labour – up to six days; or to a pecuniary fine – up to three rubles; or to hold under arrest – up to seven days; or, finally, with those not exempted from corporal punishment, to punishment with rods – up to twenty lashes. . . .

104. The volost elder and rural elder may not interfere in volost court cases and shall not be present when cases are being heard. . . .

130. The following general conditions must be observed when releasing peasants from the village community:
    - i. A peasant who wishes to leave the community, after renouncing sine die his share of the communal allotment . . . must surrender the plot of land he was using. . . .
    - iii. The family of the person released must have paid all fiscal, land and communal taxes, and in addition his own taxes must be paid up to 1 January of the following year.
    - iv. The released person must not be the subject of any uncontested private proceedings or liabilities brought before the volost administration.

v. The released person must not be under trial or investigation.
vi. The parents of the released person must give their consent to his release.
vii. Any member of the family of the released peasant who is a minor or otherwise incapable of working, and who remains in the community, must be provided with some means of support. . . .
viii. The person applying for his release must provide a certificate of acceptance from the community which he is joining. . . .

169. The allocation of fiscal and land obligations, in money and in kind, among the peasants of the rural community, is decided by the commune. . . .
187. Each rural community, whether its land is farmed communally or by the plot or household method, is jointly responsible for the strict execution of fiscal, land and communal obligations by each of its members. . . .

4. The government will cooperate in the process of the peasants obtaining both their homesteads and field allotments as property through a redemption system. This will comprise the government lending, on the security of the land obtained in this way, a fixed sum which the peasants will repay in instalments over a prolonged period. The government itself will recover both the interest on the sum lent and the repayment of the capital. The amount fixed will be paid to the landowner by means of interest-bearing bonds on which the government will pay both interest and capital. . . .
113. Peasants who acquire land through redemption must annually pay the Treasury interest at 6 per cent on the sum advanced by the government, as a substitute for the quitrent due to the landlord, until the sum in fully repaid. . . .
114. The redemption loan is repaid by means of payments made over a period of forty nine years from the date the loan was advanced. . . .

1. Peace Arbitrators, District Arbitrators' Conferences and Provincial Boards on Peasant Affairs are to be set up to sort out misunderstandings, disputes and complaints which may arise from the obligatory land relations between the landowners and the temporarily obligated peasants. . . .
23. The jurisdiction of the Peace Arbitrators includes: first, disputes, complaints and misunderstandings between landowners and temporarily obligated peasants or household serfs . . . and also

complaints by peasants and communities about volost assemblies and rural and volost officials; secondly, the witnessing of various documents drawn up between the landowners and the temporarily obligated peasants and household serfs; thirdly, certain administrative duties concerned with peasant affairs . . . and fourthly, some judicial and police matters. . . .

123. In the event that a landowner, with the voluntary agreement of the peasants and with confirmation in the approved manner, gives the peasant community part of their allotment, and if this part, including the peasants' immediate homesteads comprises no less than one quarter of the largest size of allotment set out for that locality, then the peasants who receive this gift from the landowner can renounce their use of the remaining part of the allotment which is then at the disposal of the landowner. . . .

(*PSZ*, 2nd series, vol. 36, pt. 1, nos 36657, 36659–60, 36662)

Reaction to the Emancipation Edict

This description of the reception of the emancipation edict by a member of the Tsar's bodyguard shows that government fears about widescale disturbances were unfounded. Instead the officer depicts a group of peasants presenting the Tsar with bread and salt, a traditional Russian gesture of hospitality.

* * *

On 19 February 1861 the manifesto on the emancipation of the peasantry was issued. All Russia had waited anxiously for its proclamation. The gentry, although they privately recognised that the old order was unthinkable for the future, were unable, however, to understand that the labour force which had belonged to them for centuries was leaving and that they would have to give up part of their land, of their property. The peasants, who had belonged to the landowners as their property for centuries and had worked for them for whole generations were suddenly free and independent and received rights as free men. The critical moment had come. Clashes were fearfully anticipated; it was thought the gentry would not want to give up their age-old rights, and that the peasants, when they heard they had been granted freedom would, out of ignorance, take it as an excuse not to obey the authorities. In Petersburg street disturbances were expected. But this was impossible. The gentry had lost; were they about to take to the streets in protest?

The people would have torn them to pieces. The peasants could only rejoice and pray to God for the Tsar who had given them freedom. The Sunday on which the manifesto was proclaimed went off peacefully. The day before, a printed instruction from the St Petersburg governor-general had been circulated to all regiments with details of . . . how they were to behave at the first signs of street disturbances. On the next day, I, as major-general of the imperial bodyguard, was on duty in the palace. The people who were assembled there awaiting Tsar's appearance were extremely uneasy. Some dull sound, like a shot was heard. The governor-general sent to find out what it was and it was reported to him that it was a mass of snow falling from the palace roof. (It snowed heavily the whole day). A short time later bells were heard; again a special messenger went galloping headlong and returned to report that it was the bells of St Isaac's on the occasion of the funeral of some priest.

A few days later a group of respectful old peasants together with young children assembled near the palace, and offered bread and salt to the Tsar. Later, I was a witness when the Tsar rode down Nevsky Prospekt through a thick crowds of people; many crossed themselves when they saw him and bowed low to the ground. Telegrams from nearby towns also contained reassuring views, and soon the most calming letters and despatches began to arrive from all corners of Russia.

Petersburg gave a sigh of relief. Officials had previously been sent to all the provinces to observe the proper proclamation of the manifesto and they had wide powers to put an end to disorders. There were some instances where force had to be used; but in general everything went well, and the enormous and historic revolution took place remarkably peaceably. . . .

To implement the new law and organise peasant life anew peace arbitrators were appointed. Their duty was to explain to the peasants their new position, to transfer the land to them and explain their rights and duties. To the honour of the Russian gentry it must be said that the best section of the gentry voluntarily damaged their own interests and apportioned areas of their own land to their former serfs. The Tsar gave the people freedom, the gentry gave them land, gave them a chance to live. The generosity of the gentry was unique and seen nowhere else. They were not lauded, not glorified: such was the modesty of the Russian people.

('Iz pamyatnykh zametok starogo gvardeytsa', *Ruskiy Arkhiv*, vol. 30 (1892) pp. 139–40).

Peasant Reaction

This extract from a letter by a Saratov landowner showed some of the confusions that were generated by the Emancipation Act, but at the same time reproaches the authorities for their heavy-handed attitudes to the peasantry.

* * *

The manifesto was proclaimed right across Russia, including here in the steppe. . . . Nobody could understand it. We have still not received the full text of the law. This has given the opportunity for everybody to interpret it in his own way. Confusion has begun. But first it was understood that freedom was postponed for two years. But as you know not all landlords are the same, but many are wicked. . . . It is easily understandable that when the manifesto was read, peasants belonging [to the latter sort] could not believe that all the Tsar's mercy just consisted of them having to remain under this oppression for another two years. . . . The peasants interpreted the manifesto to mean that, as they had been given freedom, there was no more labour service (completely logically, in my opinion) and stopped working for the landlords. . . .

The district administrator was sent to try to persuade them, but without success. The peasants respectfully told him 'Sir, we cannot disobey the Tsar's orders', and did not go to work. Then a provincial official came. He spoke intelligently and well. He tried to persuade the peasants and finally said that apart from the manifesto, there was a law where everything was clearly set out. The peasants asked him to show them the law. The provincial idiot answered 'I would show it to you, but I have left my keys in Saratov'. What a fool! Of course, nobody wanted to hear any more.

Then an aide-de-camp came. He did not produce the law either and explained nothing clearly. The peasants, to whom this procession of different officials was becoming suspicious, and surprised that the ADC was so unintelligent, asked him to show his passport to prove that he was who he claimed to be. He showed them his instructions and then left, without accomplishing anything.

Troops were summoned. Three battalions were brought here. The governor came and, they say, the provincial marshal of nobility. Troops began to patrol from village to village. It is true that, up to this time, according to my information, there had been no floggings, but the ADC found another means. They slaughtered chickens, sheep, calves and, if they were not working animals, cattle for the troops. The peasants, poor already, were finally and completely ruined. Do these idiots think they will strengthen the authority of the government like this? I wrote to the district marshal and advised him to adopt the simplest measure: to explain the actual law. I did not hide from him that, simply, nobody trusted him, nor the ADC nor the governor, and therefore advised him to send somebody here to do this who was trusted by the peasantry, whether it be a merchant or an intelligent peasant. But they want to make the peasants obey without any explanations. For four days in dreadful weather they had been going from village to village; they are heard but not obeyed, for they have run up against Ukranians, who say they have nothing to lose, since they have nothing; let them be ruined, but they will not go to work.

(I. A. Zhelvakova (ed.), 'Saratovskiy pomeshchik o khode reformy 19 febralya 1861 g.', in *Revolutsionnaya situatsiya v Rossii v 1859–1861 gg.* (Moscow, 1965) pp. 451–2)

The Church and Emancipation

The Orthodox Church played an important role in the emancipation, since the manifesto itself was read from church pulpits. Priests thus became the target for peasant discontent, as this report by the Archbishop of Penza demonstrates.

* * *

Rural dean Ilarion Maslovsky, the village priest of Bolshoy-Izhmora (Kerensky district) reported to me on 19 April that the village parish priests in landowners' villages were at the present time in the most difficult circumstances, for the peasants completely disbelieved the Imperial manifesto read to them about their emancipation and demanded from the priests some other manifesto marked, they said, with a cross in gold which promised them freedom. This has led to a movement amongst the peasantry which is spreading from hamlet to hamlet and from village to village. Thus, for example, on 14 April after the liturgy the village priest of Nikolsky, Nikolia Gromov, was stopped on his way from church to his house by a mass of peasants who made insistent demands for the above-mentioned manifesto and some of them were ready to insult him; he gave them the manifesto which had been read in church and left it at that. On 19 April, during the rural dean's stay in the house of the priest of Arkhangelskiy, Mikhail Mallein, a crowd of his parishioners came to the house and made persistent demands for this manifesto. However much the rural dean, together with the local priest Mallein, tried to assure them that there was no manifesto other than that read in church, and that they did not have any other, nobody wanted to believe this, assuming that the priests were either bribed or had been prevailed on by the landowners not to proclaim a manifesto advantageous to the peasantry. In such cases the silence of the priests gives the common people yet more reason for suspicion, and the words spoken by the priests are misinterpreted as having the opposite meaning which makes them most harmful for the priests, all the more so as some evil-intentioned parishioners completely falsely slander the priests.

('Tserkov i reforma 1861 g.', *Krasnyy Arkhiv*, vol. 72 (1935) p. 188)

3.5 THE IMPLEMENTATION OF THE EMANCIPATION

The brunt of the network of explaining the details of the emancipation fell on the peace arbitrators, appointed to implement the act on the ground. Ponomarev, an arbitrator working in Kharkov, here describes his time-consuming duties.

* * *

My first task was to set out my programme of action. . . .

In view of the extreme lack of knowledge and complete submissiveness of the peasantry, produced by centuries of effective slavery – this programme, naturally, had to consist of the following: at the opening of the village and the volost administrations and at the election of village and volost administrators, I explained to the peasants the rights which the Tsar had given them and the duties which they had to the state, society and landowners. . . . I instilled into the peasantry as firmly as possible that they were obliged to carry out the instructions of their elected administrators . . . on the other hand I made it clear to the elected administrators that they were not allowed to abuse their power or to indulge in arbitrary actions and must resist the temptations of office, especially bribes, under threat of arrest, fine and removal. I explained to the peasants the meaning and significance of law which they were so unaccustomed to, and the execution of which was equally compulsory for all subjects of the Tsar from the most senior officials down to the last peasant. . . . I had placed a special emphasis in all possible ways on showing the difference between the freedom given to them for their happiness and self-will, which should always, in view of its destructive consequences, be subject to more severe punishment. I demonstrated to the volost judges their high and sacred duty and made it a rule that before opening the court the Lord's Prayer, familiar to everybody, was to be said. I explained to the peasant the significance of the charters and gave a clear comparison of the relative benefits of labour service, payments in lieu and redemption payments with the cooperation of the government. Together with this I spared no effort and used all my persuasion to ensure that the peasants would not refuse their land and would not reduce the size of their holdings, but where possible would transfer their entire allotment to redemption, and I added the hope that the link of serfdom between peasant and landlord would be replaced by good neighbourliness. I supported peasant societies in their first step towards an independent life; and taught peasants to check systematically the various taxes levied upon them. I had to protect the communes from exploitation by pub landlords by keeping the latter under the threat of continuous inspection. My task was to avoid the sad necessity of using troops or corporal punishment at all costs; thus continuous trips, visits to the volosts as often as possible, and long talks with the peasants I saw as being my first duty. . . .

All of 1861 was devoted to establishing order in the village and the volost administration, and to the volost courts in my district. To this end I visited the administrations each week, especially in the volost, which gave a chance to talk to the peasants and, through endless explanations and interpretation, to achieve the calm which was so necessary for implementing the main body of the reform. Towards the end of 1861 I was already receiving fewer calls for some matter or other to be sorted out immediately. The transition from the slavelike condition of the peasantry to the complete removal of the landlords' power over them . . . represented . . . too fundamental a change for me to be able to count on the successful introduction of the land charters, even after my year-long tireless and preparatory work. And in reality no sooner had I begun this work in the spring of 1862 than I met opposition not only from the peasants, but also from large and enlightened landowners. Landowners of the middle rank, as a result of their closeness and better relations with the peasants, usually turned out to be more compliant and in any case, they were more limited in the means of influence they had to display opposition.

(N. K. Ponomarev, 'Vospominaniya mirovogo posrednika pervogo prizyva, 1861–1863 gg,', *Russkaya Starina*, vol. 74 (1891) pp. 304–17)

3.6 EMANCIPATION AND HOUSEHOLD SERFS

The Emancipation Act provided no land for the household serfs found on every estate in Russia. A Tambov landowner gives an indication of the problems faced by the household serfs, both immediately after emancipation and in the longer term.

* * *

The servants and house-serfs of Russia remained forgotten by the great law of 19 February and continued to be tied to their former masters, demanding bread for themselves and, in accordance with the new conditions of life, monetary payment. What would happen to them when the master was no longer able to feed all those who wanted to eat but were deprived of land did not concern them; they wanted to live and valued their warm places and nests. These various cooks, maids, housekeepers, poultry-girls and other serfs were not used to freely-hired work; they were used to working under the lash – and doing nothing. The whip had been taken out of the landlord's hands, he was unable to enforce discipline and moral duty and the servants, finding that they were free, gave full rein to the basic sides of their nature. They looked down on the ordinary peasants and felt themselves as of old to be in some way a necessary part of the lord's estate. In relation to the master, however, the granting of freedom replaced their previous forced fear and respect by a careless and undisciplined familiarity. They began to be rude, to threaten to leave, and began to wander off, as if rewarding themselves for their previous hardships and restraints, and along with this they tried to do nothing, or else as little as possible. . . .

By 1873 questions of food, accommodation and work were staring those servants who remained alive in the face and over the next ten years they needed a solution as the owners of the estates themselves could only provide food and repose with difficulty and hardship. The remaining stewards, housekeepers, gardeners and stablemen were scattered to different corners of the district after the break up of the gentry nest in the 1880s, and had no way of settling down for a long time. The law of 19 February had not given them their own piece of land and they had not been taught the harsh demands of real work. . . . As a result when, many years later, I took an interest in the fate of one or other servants from the estate, in most cases I received distressing news: one had taken to drink and was always seen in pubs, another had fallen into a dissolute life and was passed around the village from hand to hand. . . . Without land and removed, by the will of fate, from the noble's estate, where some sort of discipline had been imposed on them, all these people, bitterly insulted by fate, appeared to other villages as an infectious and corrupt element which had brought as much evil and harm to the peasants. Producing sadness and misery around themselves, they found no joy or contentment in themselves. Who was happier, those who died of the plague in the black days of 1873, or those who ten years later died a moral death?

(B. B. Glinsky, 'Iz letopisi sela Sergeevki', *Istoricheskiy Vestnik*, vol. 58 (1894) pp. 70–83)

3.7 THE PEASANT COMMUNE

The commune, as this landowner came to understand, continued to play a vital role in both the agricultural and administrative affairs of the Russian countryside.

* * *

. . . In long conversations with the peasants the point of communal landownership became clearer to me. It was not, as suggested by idle young men, a precious sign of the inherent socialism of our peasantry. It was the only practical compromise between the inexorable demands of the taxman and the need to give each member of the commune the possibility of earning a living for his family, through the equitable distribution of land, according to its qualities and defects. This was the most durable method of preserving the land which belonged to the commune intact and inalienable, so that it could be redistributed when necessary according to the needs and means of members of the commune. It became clear to me why the commune, rightly or wrongly, tried to keep hold of each allotment, each plot of land.

(A. G. Kaznacheev, 'Mezhdu strokami odnogo formulyarnogo spiska', *Russkaya Starina*, vol. 32 (1881) pp. 836–7)

3.8 THE IMPACT OF EMANCIPATION

The authors of these extracts, both landowners themselves, argue that emancipation by itself did nothing to improve the condition of the Russian peasant; on the contrary, they both describe a decline in the fortunes of Russian agriculture after 1861.

* * *

The Peasantry

The well-being of the peasantry temporarily improved in the first years after Emancipation, but then declined. The reasons for this were partly external and partly domestic. The former included bad harvests and the reduction in winter earnings as a result of the building of the railways. Before this, the peasants from our area had taken grain to Morshansk from not just the local land, but also from distant districts. This provided them with money and the chance to keep a reasonable number of horses. This source of income was significantly reduced with the opening of the railway. In winter there was now almost no such work. The most important internal reasons had an even stronger effect: impoverishment, family divisions, ruinous drunkenness and an incapability to keep hold of money. Nothing can be done about the family divisions. When women in a family argue, the men – willingly or not – have to split up the family, although this leads to poverty and with Emancipation the power of the women grew. . . . The pub is, if possible, an even worse evil. We fought long against the existence of the local one and eventually persuaded the peasants to close it . . . there was an end to the disgraceful communal meetings outside the pub, which were usually accompanied by three days of drunkenness. But who can prevent the peasant, if he has a spare copper, from drinking it away at a neighbouring market? . . .

The peasant's money does not just go on drink; he simply is incapable of saving. A century of serfdom, in conjunction with the happy-go-lucky Russian nature, has led to a situation where, like his master, whatever money a peasant has slips through this fingers. As a result of this we frequently come across examples of a peasant bringing his money to be looked after, or else he himself buys something unnecessary so that the money does not go on anything else. The peasant has no habit of saving and where no such habit is ingrained, then the standard of living inevitably falls. The population is growing and the amount of land for each will decrease, and is besides becoming exhausted, and the capital which should make up this deficiency is not increasing. What can come out of this but general impoverishment? . . .

As long as the peasants are not accustomed to thinking that they themselves should secure their own fate and that of their children, no sensible economic habits can be established. Only a class of individual landowners or tenant-capitalists, and not communal landholders, can be a strong village class, able to act as a source of enrichment to itself and to the country. The Emancipation was unable to solve this question; it could not accomplish two fundamental revolutions in the fate of the rural classes at once. But it did open the way to individual landownership and gave each peasant the right to buy his own allotment. The task of later legislation is to complete what has been begun and to consolidate the allotments on existing families, forbidding their transfer to new individuals. Only thus can we instil in the peasant class a concept of property, which is at the basis of all civil life. But, nothing like this has been done.

(B. N. Chicherin, *Vospominaniya. Zemstvo i Moskovskaya Duma* (Moscow, 1934) pp. 60–2

Emancipation and Agriculture

Twelve years has passed since Emancipation and for the majority the system of agriculture remains just the same. As before, they grow rye and when the peasant has a decent harvest, it has no value and nobody buys it; they grow oats, which do very badly here; they work the fields as before, hiring peasants complete with horses and tools; they mow the same poor little meadows, they keep cattle just for the manure, feed them badly and think the cattle are in good condition if they don't need to be hoisted up after the winter. The system of agriculture has not changed, everything carries on as it was before the Emancipation, under serfdom. The only differences are that the quantity of plough-land has been reduced by more than half, that cultivation is carried on even less well than before, the amount of fodder has decreased, because the meadows are not kept in good condition, are not being drained and have become overgrown; and cattle-rearing has sharply declined. When I first investigated the conditions of the surrounding farms, it became even clearer to me that it was impossible to farm like this, for I saw that in the space of twelve years most farms had already succeeded in falling into a sad state, many were completely neglected, and most landowners had got rid of their estates and gone to work for the government. In reality, going around the district and seeing decay and destruction everywhere, one might think that there had been a war here, some invasion by an enemy, but it was clear that the destruction was not violent, but gradual, that everything was decaying by itself, and was dying from exhaustion. Under serfdom we did nothing about agriculture and therefore even now little remains from that period. Its traces are still visible, however, because one still see the birch groves which were always planted near landowners' estates, and the broken dams which created ponds in the streams below the big house to give a view, for fish or for watering the animals.

(A. N. Engelgardt, *Iz derevni. 12 pisem, 1872–87* (Moscow, 1960) pp. 123–5)

Peasant Arrears in Redemption Payments and Taxes for the Fifty Provinces of European Russia, 1876–80

Groups of provinces	Sums due (rubles 000s)	Arrears (rubles 000s)	Arrears as % of sum due
Northern	8 527	3 968	46
Baltic	1 686	161	10
North Western	11 999	2 646	22
South Western	12 928	1 125	9
Industrial	24 344	5 402	22
Central Black Earth	40 574	6 443	15
Eastern	22 220	7 975	36
Southern	9 329	3 128	33
Ukraine	11 408	1 021	9
Total	143 015	31 869	22

Source: *Issledovanie ekonomicheskogo polozheniya Tsentralno-chernozemnykh guberniy* (Moscow, 1901) p. 6

3.9 RURAL MEDICINE

Living conditions for the Russian country dweller were difficult. Engelgardt, a Smolensk landowner, makes no bones about the problems of getting medical attention.

* * *

As regards medical treatment in the country, it is not just the peasant but also the less well-off landowner who is very badly served in case of illness. There is a doctor in the town, thirty versts away. If you fall ill, you must send to the town. This needs a troika or at least a pair of horses with a proper carriage and a coachman. The doctor is brought; a visit will cost 15 roubles. . . . The doctor must be taken back to the town and medicine must be brought. Reckon this up and how much will it all cost, but most important, one must have a carriage, horses and coachmen. And of course if the illness is serious, one visit will not suffice. It is obvious that the doctor is only available to rich landowners, who live the old, noble life, who have carriages, coachmen, etc., people who still maintain the old sort of establishment, people who have hung on to money or redemption bonds, people who still own forests, and still have a lot of land which they can farm, or people who, whilst living in the country, have some sort of salaried position. Less well-off landowners, for example, those who had 300 mortgaged peasants, tenants of small estates, stewards who run separate farms, priests, the proprietors of coaching inns and similar people, well-off by comparison with the peasantry, are unable to send to the town for a doctor. For the most part they make use of good, that is locally-known, unqualified doctors, drawn mainly from household servants who had run pharmacies and hospitals for rich landowners and serfdom. However these unqualified doctors are also out of the reach of the mass of our poor peasants, because they must be paid three roubles per visit and extra for medicine, making five roubles in all. Only very well-off peasants make use of these doctors. Then there is the second rank of unqualified doctors who use self-taught and every simple remedies – old men and women mainly. . . .
All that remains is a doctor come upon by chance: some quack or a medical student, visiting his relations etc. If a peasant falls ill, he stays on his feet and tries to get over it whilst he still has strength. When he has no strength left, he goes to bed. If he has some money, he sends for an unqualified doctor or some old man, and if not he simply lies there or else sends to ask for something from one of the landowners who has medicine. Some lie in bed and recover. Others die. The worst is that, after they have laid in bed and recovered, they fall ill again and rarely manage to get up a second time. This is because they are not properly recovered before they begin to work again, they catch cold (I would note, in passing, that the peasants do not have proper toilets and even very ill peasants have to walk, crawl or be carried out into the yard, no matter what the weather) and, most important, they do not get good or tolerable food of any sort.

(A. N. Engelgardt, *Iz derevni. 12 pisem, 1872–87* (Moscow, 1960) pp. 60–1)

3.10 PEASANT LIFE

Diet

Food for the peasant was simple and not always plentiful, as this description of the diet in Ryazan makes clear.

* * *

The rye-bread is noted for its high quality, but sometimes because of careless kneading and baking, it turns out indigestible; for holidays they bake pies and flat cakes from a mixture of rye and wheat flour. Cabbage soup, both on fast days and the other times, is made just from sauerkraut, with the difference that on ordinary days they sometimes add some pork fat, sour cream or plain milk. There is little notion of adding flour, butter or groats to the soup and it therefore turns out thin and unappetising and completely dark in colour. Porridge is made from buckwheat, wheat and millet, with milk and vegetable oil or with crushed hemp seeds during fasts; eating porridge is seen as a mark of being quite well-off. As regards meat, this is a great rarity on the peasant table and appears only on great holidays. Fish is eaten even less in places distant from rivers; and it is widely eaten only in the last days before Lent, on St Nicholas Day in the winter, and the Annunciation. Fish can be salted, like the different types of sturgeon or fresh, the latter being the types of small fish which are abundant in the lakes and rivers of our province: roach, perch, types of carp, and occasionally pike and bream. Vegetables are rare. The potato, which can serve as a very nourishing and tasty addition to the peasant diet, is still not generally used. . . . Peas are even less common as are beetroot and cucumbers; only cabbage is widely-used, as well as onions and radishes on fast days. The peasants hardly know any other vegetables; fruit is sold, but in northern districts they know nothing about it. Mushrooms are eaten a lot and the peasants would find it difficult to manage without them on fast days; but berries are only collected for sale. . . .

Dairy products are little used; milk and sour cream are utilised more as additions to cabbage soup and porridge. Sour milk is sometimes drunk, but more often cottage cheese is made from it, and this usually appears on the table, like fried eggs, at holidays. The peasants do not know other methods of cooking and even pancakes are an exceptional item; they are usually eaten on Shrove Tuesday and sometimes on other occasions. On great holidays and especially at Shrovetide, the quantity of food eaten, it must be said, is enormous. . . . But there are times in the year when the opposite is true and the peasants, even those whose farming is in good order, starve. The hungriest time for the people is undoubtedly the fast of St Peter (May 31–June 29); vegetables are then out of season and the cabbage which has been put aside is coming to an end, so that the usual food at this time is kvas with spring onions and cucumbers, if they are ripe. On top of all this the peasants often even have a shortage of bread then, and so are forced to take out loans or to eat rye which is unripe.

In general, peasant food is fresh and therefore healthy; it is adequately filling, but does not have a corresponding nutritional value, because almost all of it comes from the vegetable kingdom; this is also the main reason for the rapid development of scrofulous diseases. Apart from this, there are unhappy examples of poisoning and even death arising from eating salted fish . . . both because of the poor quality of the fish itself, as well as the fact that the ordinary people usually eat it raw.

The meagreness and simplicity of the peasant diet demonstrates mainly the inadequate resources which the peasants have at their disposal. They do not use cattle or poultry for food, even if they do have surplus, believing them to be vital for their farming or else as saleable to earn money. Substantial consumption of meat would be more in line with a northern climate, especially for the young, but this is not taken into consideration. As soon as children are taken from the breast, they begin to eat the same as the adults do, and are not given milk products even during fasts. . . .

Fatal incidents arising from a passion for drink are diminishing, partly because of the high price of drink and partly because the ordinary people are developing a predilection for tea. This is much drunk in the most industrialised settlements along the river Oka and on the great post roads, which contain the most prosperous section of the peasantry.

(*Materialy dlya geografii i statistiki Rossii, sobrannye ofitserami general-nogo shtaba*, Ryazanskya Guberniya (St Petersburg, 1860) pp. 397–400)

Drinking

Vodka and the village tavern were integral parts of the peasant's life.

* * *

Everyone who lives permanently in the country must be aware of the importance and popularity which the shopkeeper with his drinking establishment has amongst the local inhabitants. Everybody knows that the drinking house, to begin with, is a substitute in our villages for the non-existent schools, since the entire rural population, from the teenagers who get their first youthful impressions there, to the old men, who learn ridiculous stories and dark rumours there, pass through it. Whilst the drinking house replaces the school, at the same time it is an institution, if not the same as the volost administration, then close to it – since any event and any deal which goes on in the village is inevitably talked about there. If the peasants change their horses, if some work is to be taken on, if a new member is to be accepted into the commune, how somebody's lost plough turned up with some other villager – all these different matters somehow or other end up in the drinking-house, presided over by the landlord who is thus privy to all the petty details of public interest. In addition to this, most of the villagers, from the authorities down to the old and sick . . . are in debt to the landlord. Most of the landlord's business is done on credit, or by the peasants pawning possessions and farm produce, so there can be not the slightest doubt that the landlord and his drinking establishment are safe and insured against any sort of action. Each of the inhabitants and the village authorities sees it not just as their duty to keep in with the landlord . . . but in case of necessity even to protect him themselves.

A trading settlement, some twelve versts from my office, on the post road was my main source of experience of drinking houses and their landlords; it had some 800 inhabitants and twelve to fourteen obviously flourishing drinking establishments.

(V. N. Nazarev, 'Sovremennaya glush', *Vestnik Evropy*, vol. 34 (1871) pp. 135–6)

Literacy of the Rural Population of Selected Provinces in the First Half of the 1880s

Province	% literate
St Petersburg	19.7
Vyatka	10.3
Moscow	20.7
Kharkov	6.2
Kherson	6.2
Average of 21 Provinces	10.8

Source: A. G. Rashin, *Naselenie Rossii za 100 let* (Moscow, 1956) pp. 291

4 Urban Growth

4.1 SOME BASIC STATISTICS

Population

During this period the urban population of the Empire remained almost constant at about ten per cent of the total.

Territory	1863	1885
European Russia	61 175 900	81 725 200
Caucasus	4 157 900	7 284 500
Siberia	3 141 200	4 313 700
Steppe Region	1 484 500	1 588 500
Central Asia	–	3 738 600
Total (excluding Poland and Finland)	69 959 500	98 650 500

Source: A. G. Rashin, *Naselenie Rossii za 100 let* (Moscow, 1956), p. 26.

The Development of Heavy Industry

Year	Pig-iron smelted	Production of iron and steel	Production of coal	Production of oil
1861	18.9	11.3	20.4	–
1866	17.5	10.7	27.9	0.9
1871	20.7	14.9	50.5	3.1
1875	24.9	18.1	103.8	10.5
1881	27.4	34.6	213.3	40.0

Note: All figures are in millions of puds (1 pud = 16.3 kg).
Source: *Khrestomatiya po istorii SSSR 1861–1917* (Moscow, 1970) pp. 88–9.

Railway Growth

Year	Length of railways (km)	No. of railway employees
1861	1 404	11 100
1866	3 342	28 100
1871	9 624	70 100
1875	16 628	140 500
1881	19 957	191 300

Source: V. A. Vdovin, *Sbornik dokumentov po istorii SSSR* (Moscow, 1965) p. 173.

Comparative industrial production

Year	Germany	Great Britain	France	Russia	USA	Whole world
1860	14	34	26	8	8	14
1870	18	44	34	13	11	19
1880	25	53	43	17	17	26
1890	40	62	56	27	39	43
1900	65	79	66	61	54	60

Note: This index takes 1913 as 100.
Source: P. A. Khromov, *Ekonomicheskoe razvitie Rossii* (Moscow, 1967) p. 284.

4.2 A WORKING CLASS EMERGES

Social Origins

The Russian working class had strong rural ties, as this report of 1871 by the Moscow police chief makes clear.

* * *

At the present time cases of misunderstandings between factory workers and their employers are rising. . . .

It must be noted that we do not really have a proper factory working class and that the majority of factory workers are peasants, not then needed for agricultural work. This category of people is free from agricultural work only during the late autumn, winter and early spring, and it thus becomes clear why, every summer, when labour is especially valuable in the fields and healthy fresh air makes country life attractive, the workers almost everywhere show a strong propensity, using various excuses, to quit factories and enterprises. Formerly they were restrained by the fear of rapid on-the-spot investigation and police reprisals and the fact that they would rapidly and energetically be sent back to the factory which they had left, once the factory-owner had notified the police.

(A. M. Pankratova (ed.), *Rabochee dvizhenie v Rossii v 19 veke. Sbornik dokumentov i materialov*, vol. 2, 1861–1884, pt. 1, 1861–1874 (Moscow 1950) pp. 543–4)

Distribution of Workers in Different Forms of Employment

	Groups	No. of persons in 1860
I.	Industrial Workers	
	(a) In factories and mines	860 000
	(b) Employed in their own homes, in rural or urban industry not under (a)	800 000
	Total industrial	1 660 000
II.	Employed in building	350 000
III.	Transport	
	(a) Water	500 000
	(b) Railways	11 000
	Total transport (approx.)	511 000
IV.	Agricultural wage-earners	700 000
V.	Other persons working for wages (urban unskilled and day labourers, and apprentices in commerce, restaurants, and domestic service)	800 000
	Total non-industrial eage-earners (total II–V)	2 361 000
	Overall total	4 021 000

Source: O. Crisp, 'Labour and industrialisation in Russia', in *The Cambridge Economic History of Europe*, vol. 7, pt. 2 (Cambridge, 1978) p. 332.

4.3 WORKING CONDITIONS

Factory Life

Life was difficult for the industrial worker as this report by a factory inspector for the province of Moscow in 1882 makes clear.

* * *

Extreme arbitrariness in the imposition of fines and the resulting unregulated levels of wages has reached unbelievable proportions in some factories: in two establishments in Podolsky district, for example, ... there is a ten-ruble deduction for leaving the factory before the term of employment is up; but it is not just applied if a worker quits early, for the administration itself imposes this heavy fine on each worker who for any reason wants to leave the factory. . . . Fines can be imposed for any number of reasons and it is therefore very easy for a worker to be subject to such a deduction. Thus, for example, a one-ruble fine is imposed on workers who visit the factory office not singly, but in a group, and for a second offence the worker is dismissed – after having paid this deduction. Moreover, in one factory the attitude evidently remains that workers should be treated as serfs; wages are only paid twice a year, but even then only as much as is necessary for the worker to pay his taxes (other needs are catered for by the factory shop). Moreover, wages are not paid directly to the worker but are sent by post to his village elder or volost administration. Workers thus remain without cash for the whole year, and the substantial fines owing to the factory are recorded in their pay books, and the deductions will be made in the annual calculations at the end of each year. . . .

Of the 181 industrial enterprises which I have inspected, it appears that correct wages are being paid in only 71 factories. . . .

There are thus more than 100 factories, that is the overwhelming majority, in which wages are completely unregulated and depend completely on the whim and pocket of the boss; custom provides only for a minimum or maximum number of times during the year when things are reckoned up, that is when the debts of master and worker to each other are totted up, but payment does not always coincide with this. . . .

In Moscow and its surroundings, factory shops are a rarity and workers buy their supplies from private shops; but as, for the most part, the worker cannot obtain individual credit to any great extent, the boss or the factory administration usually indicates to the workers at which butchers and grocers they could obtain their goods by credit under the guarantee of the factory. As I discovered after questioning, the owners of many factories got a cut from the shopkeepers and canteen owners of 5–10 kopeks in the ruble. Outside Moscow and its immediate surroundings, and even in populated areas which do have shops, for example, district towns, factories as a general rule have their own shops, although this is not strictly necessary.... In places far distant from Moscow and from settlements in general, factory shops are a definite necessity, but even then, despite their being necessary for the very existence of the factory some bosses, regrettably, make too extensive use of the natural commercial monopoly in such cases and use substantial price increases as a new and significant source of income, thus further reducing the workers' wages, which, even without this, are comparatively meagre. . . .

Sleeping accommodation in Moscow factories is of two types – communal dormitories and barracks of small individual rooms. In a few comparatively small factories there are exclusively dormitories, but most factories have both types of accommodation.... Single workers sleep in dormitories, as do the married if there is a shortage of space. The separate rooms accommodate married workers; in a significant number of factories this division is not strictly observed and if in some establishments the single man and woman are separated, as are the married workers, in most there is an indifferent mixture of ages and sexes.... The furniture in the sleeping accommodation is the same everywhere, whether in dormitories or individual rooms: as a general rule there are several rows of bare plank beds and, infrequently, iron bedsteads.... The worker has to provide his own bedding and most of them sleep on their own overcoat or tunic....

But in most factories and for most workers, almost as a rule, no special sleeping accommodation is provided. This applies to all hand-weavers, no matter what they work with, cotton, wool or silk.... Weavers have to sleep on their looms.... Only in a few weaving mills is sleeping accommodation provided and there it is mostly not for the weavers, but for the other workers. The same can be said for textile printers and engravers who almost always sleep on the benches where they work. This is especially harmful for the printers, since the building where they work always has a suffocating atmosphere which is full of sometimes poisonous paint. Joiners too in general sleep on the benches where they work and for some of them there is no bed at all....

The sanitary condition of workshops is much the same as that of living accommodation, that is for the most part unsatisfactory. . . . In confectionery factory number 11, the workshops are extremely dark and dirty: most of the chocolate section is located in an extremely dark basement where all the dirt from the yard penetrates. . . . In cloth factory number 48, as in many other such factories, the air in the dyeshop was so full of steam that nothing was visible and I walked through the dye shop by touch, as if blind-fold; there was evidently no sort of ventilation.

(I. I. Yanzhul, *Fabrichniy byt Moskovskoy gubernii* (St Petersburg, 1884) pp. 81–123)

Child Labour in St Petersburg

The 1869 census of St Petersburg provides the data for this survey of the use of child labour.

* * *

In the absence of any legally-regulated minimum age for employment the hard path of work begins early for the Russian. Figures from Petersburg show that there are 656 children under 10 (427 boys and 229 girls) working and this makes up almost 1 per cent of children of this age. The Petersburg figures however present a better picture than elsewhere in Russia, either because the situation really is better there, or else because employers overstate the age of their child employees. We have always been convinced that the percentage of children working in the factories and workers of the industrial region in Russia is higher than that in Petersburg and in reality the figures collected by the Russian Technical Society confirm this impression. The number of working children increases with age: in the 11–15 age group the figure reaches 21 795 (18 056 boys and 3 739 girls) or 52 per cent of all children, and if we exclude those in private boarding schools, most of whom are not from Petersburg families, this figure rises to 61 per cent. Children under 15 make up 6.9 per cent of the independent male population and 3.6 per cent of the female. . . .

Child labour is used most in manufacturing industry, where boys under 15 comprise 10.6 per cent and girls 7.1 per cent of the work force, in trade where the figures are 10.3 per cent and 0.8 per cent; transport – 4.8 per cent and 0.2 per cent and finally, personal servants – 1.8 per cent and 2.6 per cent.

Closer analysis of the figures reveals that most children are part-apprentice, part-worker in various small workshops, rather than in large factories. This does not, however, diminish the significance of the figures since the question remains as to whether, in our entrepreneurial system, work in a small workshop or in a large factory leads to greater physical exhaustion and moral corruption. Information collected by the Russian Technical Society shows that children who work in factories live mostly with their parents and many of them go to school; but most children apprenticed to a small workshop are dumped in the capital by parents who live far away, and come under the dubious educational influence of the workshop at an early age. Cases of suicide due to cruel treatment by masters of their apprentices are common in Petersburg life.

(Yu. Yanson, 'Naselenie Peterburga i ego ekonomicheskiy i sotsialnyy sostav po perepisi 1869 goda', *Vestnik Evropy*, vol. 56 (1875) pp. 61–3)

4.4 URBAN CHANGE

A Vanished Moscow

Chicherin's lament for the passing of noble Moscow describes the city as he saw it at the end of the 1870s.

* * *

Moscow at the time we moved there was no longer the Moscow of the 1840s and '50s. The gentry city had turned into an industrial centre. In the old days it had fully deserved to be called the heart of Russia. From all over Russia the most prosperous representatives of the landed class had assembled here and it was they who dominated the wide expanses of our country. Here, in an independent environment, far from the corrupt influence of the court, the feelings and thoughts of the best section of the Russian gentry, its fervent patriotism and its enlightened aims have been displayed. Educated and gifted people, full of character and an adornment to society came to the fore here. But now Moscow had ceased to be a meeting place for the gentry. Landowners of the middle rank, occupied with economic and social matters, remained in the country; the more prosperous used the convenience of the railways and freedom of travel to live abroad. In the capital, more than in the provinces, there was a feeling of improverishment. The English Club had to go looking for members and became a refuge of unbearable tedium. Social life too declined; there were none of those endless celebrations I had witnessed in my youth. Balls became a rarity; they were primarily populated by debutantes who were having difficulty finding a fiancé. Escorts were required not just at university, but even at school. The nobles' houses were, one after the other, acquired by rich merchants who came to the fore in place of the shattered aristocratic class. But this was a poor exchange. The merchants were on a par with the old nobility neither in education, nor in the refinement of their morals, nor in the level of their aims and interests. One society had gone before another had been able to take shape.

(B. N. Chicherin, *Vospominaniya. Zemstva i Moskovskaya Duma* (Moscow, 1934) p. 66)

Poverty

A different perception of Moscow is provided by the great novelist Leo Tolstoy in an account which is contemporary with that of Chicherin.

* * *

I had a desire to see all this poverty which I had heard about. . . .

And so on a freezing and windy December day I set off towards the centre of this urban poverty, the Khitrov market. This was an ordinary working day, around four in the afternoon. As I got close to the market I began to notice more and more people in clothes which were old and obviously not their own, and in even stranger footwear, people with that special unhealthy colour to their faces and, most important, none of them took any interest in their surroundings. . . . They were all going in the same direction. Although I did not know the way I had no need to ask, but followed them into the market where there were the same sort of women in ragged coats, jackets and footwear and, despite their abnormal clothing, young and old sat about easily, sold things, walked about and cursed. . . . The further I walked, the more people there were going in the same direction. Going through the market and along the street I caught up with two women: one old and the other young. They were dressed in some ragged, grey garments and were talking as they walked along.

After each necessary word they inserted one or two unnecessary and most improper words. They were not drunk, but concerned about something and men near them did not pay the slightest attention to what was for me a strange way of talking. In this area evidently everybody spoke like this. On the left were the private doss-houses, and some went into them, others continuing on further. Going uphill we arrived at a big building on a corner. Most of the people who were with me stopped here. ... This was the Lyapinsky free doss-house and a crowd of people were waiting to be let in to spend the night there. At five o'clock the doors would open and they would be admitted. Nearly all the people I had been following had come here. ...

Nearest to me was a peasant with a swollen face and a red beard, wearing only a torn jacket and worn galoshes on his bare feet. It was eight degrees below freezing. ... I asked him where he was from: he answered willingly and began to talk and others gathered around. He was from Smolensk and had come to look for work so that he could buy food and pay his taxes. ... He told me of his adventures. His story was the same as almost all the others: he had been a worker but the job had come to an end and his money and identity card had been stolen in the doss-house. Now he could not leave Moscow. He told us how he spent his days trying to keep warm in taverns ... sometimes he was given food, sometimes he was chased out; he spent the night here free in the Lyapinsky doss-house. All he was waiting for was for the police to come around: as he had no identity card he would be arrested and then sent back to his village. ... 'They say the police will come around on Thursday, then I'll be caught. I've only got to manage till Thursday'. (For him prison ... was the promised land). ... One of the men asked for money and I gave him some. A second and a third did so and a crowd surrounded me. There was confusion and pushing. ...

The doss-house was enormous. It comprised four sections: the upper storeys housed the men, the lower the women. I went first into the women's section; a huge room filled with bunks similar to those in third-class railway carriages. The bunks were two-storey and strange, ragged women, young and old, came in and occupied the places. ... Some of the elderly women crossed themselves and prayed for those who had set up this shelter. I went upstairs to where the men were arranging themselves and I saw one of those to whom I had given money, but I felt ashamed when I caught sight of him and hurried out of the room. And with a feeling that I had committed a dreadful offence I left the building and walked home. At home I walked up a carpeted staircase ... and when I had taken my fur coat off, I sat down to a five-course dinner served by two waiters in tails, white tie and white gloves.

(L. N. Tolstoy, 'Tak chto zhe nam delat?', in *Sobranie Sochineniy*, vol. 16 (Moscow, 1964) pp. 165–8)

St Petersburg: Population and Social Structure

Based on the 1869 census, this extract gives a detailed account of the social and economic composition of the population of Russia's capital city.

* * *

The 1869 census gave the following figures for population [of St Petersburg]: 377 380 men and 289 827 women, making 667 207 in total. ... From the economic and social point of view, the following main groups can be identified:
1. Those with an earned income or who have their own means of support;
2. Those dependent on others – children, old people, prisoners, those living on charity etc.;
3. Those without definite means of support – and who, for the most part, have no means of support: the so-called 'dangerous classes', including prostitutes.

Our 'dangerous class' is comprised of 788 males and 1557 women without definite means of support, 1815 prostitutes working in brothels and individually and 162 brothel-keepers. This makes a total of 788 men and 3534 women, 4322 in all (0.6 per cent of the population), but this number is undoubtedly much greater in reality, especially the number of women, since the 1815 registered prostitutes are hardly one-third or one-quarter of the total for whom this is the main or a subsidiary occupation, but who also work as seamstresses, housemaids, factory workers, etc.

The second group includes:

	Males	*Females*
Teachers in private boarding schools	6 748	5 098
Teachers living away from their parents	4 846	218
Persons living in almshouses	1 094	5 348
Persons living on benefits from charitable institutions and private individuals	817	4 318
Persons ill in hospital	3 700	2 268
Prisoners	1 893	201
Persons receiving income from a self-employed head of a family	59 783	145 693
Total:	78 881	163 144
Grand total:	242 025	

Finally, the first group is comprised of 294 579 men and 121 330 women, a total of 415 909 people who live on income from property or who work in the widest sense of the word. . . .

The majority of the independent population falls into four groups:
1. Persons with an unearned income;
2. White-collar workers;
3. Industrial workers;
4. Servants . . .

The numbers of those living on an unearned income is as follows:

	Males	Females
Property owners	2 111	2 911
Pensioners	3 525	6 108
Persons living on capital	2 122	4 083

This makes a total of 7758 men and 13 092 women, 20 850 in all, which comprises 3.1% of the (settled) population. . . .

The white-collar workers are composed of the most varied elements. They include officials, lawyers, scientists, writers, teachers, doctors, clergy, etc. as follows:

	Males	Females	Percentage of population
Army officers	5 315		
Naval officers	1 070		
Lower ranks of both services	31 626		
Total: =	38 010		5.7
Officials of the civil administration and public service	13 673	26	2
Royal court officials	2 770	108	0.4
Lawyers, etc.	2 326	Nil	0.3
Medical personnel	2 350	2 090	0.7
Teachers	1 449	2 657	0.6
Persons engaged in science, literature, art	2 663	845	0.5
Clergy and church employees	1 520	323	0.3
Total:	65 161	6 049	
Grand total:		71 210	10.7

These groups make up 17.1% of the independent population. . . .
(Yu. Yanson, 'Naselenie Peterburga i ego ekonomicheskiy i sotsialnyy sostav po perepisi 1869 goda', *Vestnik Evropy*, vol. 555 (1875) pp. 610–17)

Literacy of the Urban Population

The compiler of this table estimates that slightly more than one-third of the total urban population of Russia in the early 1870s was literate.

Town	Year of census	% literate		
		Men	Women	Overall
St Petersburg	1869	62.0	46.4	55.6
Kiev	1874	52.9	33.2	44.3
Moscow	1871	49.5	34.1	43.2
Kharkov	1879	47.3	31.3	40.0
Kazan	1863	39.0	30.6	35.4
Odessa	1873	35.7	22.4	30.9

Source: A. G. Rashin, *Naselenie Rossii za 100 let* (Moscow, 1957) pp. 295–6.

The Municipal Statute, 16 June 1870

1. The municipal public administration directs the municipal economy and provides public services while the provincial governor supervises the lawful execution of these matters. . . .
2. The jurisdiction of the municipal public administration includes:
    (a) The organisation of the administration and the municipal economy. . . .
    (b) The provision of outdoor public services in the city, namely . . . the building and maintenance of roads, . . . municipal gardens . . . bridges . . . water supply and the lighting of the town.
    (c) The welfare of the city inhabitants: the provision of public food supply, the organisation of markets and bazaars; . . . the maintenance of public health, the adoption of preventative

measures against fires and other disasters, and protection against losses incurred through them; the safeguarding and development of local trade and industry, the organisation of port facilities, stock exchanges and credit institutions. . . .

(d) The organisation and management, at the expense of the city, of charitable institutions and hospitals; . . . participation in public education . . . and likewise the organisation of theatres, libraries, museums and other similar institutions.

(e) The presentation to the government of information and opinions on subjects relating to local needs and the well-being of the city. . . .

11. A Provincial Board for Municipal Affairs is to be set up in each province to supervise the activities of the municipal public administration. It is to be under the chairmanship of the governor and will include the senior provincial officials, the chairman of the provincial zemstvo executive board and the mayor of the provincial capital. . . .

16. Municipal electoral assemblies take place every four years to elect members to the municipal council. . . .

17. Every resident of the city, whatever his legal status, has the right to vote to elect council members: 1) if he is a Russian subject; 2) if he is at least twenty five years of age; 3) if, these conditions being met, he owns property within the city that is liable to taxation by the city, or has a commercial or industrial establishment under a merchant's licence or, having lived in the city for two years, is a taxpayer on merchants' licences. . . .

24. Three electoral assemblies are formed in each city from those inhabitants who have the right to vote in elections in order to elect duma members . . . and each of these elects one-third of the total number of members. . . . The first category is composed of those electors who have the highest assessments for city taxation and who together pay one-third of the total taxes paid by all electors; the second category is made up of the electors with the next highest taxation assessments who likewise together pay one-third of all taxes; the third category includes all remaining electors. . . .

48. The municipal council is composed of members elected for four years, under the chairmanship of the city mayor. . . . In cities where the number of electors is less than 300, the city council shall have 30 members. For each additional 150 electors, the council shall include six more members, up to a maximum of seventy.

70. The municipal executive board is chaired by the city mayor. . . .

82. The posts of city mayor, members of the municipal executive board, and council secretary are filled through election by the municipal council. . . .
92. Persons elected to the post of mayor of provincial capitals are confirmed in office by the Minister of Internal Affairs and in other cities by the provincial governor. . . .
150. Complaints against unlawful decisions of the municipal council are brought before the provincial governor who transmits them to the Provincial Board for Municipal Affairs for a decision. Complaints against decisions of this Board are brought before the Senate.

(*PSZ,* 2nd series, vol. 45m pt. 1, no. 49498)

5 Society and the Regime

5.1 THE SOCIAL ELITE

Tyutcheva, a member of the suite of the Empresses of both Nicholas I and Alexander II, saw the Slavophiles as the only serious members of the Russian social élite. She herself was married to Ivan Aksakov, a leading Slavophile author, and she acted as the unofficial representative of Slavophile and Panslav opinions at the imperial court.

* * *

We have two types of cultured people. There are those who read foreign newspapers and French novels, or else read nothing at all. They go to a ball or a reception every night and, dutifully every winter, get carried away by the prima donna or tenor of the Italian opera. They go to Germany on the first boat in the spring to take the waters and, at last, find their equilibrium in Paris. The second type of people are those who only go to balls or receptions if it is absolutely necessary. They read Russian journals and write notes in Russian which will never be published. They discuss the emancipation of the serfs and the freedom of the press from all angles. From time to time they travel to their estates and they hold the company of women in contempt. These men are usually called Slavophiles, but this term covers endless shades of opinion.... The people who belong to the first category, on the other hand, are easy to define as a whole: they are harmless and do not arouse any displeasure on the part of the chief of the secret police, Prince Dolgorukiy, himself a harmless and well-intentioned man.

(A. F. Tyutcheva, *Pri dvore dvukh imperatorov. Vospominaniya, Dnevnik, 1853–82* (Moscow, 1928–9) pt 2, pp. 142–3

5.2 HERZEN ON RUSSIA AND EUROPE

The debate about the relationship between Russia and Europe continued during the 1850s. Alexander Herzen who lived in emigration from 1847 until his death in 1870, here, in a letter written to the novelist Turgenev in 1857, gives his views.

* * *

You love European ideas – as I do – these are the ideas of the whole of history. . . . Without them we would fall into Asiatic quietism, into African inertia. With them, and only with them, can Russia come into that great inheritance which falls to her. . . .

I do not consider the question about the future of Europe to be finally decided, but . . . being prejudiced in favour of the West, rather than against it, and having studied it for ten years not from theories and books, but in the clubs and the streets, in the focus of its entire political and social life, I must say that I see no imminent or good way out. On the one hand there is the unhealthy and one-sided development of industry, the concentration of all wealth – moral and material – in the hands of the middle class, the fact that the middle class has gained control of the church and the government, of machines and schools, that the troops are obedient to it and the judges decide in its favour; on the other hand, there is the lack of development of the masses, the immaturity and weakness of the revolutionary party. I do not foresee the rapid fall of the petty bourgeoisie and the removal of the old state structure without the most terrible and bloody struggle. . . .

But outside Europe there are only two energetic regions – America and Russia. . . .

The growth of Russia has been impressive, but it is far from finished, and Russia has hardly reached her natural limits. This is clear, beyond geographical considerations, from the endless arrogance of the government, from its permanent aim of seizing some small piece of territory. But Russia's expansion is proceeding differently to that of America; she is not a colony, not a movement of peoples, not an invasion, but a distinctive world, moving in all directions and firmly occupying its own land. . . .

Russia appears as an absolutely special world, with its *own* natural way of life, its *own* physiological character – not European not Asiatic, but Slavonic. She participates in the fate of Europe, but without its historical traditions, free from its obligations to the past. . . . Nowhere do we have those deeply ingrained prejudices which in Western man have, like paralysis, taken over half of his organs. At the basis of Russian popular life lies the village commune with its division of fields, its communist ownership of land and elected administration. . . . This is all in a depressed and distorted condition, but it is still alive and has survived worse times. . . .

The Russian state has been consolidated by terrible means: it has driven the Russian people to establish an enormous empire through slavery, flogging and executions. . . . It is pointless to be angry at the past. . . . On our expanding, simple soil there is nothing but the conservative – the village commune – that is worth preserving. . . .

The state and serfdom have by themselves preserved our ancestral commune. . . . Communal ownership of land, the commune and elections comprise the soil from which a new social life can develop, which, like our black earth, is almost non-existent in Europe. . . .

We do not seek help from the government but desire only that it does not interfere. The West, on the contrary, has so many riches that it is unable to use them. . . . It is stingy with them and conservative, like any property owner. We have nothing to look after. Of course, our poverty does not by itself give us the right to a different future, and long slavery does not give us the right to freedom; but just here, moving from opposed premises to opposed aims, I meet with some of the ideas of the Slavophiles.

I believe in the ability of the Russian people. I see from the winter shoots what sort of harvest there can be. I see in the poor and oppressed phenomena of the Russian people's life a means unrecognised by it to achieve that social ideal which European thought has already consciously reached.

(A. I. Herzen, 'Eshche variatsiya na staruyu temu', *Sobranie sochineniy v tridtsati tomakh*, vol. 12 (Moscow, 1957) pp. 425–31)

5.3 'YOUNG RUSSIA'

This violent appeal was produced in 1862, whilst the author, P. G. Zaichnevsky, was in prison.

* * *

Russia is entering the revolutionary period of its existence. If you trace the life of all social groups you will see that society is now becoming divided into two sections with diametrically opposed interests and, consequently, hostile to each other.

From below a dull and suppressed rumbling is heard from the people, a people repressed and robbed by everybody who has even a little power in their hands. . . .

Above, there stands a small group of satisfied and happy people. These are the landowners. . . . At their head is the Tsar. He could not exist without them, nor they without him. If one falls, the other is destroyed as well. . . .

The way out of this oppressive and terrifying situation which is destroying contemporary man and which he wastes his best strengths struggling with – the only way out is revolution, bloody and inexorable, revolution which will radically change all the foundations of contemporary society with exception and destroy the supporters of the present order.

We are not afraid of it, although we know that rivers of blood will flow, that innocent victims will perhaps die; we foresee all this, and all the same we welcome its approach. We are ready to sacrifice our own lives if only the long-desired revolution would come more quickly! . . .

We demand the transformation of the present despotic administration into a republican-federative union of regions, in which all power should pass into the hands of National Regional Assemblies. . . .

Each region should be comprised of agricultural communes and their members should have equal rights. . . .

The land assigned to each member of the commune will be granted . . . only for a defined period of time, at the end of which the commune will redistribute the land. . . . We demand that all judicial authorities be elected by the people themselves. . . .

We demand that, as well as the National Assembly, made up of delegates from all of Russia . . . there should be Regional Assemblies in the chief town of each region, made up purely of representatives from that region.

The National Assembly will decide all questions of foreign policy, investigate inter-regional disputes, pass laws, check on the execution of earlier decisions, appoint regional administrators, and determine the general level of taxation. The Regional Assemblies will decide on matters which concern only their regions. . . .

We demand a proper distribution of taxation; we want its full weight to fall not on the poorer section of society, but on the wealthy. . . .

We demand the establishment of public factories which should be run by individuals selected from society. . . .

We demand public education for children, and that their upkeep should be at the expense of society until the end of their education. We also demand that the sick and old be maintained at society's expense. . . .

We demand the total emancipation of women and that they receive all the political and civil rights which men will have; we demand the abolition of marriage as a phenomenon which is, in the highest degree, immoral and unthinkable if there is complete equality of the sexes, and consequently, the destruction of the family. . . .

We demand the destruction of the chief den of iniquity – monasteries and nunneries. . . . Their property, as that of all churches, should be given over to the benefit of the state. . . .

We demand a substantial increase in soldiers' wages and the reduction in the period of military service. . . .

We demand complete independence for Poland and Lithuania, and for regions which express a desire not to remain united with Russia. . . .

Where are those elements whom we want to unite, who is on our side?

We are relying on the people; they will be with us, especially the Old Believers. . . . The downtrodden and robbed peasants will stand together with us for their rights and it will be they who will decide the matter. The initiative, however, will belong not to them, but to the troops and to our young people.

We are counting on the troops, counting on officers angered by the despotism of the Court. . . .

But our main hope is with young people. . . .

Soon, soon will come the day when we will unfold the great banner of the future, the red banner with the great shout: Long live the social and democratic Russian republic!

(V. I. Burtsev (ed.), *Za sto let* (London, 1897) pp. 40–5)

5.4 PISAREV AND 'REALISM'

Pisarev's 'realists', described in his article of 1864, were to aim at criticism and independent action – others labelled them as 'nihilists'.

* * *

The realist is a thinking worker, carrying out his labour with love. From this definition the reader will see clearly that at the present time only representatives of intellectual work can be realists. Of course the work of those men who feed and clothe us is useful in the highest degree, but these people are not in the least realists. The present organisation of material labour, and the present situation of the unskilled working class in the entire world mean that these people are nothing more than machines, differing from wooden and iron machines only in the unfortunate capacity to feel exhaustion, hunger and pain. At the moment these people, with complete justification, detest their work and spend no time on thought. They comprise a passive material which has been much worked on by friends of humanity, but it offers very little help itself and up to now has not taken any definite form. . . . The most real work which brings the most tangible and unarguable benefit remains outside the field of realism, outside the field of critical reason, in these cellars of society where not a single ray of human thought penetrates. What can we do with them? For the moment we must leave them in peace and turn to the phenomena of intellectual work which can be considered allowable and useful only when, directly or indirectly, it leads to the creation of new worlds from the primeval fog which fills the dirty cellars.

Of all the realists only natural scientists, who move forward the limits of science by making new discoveries, work for humanity in general, without relation to individual nationalities and the differing conditions of place and time. The remaining realists also work for humanity, but the tasks and methods of their activity change with circumstances and adapt to the demands of individual human societies. . . .

To strengthen and elevate the human personality, intellectual work must be useful, that is it should not only be directed towards a definite intellectual aim, but it should, as well, achieve this aim.

(D. I. Pisarev, 'Realisty', *Sochineniya v chetyrekh tomakh*, vol. 2 (Moscow, 1956) pp. 67–9)

5.5 KARAKOZOV'S ASSASSINATION ATTEMPT, 1866

Preparation

This description of Karakozov's aims is from the report of the Official Investigative Commission into the assassination attempt.

* * *

Whilst living in Moscow, Karakozov belonged to a secret society founded there mainly from occasional and some full-time students of the university and the agricultural academy, as well as some school pupils and others.

This society . . . aimed at spreading socialist teaching, destroying the basis of public morality, weakening faith in the foundations of religion and at overthrowing the existing order of the state by means of revolution.

The means for this were to be:
(a) Propaganda amongst the rural population; with a declaration that land is the property of the entire people;
(b) Stirring up the peasants against the landowners, the gentry, and against authority in general;
(c) The establishment of various schools, workshops, cooperatives . . . and other associations to thus get closer to the people and inculcate them with the pernicious teachings of socialism;
(d) The establishment in the provinces of libraries, free schools and various societies, on the basis of communism, which in the hands of members of the main society could more easily attract and prepare new members. . . .
(e) The dissemination amongst the people of socialist teaching by seminary staff and by village teachers and
(f) Propaganda in the Volga region using the ease of river communications. . . .

The individuals comprising the society had two trends: some aimed, by means of socialist propaganda and intimacy with the people, to achieve gradually a revolution in the state with the overthrow of the legal government; others wanted to achieve their aims more quickly and carry out a revolution, and they recognised that they would sooner or later resort to the most extreme measure – regicide. Amongst these latter was numbered Karakozov and he proposed to carry out this dreadful crime immediately.

(V. I. Burtsev (ed.), *Za sto let* (London, 1897) pp. 85–7).

The Government's Reaction

The government also moved to investigate the deeper causes of discontent: this report, written by P.A. Shuvalov, the head of the secret police, sets out the measures he believed would quell unrest.

* * *

The chief steps which need to be taken to strengthen the foundations of the social order, which otherwise could be easily shaken, are: to restore authority, to reform the police, to change the policy of the Ministry of Education and to support landowning elements, and therefore, the gentry. To restore authority we must put a stop to the attacks by the press and the hostile outbursts by gentry and Zemstvo assemblies which have recently developed against the government, its principles and representatives. . . .

The following measures should be firmly implemented to remove the pretensions of journalists: warnings should be issued to periodicals which attack the foundations of government and they should then be closed down. . . . If these measures proved to be inadequate, then it will be necessary to amend the Press Law which has, in its initial phase, already demonstrated its bankruptcy. Freedom of the press is incompatible with our system of government; it is feasible only in a constitutional state where it is supplementary to freedom of speech. . . . Where there is no freedom of speech, freedom of the press poses too great a danger as an anti-government weapon, since the government cannot enter into daily polemics but stands as a silent opponent, forced to concede in an unequal struggle.

Hostile demonstrations by various meetings must be limited and they must be taught respect and a degree of fear of the government by making their leaders responsible for their policy. A situation in which the government is assailed from all sides with complete impunity and in which demands are made which are contrary to its foundations can no longer be tolerated, since such a situation will lead rapidly to an alteration of the basis on which autocracy rests.

It is further necessary for the censorship authorities to be more clear and energetic in making their provincial representatives aware of the policy which they should be implementing and those who do not obey their orders should be dismissed. Each government employee cannot be allowed to have his own particular view. . . .

Investigation into the crime of 4 April has revealed the complete disorganisation of the capital's police down to its very foundations. It has been only a passive spectator as evil elements and aspirations have developed among us. . . . The main aim of reform will be, as far as possible, to introduce the political police in regions where they do not already exist and to concentrate the existing police in the Third Section of H. M. Chancellery. This will enable their activities to be unified and the whole empire can then be uniformly examined to discover exactly which movements are hostile to the government and what means should be employed to combat them. . . .

The development of educational institutions in the last ten years, instead of producing good results, has on the contrary created a generation infected by ultra-democratism, socialism and nihilism. The harm done by each of these movements is made all the more dangerous as their adherents see their aim in life as being to spread propaganda amongst the young. . . . These people become harmful members of society . . . able to disturb the social order of the state. There is no doubt that the root of the evil is chiefly in the political and moral beliefs of those people who have the education of the younger generation in their hands; many of them themselves implant these harmful seeds in the young. There are university faculties and even entire grammar schools, for example those in Penza, Saratov and Kazan whose evil spirit has gained them a regrettable notoriety. It is not obvious that effective measures have been taken to eradicate this evil. The composition of the teaching staff and of the educational administration should therefore be substantially changed and one cannot avoid the lamentable conclusion that *to halt the education for a period would be better* than to turn out the semi-educated and deformed students which have now attracted the attention of the government. . . .

The gentry are offended that their demands, especially those which concern their material-well-being, are treated with indifference by the ministries, that insufficient attention is paid to these demands and that they are sometimes rejected after personal review by ministers. . . . Any spirit of enterprise has disappeared; all property owners are abandoning their holdings and everybody is tired of continual changes and is asking the government for a more peaceful and more conservative era. . . .

As a result of this there has been a loss of confidence in the government by the landowing class. Constitutional tendencies have appeared, as has a desire to acquire for the gentry themselves some of the rights which belong to the supreme authority. This has come about not out of revolutionary aspirations, but with the aim of self-preservation. When the Zemstvo assemblies finally opened, the gentry came together with representatives of other classes and in this new environment they were able to acquire the social influence which formerly they had been given by the government. This influence is clearly evident in the fact that the gentry make up the majority of anti-government speakers in the Zemstvo assemblies.

The gentry is, however, the best weapon for opposing democracy and there is no better means of opposing socialism and revolutionary movements than through the conservative element. The government by itself is in no condition to begin a nationwide struggle with these harmful groups without the help of this element. When the government resolutely adopts such a policy, when it gives the gentry proof of its trust, then we shall see that *the majority of those adherents to constitutional ideas will forget their past dissensions, will be happy to return to their natural element*, and will closely surround the Sovereign, to serve him sincerely and unconditionally.

('Nezabvennye mysli nezabvennykh lyudey', *Byloe*, 1907, no. 1, pp. 237–41)

5.6 BAKUNIN'S ANARCHISM

Bakunin lived outside Russia for most of his life. His influence on a younger generation of Russian revolutionaries was, however, significant through writings such as this programme for action published in 1868.

* * *

Our Programme

We desire the complete intellectual, social-economic and political liberation of the people.
I. Intellectual freedom, because without it political and social freedom can be neither complete nor stable. Belief in God, belief in the immortality of the soul and in any sort of idealism in general serves, on the one hand, as an indispensable support and justification for despotism, for every sort of privilege and for the exploitation of the people, whilst on the other hand, it demoralises the people themselves . . . and deprives them of the energy necessary to win their natural rights and to attain a free and happy life.

It clearly follows from this that we are supporters of atheism and materialism.
II. The social-economic freedom of the people, without which any freedom would be loathsome, and an idle lie. . . . All political and civil organisations which have existed and which exist now in the world are supported on the following main foundations: on conquest, on the right of hereditary property, on the family rights of the father and husband and on the sanctification of all these by religion; together these make up the essence of the state. A necessary result of the whole state structure has been the servile subjection of unskilled labourers and the ignorant majority to the so-called educated exploiting minority. The state is unthinkable without political and legal privileges, basd on economic privilege.

As we desire the real and final liberation of the people, we want:
1. The abolition of the right of hereditary property.
2. Equal rights for women, both political and social-economic:

consequently we desire the destruction of family rights and of marriage, both religious and civil, which is inextricably linked to the right of inheritance. . . .

We advance these fundamental propositions as the basis of economic truth:

Land belongs only to those who work it with their hands – to agricultural communes. The capital and all tools of work belong to the workers, to workers' associations.

III. All future political organisation should be a free federation of free workers, both agricultural and industrial.

And therefore in the name of political liberation, we want, first of all, to see the final destruction of the state, we want the eradication of the whole state system with all its religious, political, military- and civil – bureaucratic, legal, educational and financial–economic institutions.

We want complete freedom for all peoples now repressed by the empire, with the right of complete self-determination, on the basis of their own instincts, needs and will. Federations can develop from below and those of them who want to be members of the Russian people can together create a truly free and happy society in friendly and federative union with such societies in Europe and the whole world.

(M. A. Bakunin, *Izbrannye sochineniya*, vol. 1 (London, 1915) pp. 335–7)

5.7 THE MOSCOW MUNICIPAL DUMA ASKS FOR REFORM

Signed by 110 member of the newly established Moscow city Duma, the address they presented to the Tsar in November 1870 aroused severe displeasure on the part of the Tsar.

* * *

The Address of November 1870

Each of Your great reforms, whether completed or still under way, serves as a source of strength for Russia and Your Majesty. Nobody has gained such rights to the gratitude of the people as You, Sovereign and the people have shown such warm gratitude to nobody else. It has received this gift from You and it continues to see You as the most reliable protector of the liberties it has acquired, standing henceforth as its daily bread. Only from You does it expect completion of the beneficial undertakings you have embarked upon. As a first step it is waiting for more latitude for opinions and the printed word: without this the people's spirit will flag and there will be no sincerity or truth in its relations with authority. It then wants religious freedom, without which preaching itself is ineffective, and finally freedom of conscience, the most valuable treasure for the human spirit.

Sovereign! Internal and external affairs are inextricably linked. The guarantee of success in the external field lies in the strength of the people's self-consciousness and self-respect which the state introduces into all areas of life. The state organism will be strengthened only by the unwavering service to the foundations of nationality. This is the only means of pulling together the borderlands and of creating that unity which has been the unchanging historic bidding of You and our predecessors and the permanent banner of Moscow since the beginning of its existence. Under this banner, Sovereign, all classes of society will muster at your first summons without any distinction of calling, as a harmonious host in unshakeable trust in God's mercy, in the rightness of our cause and in You. Trust in his people by the Tsar, rational self-control in freedom and honourable obedience by the people, a mutual and unbreakable link between the Tsar and the people, founded on the contact of the national spirit and on the harmony of aims and beliefs – this is our strength; this is what will help Russia to fulfil her great historical mission. . . .

(S. N. Sukhotin, 'Iz pamyatnykh tetradey S. N. Sukhotina', *Russkiy Arkhiv*, vol. 32 (1894) pt 2, p. 248)

Imperial Reaction

I told the Empress that the members of the Duma were convinced of the need to present the address and they themselves understood how timely it was. . . . They did not want the address to be just a compilation of official phrases, but for it to be the expression of a vigorous appeal by the people to their sovereign together with a feeling of devotion and gratitude for all the beneficial reforms implemented during his reign. At the same time, they were submitting to the steps of the throne the desires, needs and aims which Russia expects and wants to expect to be fulfilled only by its sovereign. These gentlemen in their address wanted only to express their devotion and loyalty to the Tsar and have been deeply surprised and grieved that they had aroused his displeasure. The Empress replied that nobody in Russian had the right to raise questions of social organisation which were outside its competence and that the Duma had acted illegally by raising the questions of freedom of the press and the church in its address. I replied that, in reality, the Duma could be censured from this point of view, but one could argue in its justification that as public opinion had no legal way of reaching the Tsar, then it was forgivable for the Duma to select a path which was outside the law, in order to express the aims and fears of the country. The restrictions of the press are such that most questions which agitate public opinion at the moment cannot be freely discussed. I pointed out that they were not asking for freedom of the press, but only 'more latitude for the printed word'; that there was a definite belief in the necessity of some form of discussion of questions in the interests of the government itself; that, at the stage of development which our society had reached, it was impossible to suppress an attentive attitude and interest in questions of internal and external politics, and that if the government attempts, as is rumoured at the moment, to deprive the press of all freedom, it will thus itself close a safety valve and will open the way for an endless stream of false rumours and interpretations, suppressed spite and secret intrigues which will ripen in the dark and silence. All this would sooner or later lead to explosions which could not be prevented because they would not be foreseen and, in view of all this, anybody who is devoted to the government should see it as his duty to take up these important questions with the authorities. I further added that, in referring to freedom of conscience and of the church, they thought they were discussing a policy which the Sovereign himself felt was desirable, since during his reign all measures of religious persecution had, in practice, come to an end. Nevertheless, the laws which provided for these measures were still in existence and again could always become a weapon of fanaticism and intolerance; by their very existence they were a stain and disgrace on Russia itself, on a civilised Europe. To all this the Empress replied that the Sovereign had many solid reasons for being discontented with the press, that it sometimes caused him difficulties in his foreign policy with Europe and it aroused national passions inside Russia; to this I retorted that it was more correct to say that the press drew attention to an evil, rather than to blame it for creating the evil.

(A. F. Tyutcheva, *Pri dvore dvukh imperatorov. Vospominaniya, Dnevnik 1853–1882* (Moscow, 1928–29) pt 2, pp. 214–15)

5.8 POPULISM: 'GOING TO THE PEOPLE'

These two extracts were both written in the summer of 1874: the first by a village schoolteacher in Vyatka, the second after a visit to villages in

Orenburg. Both writers show disillusionment with the reaction of the peasants to their work.

* * *

... You know, of course, the aim which I came here with (to get to know life), but this aim has not been fulfilled. I devote almost my whole day to the school, so that I have absolutely no time to meet the peasants and to go to see them. And there isn't much to say to the old women, because ... all they talk about is who has been where and why ... so that I find no interest in speaking to them. It is different with the men – they are very interesting to talk to, but again there is a snag, in that they are permanently away, and if they are at home then they are always at work somewhere outside the house, and only return home in the evening when it is too late to visit them – and as well as this they are tired and exhausted.... I can't talk to them either since I find a permanent gap in my knowledge when I try to prove anything to them. I am unable to dissuade them, for example, even from superstitions (which they are all full of) because they put forward facts which they themselves have witnessed or experienced and I simply have to give into them. ...
Of course I read with my pupils, but again what for? At least some of my pupils like just to read about nature and nothing else, but they do not like literature in which social questions would, to some extent, be considered.... But the St Petersburg people still send us questions which we could put to our pupils when they have read such books, questions, of course, of a social nature and I have already said that the pupils pay no attention to them.... Thus it ends up that I am just a teacher and nothing more, and the aim which I came here with will not be fulfilled, i.e., I have not got a thorough knowledge of peasant life and peasant ideas.... Tell me for God's sake what I am to do? I have nevertheless decided that a good person will always do something to fulfil his aim and yet I cannot do anything!
Of course there is partly the benefit of staying in the countryside, but this benefit is insignificant compared with the aims I came here with.

(*Revolyutsionnoe narodnichestvo 70-kh godov XIX veka*, vol. 1 (Moscow, 1964) pp. 266–7)

* * *

The first thing I noticed amongst the peasants was the absence of solidarity among them; you notice this as well, many notice it;

accordingly it is a universal fact. Solidarity is the only remedy; a lack of solidarity means a lack of all remedies. The second thing which surprised me was the lack of sharp differences between the exploiter and the exploited amongst the peasantry: today's landless peasant could easily become tomorrow's exploiter. . . . Justice demands that I say that I came across many fine features amongst the peasantry: in particular sensible ideas about property, the honour of productive work and contempt for trade.

(Ibid., pp. 278)

5.9 LAND AND LIBERTY

Both these extracts relating to the Land and Liberty group – *Zemlya i Volya* – were written in 1878.

Programme

This programme, from May 1878, stresses both the Populist nature of the movement as well as the need for effective organisation.

* * *

1. . . . We should demand the transfer of all land to the rural workers and its equal distribution. . . .
2. An aspiration to complete communal self-government exists in the Russian people. Each association of communes should itself define which functions it will give to the administration. . . .
3. Religious toleration and, in general, a desire for religious freedom are noticeable in the Russian people; therefore we should aim at complete freedom of belief.
4. The present Russian empire also includes areas and nationalities which are ready to secede at the first possible moment. . . . Consequently, our duty is to help in the division of the Russian empire according to local wishes.

Thus the formula 'Land and Liberty' . . . now serves as the best expression of the people's views on the ownership of land and the organisation of their community. . . .

It is self-evidently clear that this formula can only be brought to life by means of violent revolution and this as quickly as possible, since the development of capitalism . . . is threatening to destroy the commune. Thus, our immediate practical tasks are:

A. Organisational section
(a) A tight and well-organised organisation of ready-prepared revolutionaries.
(b) Closer contact and even a merger with groups of a religious–revolutionary character which are opposed to the government. . . .
(c) The establishment of the closest and most durable contacts in localities where discontent is strongest. . . .

The activity of the people who implement these points should aim at emphasising and developing the people's aspirations and should consist of agitation in the widest sense of the word, beginning with legal protest against local authorities and concluding with armed uprising, i.e. revolt. . . .

(b) The establishment of links with the liberals with the aim of exploiting them for our own benefit. . . .

B. Disorganisational section
(a) The establishment of contacts and of our organisation amongst the troops. . . .
(b) The recruitment of people serving in government establishments.
(c) The systematic destruction of the most harmful or prominent people in the government and, in general, of the people who control the order which we hate.

(*Revolyutsionnoe narodnichestvo 70-kh godov XIX veka*, vol. 2 (Moscow–Leningrad, 1965) pp. 31–3)

Terrorism

This justification of terrorism, written by one of the perpetrators of the assassination of General Mezentsov, head of the Third Section, Kravchinsky, was written in the summer of 1878.

* * *

We are socialists. Our aim is the destruction of the existing economic order, the abolition of economic inequality which in our conviction comprises the root of all human suffering. Therefore political forms alone do not matter to us. As Russians we were, at first, inclined to refrain from political struggle and even more from any violent measures more than any other nation, since neither our previous history nor our upbringing has schooled us in them. The government itself has pushed us onto the path which we have followed. The government itself has put daggers and revolvers into our hands.

Murder is a terrible thing. . . . It is the Russian government which has driven us, socialists, devoted to the work of liberating the suffering people and condemning ourselves to any hardship so as to avoid it for others, the Russian government itself has driven us to a decision to embark on a whole series of murders and to make a system of it.

It has driven us to this by its cynical toying with tens and hundreds of human lives and the insolent contempt for any law whatsoever which it has always displayed in its relations to us. . . .

Gentleman of the government, policemen, administrators this is our last word to you:

You are representatives of authority; we are opponents of any enslavement of man by man, therefore you are our enemies and there can be no reconciliation between us. You must be destroyed and you will be destroyed! But we do not believe that political slavery gives birth to economic slavery but rather the contrary. We are convinced that the destruction of economic inequality will bring about the destruction of the poverty of the people and with it also the ignorance, superstition and prejudice with which all authority supports itself. This is why we are reminded to leave you, the governing class, in peace as much as possible. Our real enemy is the bourgeoisie which is now hiding behind you, although it hates you because you have tied its hands. You are an outsider! If you do not prevent us from fighting our real enemies we will leave you in peace. You can sleep peacefully until the overthrow of the present economic order. . . .

Until that time, and whilst you keep the present savage lawlessness in existence, our dark court will permanently hang over you like the sword of Damocles and death will be the answer to each of your attacks against us.

(S. M. Kravchinsky, *Smert za smert* (Petrograd, 1920) pp. 13–19)

5.10 BLACK REPARTITION

Black Repartition, one of the two groups resulting from the split in Land and Liberty in 1879, stressed the need for land to be equally distributed amongst the peasants. This extract from the first issue of the group's newspaper was written in January 1880 by G. V. Plekhanov.

* * *

... Russia's whole internal history, is in our view, nothing more than a long tale, full of tragic elements, of the struggle for life and death between the completely opposed principles of popular-communal and state-individual life. ...

Free communal organisation and self-government; the granting to all members of the commune, firstly, of the right to free use of land ... then, with an increase in population, of equal allotments of land; ... work, as the only source of the right to property; equal rights for all who participate in the discussion of social questions and the free ... association of communes in larger units. ... These are the foundations, the principles of social life which the people have so jealously protected and which, summed up in the battle cry 'Land and Liberty' at times when the cup of popular suffering has overflowed, have possessed the magical ability to excite the minds of the masses. ...

Our views on the practical tasks of our party are composed of two components – general scientific indicators and the special conditions of Russian history and of contemporary reality. We recognise socialism as science's last word about human society, and on the strength of this we consider the triumph of collectivism in the field of ownership and labour as the alpha and omega of progress in the economic structure of society. ... We remember that each step on the path of this development is determined strictly by society's previous history and by its condition at a given moment – in short, by the entire sum of the dynamics and statics of the society in question. But we are also convinced ... that any social activist should aim to make the maximum of necessary and possible reforms to society, in short, that every public figure should be a radical. Economic relations in society are considered by us to be the basis of all others, as the fundamental cause not only of all the phenomena of political life, but also of the intellectual and moral stance of its members. In our opinion, radicalism should first of all be economic radicalism. The efforts of a radical reformer should be directed, in the main, to bringing about maximum change for the better in the social-economic structure, without worrying whether this change can be brought about peacefully or only in the fact of violent opposition from people interested in the preservation of the old order. ...

But to bring about this maximum of reforms we must firstly turn our efforts to the destruction of the state structure which already exists in our homeland. The whole of the people's work is enslaved to the state. Land shortage, created by the state by means of expropriating lands from the people, has created a body of farm labourers artificially torn from their native hearth and field, and from whom factories and works acquire workers. . . . The state supports the kulaks and usurious capitalism in the countryside. . . .

The social-revolutionary party should lead the people from passively waiting for 'black repartition' from above, to demanding actively 'Land and Liberty' from below by inciting the people to active struggle with the state, by instilling independence and activism in them, by organising them for struggle, using each small opportunity to arouse popular discontent and instilling in the people correct opinions about existing social relations and those desirable in the future by means of propaganda through word and deed. This is the task and the possible limits of its influence on the people.

(*Revolyutsionnoe narodnichestvo 70-kh godov XIX veka*, vol. 2 (Moscow–Leningrad, 1965) pp. 139–44)

5.11 NARODNAYA VOLYA – THE PEOPLE'S WILL

The second group resulting from the split in Land and Liberty was The People's Will – *Narodnaya Volya*.

Aims

This description of its aims and activity was written in June 1880 whilst the author, A. A. Kvyatovsky, was in prison accused of complicity in an attempt to place a bomb in the Winter Palace. He was later executed.

* * *

No party in the world, however large it might be, in the conditions in which Russia is – in short – powerless, is in a position to change the people's outlook on the world, as it has been built up over the centuries. Only life itself can make such a change. Therefore the task at the present time is *to assist in fulfilling the ideas and aspirations which the people already hold.*

We by conviction are *anarchists*. Not in the vulgar, abusive sense of the word which it is usually given in ordinary conversation and in our legal literature; but in the beautiful and elevated meaning which relates to the concept of an ideal future social structure, where the supreme intellectual and moral development of man completely removes the need for any coercive social forces, where the development of solidarity and of social instincts of itself does not allow for the appearance of anti-social feelings in man. This is an ideal, and an ideal of course, which is far distant.

We are *socialists* – for we recognise work as being the sole criterion for the distribution of the goods of production. In the practical tasks which we set ourselves, we are anarchists insofar as the people themselves are anarchists: we are socialists insofar as the people is socialist in its ideals and aspirations.

We are *revolutionaries* because however much we are opposed to revolution for the sake of revolution, to violence for the sake of violence, on the basis of historical experience we foresee that it is unlikely that the people's aspirations and desires will be fulfilled by peaceful means, however desirable this may be, and the people will have to stand up for their rights.

Thus the aim which *the populist party* sets itself is to implement the people's desires and aspirations however the people's consciousness sees them. These desires and aspirations can be formulated thus. *Land*, as state property, as a necessary condition of work, should be in the hands of the people in quantities corresponding to their demands and needs. *A reduction in the burdens and the inequality of taxation* which, thanks to extortionists, have now grown ten-fold. *The abolition of administrative oppression and arbitrariness* and therefore *the full development of self-government* – the fufilment of these of the people's desires will result in a situation which is, of course, far from the ideal social structure, but in any case it will give society a chance to develop freely from the features present in its every day and social order, in the direction of this ideal. *The means* to fulfil this aim are as follows: the countryside is the centre of our activity; the party should aim to settle its members across a more or less *extensive region*. This should be a firm and protracted process. The first and most important task of the populist is to gain the respect and trust of the people, and thus, influence over them. In short, to himself become . . . a citizen of the area. The way in which this can be done will vary. Some convenient job can be taken (secretary, teacher, medical assistant, manager of agricultural enterprises and factories, trader, worker) as long as it, in itself, does not go against the aims of the populist and does not arouse distrust of him (that is any administrative post). Subsequently, a practical plan of action must be drawn up in each area depending on the particular conditions there, with the aim of giving rise to active expression by the people of its aspirations and desires.

Local revolts are not the sole and absolute means of arousing such expressions of the people's demands and desires. Everything depends . . . on local conditions. And as practice has shown there have been sufficient methods in which activity can be carried on legally.

('Avtobiograficheskoe zayavlenie A. A. Kvyatovskogo', *Krasnyy Arkhiv*, vol. 14 (1926) pp. 163–5)

Alexander II's Assassination

This statement was issued by the Executive Committee of The People's Will after the successful assassination of Alexander II on 1 March 1881.

* * *

1 March 1881.

. . . Today, 1 March 1881, in accordance with the decision of the Executive Committee, . . . Alexander II has been executed by two agents of the Executive Committee. . . .

Two years of striving and heavy sacrifice has been crowned with success. Henceforth all Russia can be certain that an intense and dogged struggle is capable of overcoming even the centuries-old despotism of the Romanovs.

The Executive Committee considers it necessary to make a public reminder that it had given more than one warning to the now deceased tyrant, and had exhorted him several times to put an end to his murderous arbitrariness and return Russia's natural rights to her. Everyone knows that the tyrant took no notice of any of these warnings and continued his previous policy. . . . The Executive Committee decided to execute the despot at all costs. This was carried out on 1 March.

We remind the new Tsar, Alexander III, that historical justice exists for him and for everybody. Russia, worn out by famine, exhausted by arbitrary administration, continuously losing its sons on the gallows, in hard labour, in exile, in oppressive inactivity forced on them by the existing regime – *Russia cannot live like this any longer.* . . . We remind

Alexander III that any violator of the will of the people is their enemy
... and a tyrant.... The death of Alexander II has shown what sort of
retribution such a role deserves.

(*Revolyutsionnoe narodnichestvo 70-kh godov XIX veka*, vol. 2 (Moscow–Leningrad, 1965) pp. 232–3.

6 Foreign Policy

6.1 THE END OF THE CRIMEAN WAR

This is part of a report written by the head of the Third Section in January 1856.

* * *

Observation of the general temper of the people at this time of severe trial gives a most reassuring picture: all Russia proper is ready to make the very greatest sacrifices and, in a spirit of reverent devotion to its homeland and its sovereign, is ready to carry out everything which he, in his wisdom, orders.

All the same it must be noted that the war is a heavy burden on Russia: conscription, local militia and disrupted trade have increased poverty. Although the Russian people are prepared to endure further hardships, if the government, whilst maintaining its steadfastness and its dignity, made an honourable peace, this would be greeted by general joy in the empire.

('III otdelenie i Krymskaya voina', *Krasnyy Arkhiv*, vol. 3 (1923) p. 294)

6.2 POLAND AND FOREIGN RELATIONS

The Russo-Prussian Convention of 8/20 February 1863

The Polish rebellion was recognised as a threat to both Russia and Prussia; hence the agreement of February 1863 on joint action.

* * *

The Russian and Prussian courts note that the events which are taking place in Poland have inflicted serious damage on both public and private property and may, as well, cause disturbances in the Prussian border provinces. They have agreed:

By request of the commander of the Russian army in Poland or of the general . . . of the Prussian army corps and also by request of the local authorities of both countries to the commanders of Russian and Prussian attachments, mutual cooperation may be shown and, in case of necessity, the frontier may be crossed to pursue rebels who have crossed from one country into the other. . . .

Secret Article: the Russian and Prussian courts agreed to inform each other, through military and civil channels, of all signs of political intrigues both in Poland and in Poznan.

(V. G. Revunenkov, *Polskoe vosstanie 1863 g. i evropeyskaya diplomatiya* (Moscow, 1957) p. 134)

Influencing Foreign Opinion

It was important for the Russian government to put its point of view across in foreign countries. The first part of this extract is a report written to the Minister of War in June 1863, recommending what action could be taken.

* * *

It is known that the Polish party spends enormous sums on attracting all the organs of public opinion in Western Europe to its side and that it organised what could be called a whole factory for news and articles, which pours floods of the most loathsome slanders onto Russia. . . .

This situation which is extremely unfavourable for us must, as far as possible, be eliminated by publishing in Europe both original articles in foreign languages on Polish affairs and translations of the best work of the Russian press on this topic. . . .

It would be sufficient to assign . . . 10 000 rubles . . . to be spent on the printing of original and translated essays and articles on the Polish question. . . .

This was not completely successful and in 1864 further proposals were made.

The publication of pamphlets in foreign languages has not, however, completely achieved its aims. It would be more desirable to produce a periodical publication in foreign languages, with the aim of it then being used by foreign newspapers. . . .

It is instead proposed to circulate a lithographed newsheet in French, German and English under the title *Correspondence Russe*.

By the end of 1864 the following report could be presented to the government.

This was published secretly . . . and distributed exclusively to the editors of foreign newspapers. *Moskovskie Vedomosti*, when it met references to this publication in foreign newspapers, called it some sort of underground newspaper. . . .

The foreign press which was so hostile to Russia in 1863 is now much more restrained and we can boast that this favourable change has, to a significant degree, been brought about by this lithographed publication.

This publication is now brought out regularly and systematically. Its twenty-eighth number appeared in French, English and German. . . .

In all, eighty two newspapers in different countries have received our reports directly or indirectly and have utilised them. . . .

In England our publication is regularly distributed to eighteen papers, fourteen of which are published in London. For four months now, not one article written by Polish immigrants who are so numerous in London, has been accepted. . . . If we remember the nature of the English press even last summer, if we think of the continuous intrigues of discontented Poles who still try to arouse England with the aim of raising a movement against Russia, then the success we have achieved seems highly satisfactory.

(S. P. Zykov, 'Nabroski iz moey zhizni', *Russkaya Starina*, vol. 143 (1910) pp. 22–31)

6.3 GORCHAKOV'S RENUNCIATION OF THE TREATY OF PARIS

Russia found the restrictions placed upon her by the Treaty of Paris increasingly irksome: in October 1870 Gorchakov, the Russian Minister of Foreign Affairs, issued the following circular to Russia's diplomatic representatives abroad.

*   *   *

The numerous recent contraventions of treaties considered as the basis of the Eastern balance of power have made it necessary for the Russian cabinet to consider carefully the importance of these treaties in relation to Russia's political position.

Of these the Treaty (of Paris) of 18/30 March 1856 has the most direct impact on Russia.

Annexed to the treaty was a separate convention between the two powers with a Black Sea coastline, by which Russia was compelled to reduce her naval forces to the very bare minimum.

On the other hand, the treaty established the basic concept of the neutrality of the Black Sea.

The signatory powers to the treaty considered that this should remove any possibility of clashes between Russia and Turkey and between those and other naval powers. It was also intended to increase the number of countries that would benefit by this neutrality . . . and thus, to protect Russia from any danger of attack. The experience of the last fifteen years has demonstrated that this concept, on which the security of Russia's border along its whole length in this area depends, has only theoretical significance.

In fact, at the same time as Russia has disarmed in the Black Sea and has . . . undertaken not to embark on any real measures of naval defence in adjacent seas or ports, Turkey has retained her right to maintain unlimited naval forces in the Archipelago and Straits; France and England can as before concentrate their squadrons in the Mediterranean.

As well as this . . . access to the Black Sea is formally and permanently prohibited to naval vessels of all states, including those bordering on it; but according to the convention on the Straits, passage through the Straits is forbidden to naval vessles only in time of peace. This contradiction means that the shores of the Russian empire are open to attack, even from a less powerful state, as long as it uses naval forces, against which Russia can only set a small number of unsubstantial vessels.

However the treaty of 18/30 March 1856 has not been exempt from the breaches which most European treaties have suffered. . . .

Under different excuses passage through the Straits has been granted to foreign naval vessels on several occasions and whole squadrons have entered the Black Sea. The presence of these vessels has been an infringement of the total neutrality of these waters.

The gradual weakening of the guarantees provided for by the treaty, in particular the pledge of real neutrality for the Black Sea, and the construction of ironclads which were not known and not considered when the 1856 treaty was concluded, have increased the dangers for Russia in case of war and have significantly exacerbated the inequality in naval forces which is now very obvious. . . .

The Tsar . . . declares that he can no longer consider himself bound by the undertakings in the treaty of 18/30 March 1856, insofar as they limit his sovereign rights in the Black Sea. . . .

You will make every effort to make it clear that the Tsar has in view solely the security and dignity of his empire. He has no intention of reopening the Eastern Question. . . . He desires only to preserve and strengthen peace. He continues as before to recognise completely the main foundations of the 1856 treaty which defines the place of Turkey amongst the European states.

(*Sbornik dogovorov Rossii s drugimi gosudarstvami, 1856–1917* (Moscow, 1956) pp. 103–7)

6.4 EUROPEAN SECURITY

During the early 1870s the League of Three Emperors was established.

Russo-German Military Convention, 24 April/6 May 1873

This convention, made between the chief of the German General Staff and the Russian Field Marshal Berg, was not endorsed by Bismarck and was never invoked.

* * *

... If any European power attacks either of the two Empires, the latter will receive help in the form of an army of 200 000 battle-ready troops as soon as possible.

This military convention is concluded in a spirit which excludes hostility to any other nation and to any other government.

('Russko-germanskie otnosheniya', *Krasnyy Arkhiv*, vol. 1 (1922) p. 29)

Russo-Austrian Military Convention, 25 May/6 June 1873

The Russo-Austrian military convention, made directly by the two emperors themselves was later endorsed by the German emperor.

* * *

... In the case of an attack from a third power which threatens European peace, Their Majesties jointly undertake, without seeking or concluding new alliances, to consult with each other as to the actions which they should jointly pursue.

If military action is necessary as a result of this agreement, this will be in accordance with a separate convention with Their Majesties will conclude. . . .

('Russko-germanskie otnosheniya', *Krasnyy Arkhiv*, vol. 1 (1922) p. 31)

Russo-German Relations 1879

This extract from a long note written in 1879 by P. A. Saburov, Russian Ambassador to Greece and from 1880 to Germany, argues for a resumption of Russian friendship with Germany.

* * *

The Triple Alliance is doomed. This agreement . . . has turned out to contain more disappointments than real results for us. It has even done us definite harm; the accession of the third party has spoilt our direct relations with Germany. Germany would, of course, have been more useful to us if she had stayed to one side in any disagreements between us and Austria.

All our achievements are due solely to ourselves, to our brave troops and to the persistence of the emperor. It is true that the Triple Alliance has done us a definite service: it held Austria in check during the war and, thus, covered our army's flank and rear. But this service has subsequently been negated by so many disappointments that nothing could encourage us to keep to the system of the Triple Alliance.

Rather, we do not intend to conclude alliances now. We are living not on the eve, but at the end of a war, a war which has led to the emergence of new and still fluid political combinations which, if our diplomacy does not beware, could crystallise. Specifically, the cabinets of the great powers are drawing noticeably closer – excluding ourselves. Therefore our task now is to prevent this situation crystallising, but this is impossible if we will stand alone. We must locate the point on which our diplomacy should be concentrated so as to break the chain of European agreements. In other words, to which power should we draw close in order to restore the European balance of power, a system which allows us to retain our share of influence and activity, to France? or to Germany?

Any rapprochement with France must be based on the assumption that rivalry between France and Germany will continue. France needs our friendship only for the sake of *revanche* and it would be risky to depend too much on the continuation of this rivalry . . . for France would cease to have need of us if she was satisified with the acquisition of some territory or with the return of Alsace-Lorraine.

For this reason I consider advances by us to France to be highly dangerous, even if we were to embark on them solely in the hope of seeing Bismarck return to our side, humble and repentant. We would achieve absolutely the opposite result with this man. We would only strengthen his inclination to listen to the advice which would, very likely, be given from London and Vienna with the aim of finding a way to reduce French desire for *revanche* by means of some new territorial combination. Our patriotic instinct should tell us that the basic aim of these diplomatic efforts by our European opponents, both in London and Vienna, is to see the reconciliation of France and Germany, and thus to take away the best card which we have ever had in our hand.

This is sufficient to indicate the direction our efforts should take. In politics the old ideas are often the best. This includes friendships with Prussia, now – Germany, and whatever misunderstandings there have been recently, they are far from outweighing the advantages which this friendship provides. These are as follows:

1. Whilst Bismarck is sure of us, whilst his rear is covered, he will not fear a second conflict with France and, of course, will not think of parting with Alsace-Lorraine. Thus, the continuation of the enmity between Germany and France for an indefinite period depends solely on us . . .
2. A year has passed since we saw a growing rapprochement between Berlin and Vienna. This is the direct result of our strained relations with Germany. Bismarck supports this rapprochement now only in the absence of anything better, and we can put an end to it when we want to. Bismarck is not fussy about taking such a course since he looks for advantage wherever he can find it. . . . He does not need to be taught to look to Vienna for a source of support which Petersburg cannot provide.
3. The friendship of Prussia has been of invaluable service to us for a century, as it has protected our most important border. It would have cost us millions over this period to defend this border against a hostile Prussia. But a friendly Prussia, on the other hand, puts us in the most privileged position of being the only European power which has nothing to fear in the way of attack and can disarm without fear of punishment. . . .

(Ibid, pp. 79–83)

The League of Three Emperors, 1881

By June 1881 the full alliance of Russia, Germany and Austria–Hungary was resurrected.

* * *

Article I
Should one of the . . . Parties be at war with a fourth Great Power, the remaining two will maintain an attitude of benevolent neutrality and will attempt to localise the conflict.

This condition is also applicable in the case of war between one of the three Powers and Turkey, but only if a preliminary agreement has been concluded between the three Powers to deal with the results of such war. . . .

Article II
Russia, in agreement with Germany, firmly declares that she will respect the interests of Austria–Hungary which arise from her new position, as provided for by the Treaty of Berlin.

All three Courts, desirous of avoiding any disagreements between them, are obliged to take the interests of the contracting parties in the Balkans into mutual considersation. Furthermore, they give a mutual promise that any changes in the territorial *status quo* of Turkey in Europe will take place only with their mutual agreement. . . .

Article III
All three Courts recognise the European significance and mutual responsibility of the principle of closing the Bosphorus and the Dardenelles. . . .

They will jointly ensure that Turkey does not allow any exceptions to this rule in the interests of any government, by permitting part of its empire – into which the Straits lead – to be used for military operations by a warring power. . . .

It has been agreed:
1. Bosnia and Hercegovina
Austria–Hungary retains the right to annex these two provinces at a suitable moment. . . .
3. Eastern Rumelia
All three Powers jointly recognise that the possibility of the occupation of Eastern Rumelia or the Balkans would pose a great danger to general

peace. If necessary they will use their efforts to deflect the Porte from such a step. . . .

4. Bulgaria

None of the three powers will oppose a possible unification of Bulgaria with Eastern Rumelia inside the territorial limits given them by the Treaty of Berlin. . . . They jointly agree to restrain the Bulgars from any aggressive actions in relation to neighbouring provinces, in particular Macedonia, and declare to the Bulgars that in such a case they act at their own risk. . . .

(Ibid., pp. 131–5)

6.5 FORWARD POLICY IN THE BALKANS

N. P. Ignatev, Russian diplomatic representative in Constantinople from 1864 to 1877 and a convinced Panslavist, here sets out the aims which he pursued in his diplomacy. He had been the Director of the Asian Department of the Ministry of Foreign Affairs in the early 1860s and was Minister of Internal Affairs from 1881–82.

* * *

I was convinced that our diplomacy should pursue three invariable aims:
1. The abrogation of the Treaty of Paris. The honour and dignity of Russia should be satisfied by restoring her rights to ownership of the Black Sea coast and her dominance in the Black Sea itself by the return or areas ceded in 1856. . . .

Gorchakov also aimed at removing the humiliating conditions of the Treaty of Paris, but the basic difference between our views was that he believed in Europe, in the 'Concert of Europe', he thirsted after conferences and congresses and he preferred fine-sounding phrases and brilliant diplomatic fictions to real practical action, not so impressive, but dogged, insistent and thorough. I suggested that we should first build battleships in the Black Sea and acquire a fleet and then make a direct agreement with Turkey.

. . . My chief aim has always been, despite the traditions of the Ministry of Foreign Affairs, a direct agreement with Turkey. This would avoid new obligations to other powers, especially England and Austria, in relation to Eastern questions. . . . I deeply mistrusted Europe and European conferences and recognised that in relation to the Eastern

Question all the powers were more or less hostile to us: in this climate it was all the easier to construct coalitions and alliances against us. . . .
2. Russia is cramped in the Black Sea and she should, directly or indirectly, own the exit, that is, the Straits, as much to protect the security and welfare of the south of Russia as for political and economic reasons. Russia must become the master in Constantinople by one of two methods: either by a Russian becoming the governor of the city and the Straits . . . or by seizing the area which would arouse opposition from Europe and non-cooperation from the local administration. There is no other way to ensure permanent protection of Russian interests and at the same time to solve the Eastern question. . . .

Our influence should be dominant in the affairs of Turkey. If we lived in friendship with the Sultan and were in charge of his ministers, we would be able to prepare the Orthodox Christians for autonomy and to make Turkey harmless to us. With the right to govern the Straits, the Sultans in Constantinople could be left to live out their time until they were unnecessary. This radical solution to the Eastern Question which, would leave the Straits in our possession and give us corresponding influence on the Bulgars, Greeks, Serbs and Armenians, would appear to be least harmful to the interests of England, France, Italy, Austria–Hungary and Germany.

(N. P. Ignatev, 'Zapiski', *Istoricheskiy Vestnik*, vol. 135 (1914) pp. 50–4)

6.6 THE BALKAN WAR, 1877–78

Origins

This speech by Alexander II in the autumn of 1876 showed that he was prepared for Russia to embark on war with Turkey. Despite the meetings in Constantinople which the Tsar mentions, war broke out in the spring of 1877.

* * *

You are already aware that Turkey has submitted to my demands for the rapid conclusion of a truce which will put an end to the fruitless slaughter in Serbia and Montenegro. In this unequal struggle the people of Montenegro have shown themselves, as always, to be true heroes.

Unfortunately, one cannot say the same for the Serbs, despite the presence in their ranks of our volunteers, many of whom have spilt their blood for the Slav cause. I know that, together with me, all Russia will show the keenest sympathy for the sufferings of our brothers in faith and ancestry; but for me the real interests of Russia are dearest of all and I want to spare Russian blood as far as possible. This is why I have tried and am continuing to try to achieve a real improvement in the life of all Christians in the Balkans by peaceful means. Meetings should soon begin in Constantinople between the representatives of the six Great Powers to set out conditions for peace. I desire greatly that we can reach a general agreement. If this does not take place, and I foresee that we shall not obtain the guarantees necessary to provide for the implementation of everything which we have the right to demand from the Porte, then I firmly intend to act independently and, in such a case, I am sure that all Russia will respond to my summons, when I consider it necessary and the honour of Russia demands it.

(S. S. Tatishchev, *Imperator Aleksandr II. Ego zhizn i tsarstvovanie*, vol. 2 (St Petersburg, 1903) pp. 335–6)

San Stefano

The armistice in January 1878, from which this extract is taken, was the basis for the Treaty of San Stefano of March 1878.

* * *

1. ... Bulgaria, inside the frontiers defined by the majority of the Bulgarian population and, in any case, not less than the frontiers set out at the Constantinople conference, will be elevated to an independent princedom. ... The Ottoman army will no longer be located there.
2. The independence of Montenegro will be recognised. ...
3. The independence of Romania and Serbia will be recognised. Romania will be provided with adequate recompense in land, and there will be amendments to the frontiers of Serbia.
4. Bosnia and Hercegovina will be granted autonomous administration. ...
5. The Porte will accept his responsibility to compensate Russia for her expenditure on the war and the losses which she has suffered.

(*Rossiya i natsionalno-osvobitelnaya borba na Balkanakh, 1875–1878* (Moscow, 1978) p. 360)

The Congress of Berlin

P. A. Shuvalov, Russian ambassador in London in the late 1870s, looks back on the problems involved in summoning the Congress of Berlin. Despite Russian objections, the Congress opened in June 1878.

* * *

I was never a supporter of the Congress. The idea for it . . . hovered in the air from the very beginning of the war, especially as a result of the many declarations which the Russian cabinet addressed to Europe. . . . Apart from the responsibilities to Germany and Austria–Hungary which compelled us to come to an agreement with these powers as to the results of the war, we tirelessly repeated that we were defending European interests . . . and that, in consequence, the war would be settled on the basis of general agreement. But later, with the San Stefano truce, we tried to move away from this principle.

I approached the Congress with trepidation for the following reasons. . . .

We held an excellent card for the entire crisis: the concealed disagreement between Austria–Hungary and England. . . .

This had an important influence on the development of the Eastern crisis. If London and Vienna could have reached agreement from the beginning and if they had declared that they would not permit war, then the possibility of war would have been excluded. The presence of the English fleet in the Baltic and Black Seas would have splintered our forces and the movement of the English army would have threatened our lines of communication and hindered our crossing of the Danube. . . .

I feared the Congress. I foresaw that the agreement which the English and Austrians had been unable to achieve at a distance could easily be concluded in Berlin and that this agreement would be directed against us. . . .

Meanwhile, all the official communications I received from St Petersburg indicated that there they were thirsting for the Congress, flattering themselves with the idea that Europe would sanction the San Stefano treaty without objection. As a result of this I was instructed to facilitate the summoning of the Congress. . . .

We wanted the Congress to be summoned, but did not want do discuss what was demanded, completely justifiably, by the other cabinets, namely its principles and the limits of its competence. . . . We certainly did not want to submit the articles of the San Stefano treaty, other than those of a general nature, for European discussion. Neither the English nor the Austrians could agree to this. As well, we did not want Europe to understand our strategy . . . and we fell back on fine words. . . .

England demanded that the San Stefano treaty be presented in its entirety to the Congress and that each of its articles be subject to discussion.

We thus ended up in an impasse. Neither country could withdraw from its position without harming its dignity. The summoning of the Congress became impossible; military preparation intensified in England.

('P. A. Shuvalov o Berlinskom kongresse 1878 g', *Krasnyy Arkhiv*, vol. 59 (1933) pp. 91–3)

Public Opinion and the Congress of Berlin

This extract from an article in the newspaper *Nedelya* expects Russia to consolidate her position in the Balkans at the Congress of Berlin.

* * *

. . . What should Russia's tasks and aims be [at the Congress of Berlin]? The war with Turkey was begun to liberate the Christians of the Balkan peninsula from an alien and hated regime. The successful outcome of our military action gives us the right to expect that we will achieve this aim – the sole aim which Russia declared frankly from the very beginning of the war. Consequently, all the efforts of Russian diplomacy should be directed towards finally removing Turkish domination over the Christian population of the Balkans and achieving a situation in which Christians will have the chance to live and develop independently and peacefully. . . .

In the practical sphere a demand should be made for real and lasting guarantees which would eliminate for a substantial period, if not permanently, any possibility of a repetition of the events of the last two years.

But even this is insufficient. Turkish domination over the Christian provinces . . . could very easily be replaced by a different type which, although more civilised, would still be alien oppression – whether it was in the form of English administration in southern Bulgaria or Austrian 'guardianship' in Bosnia and Hercegovina.... This is why it seems to us that the aims of Russian policy should be broadened and that instead of the liberation of the Christians from the Muslim yoke, Russia should proclaim its slogan to be their liberation from any alien dominance and oppression. This aim, of course, can be achieved by organising the internal and public life of the new provinces so that they correspond as much as possible to the real needs of the population. Thus Russia's liberating mission can be fulfilled to its full extent and Russia will be able to conclude this battle which it took on itself, having completely compensated itself for all its sacrifices and efforts.

(*Rossiya i natsionalno-osvoboditelnaya borba no Balkanakh, 1875–1878* (Moscow, 1978) pp. 383–4)

6.7 EXPANSION IN CENTRAL ASIA

Gorchakov's Justification

Russian moves into Turkestan in 1864 were justified by Gorchakov, Minister of Foreign Affairs, in this circular to the European powers.

* * *

The position of Russia in Central Asia is the same as the position of any civilised state which comes into contact with a semi-barbarous people, nomads without affixed social organisation. In such cases the interests of frontier security and of trade relations always require that the more civilised state acquires a certain power over its neighbours, whose wild and turbulent customs make them extremely awkward. It begins by curbing raids and robberies and in order to limit these, the neighbouring peoples usually have to be subjected to some degree of control. When this result has been achieved, these peoples acquire more peaceful customs, but they in their turn are subject to attacks by yet more distant tribes. The state is obliged to defend them from these incursions and to punish those who carried them out. This creates the necessity of periodic and prolonged expeditions against a distant enemy, whose social structure makes him difficult to catch. If a state restricts itself to punishing the plunderers and then withdraws, the lesson will soon be forgotten and the retreat will be attributed to weakness; Asiatic peoples, for the most part, respect only visible and tangible strengths; the moral force of reason and of the advantages of education still has hardly any impact on them. Therefore, the work has to be continually restarted. A number of fortified points are set up amongst a hostile people so as to put a rapid end to these endless disturbances; authority is set over them and this, little by little and with more or less force, makes them submit. After this second mission, however, other and yet more distant peoples soon begin to pose just the same dangers and require the same measures of restraint. Thus the state must decide on a definite course of action: either to refrain from this unending work and to condemn its frontiers to endless disturbances which will make well-being, security and education impossible there, or to move further and further forward into the depths of uncivilised countries, where with each step taken, the distances increased the difficulties and burdens for the state. This has been the fate of all states in such conditions. The United States in America, France in Africa, Holland in her colonies, England in the East Indies – they have all been trapped on this path of forward movement, motivated less by ambition than by extreme necessity, and where the greatest difficulty is in being able to stop.

(S. S. Tatishchev, *Imperator Aleksandr II: Ego zhizn i tsarstvovanie*, vol. 2 (St Petersburg, 1903) pp. 115–116)

Practical Policy

This report of June 1866 to the military governor of Turkestan sets out practical steps which Russia should take to consolidate her position in Central Asia.

* * *

Russia must: 1. secure her dominance on the banks of the Amu-Darya; 2. not permit the influence of any other European power to become established in Bukhara; 3. guarantee the life and property of its citizens and, as far as possible, of the inhabitants of Central Asia; 4. expand her trade. The main thrust of our future activity is to attain these goals in the easiest and cheapest manner. Russia should not annex Bukhara nor is it necessary to make or turn Bukhara into a vassel state. Both courses would require great expense by Russia and would result in us being restricted in our future actions. Therefore it would be more useful and advantageous *to have Bukhara as an independent ally, whose loyalty and devotion would be guaranteed in the most durable way.* But since this cannot be achieved through negotiations or treaties we must take more effective measures which would make the Emir completely dependent on Russia. Careful examination of all the circumstances in Central Asia leads me to the firm conviction that the following measures should be taken:

1. Russia must gain control of Dzhizak as the key to the whole Zaryarzsha valley. If this area is in our hands, we will always be able to exert a dominant influence over all the affairs of Bukhara.
2. *We must protect the person of the Emir* from his various enemies at home. This is a matter of the first importance, in order permanently to win the Emirs over to Russia. . . . The Emirs fully recognise the need to have more or less organised troops . . . and it would not be at all surprising if English officers soon appeared in Bukhara. Therefore it would be extremely useful to anticipate the wish of the Empire and provide him not only with officers, but even with Russian escorts to protect his person. . . .
3. *It would be useful subsequently to establish a customs union of Russia and the Central Asian khanates.* . . . The removal of this barrier between Russia and Central Asia will be of great assistance in developing our trade and in permanently consolidating our dominance in Central Asia. . . .
4. *We must rapidly extend the trade route from the Krasnovodsk gulf to the mouth of the Amu-Darya river.* Political, trade and military consideration all dictate that Central Asia be drawn closer to Russia, so that communications between them can be much more rapid and less expensive. . . .

The centuries-old structure of the Muslim states cannot be transformed into a European pattern by any persuasion, advice or threats from Russia. There is no middle way, but only two alternatives: either to seize the Central Asian khanates or to organise the khans so that they do not dare to make a move without Russia's consent.

(*Zapiska o znachenii Bukharskogo khanstva dlya Rossii i neobkhodimosti prinyatiya reshitelnykh mer dlya prochnogo vodvoreniya nashego vliyaniya v Srednoy Azii* (St Petersburg, 1867) pp. 34–8)

7 Education and Culture

7.1 Educational Statistics

Table 7.1 Statistics on secondary school pupils at 1 January 1865

Religion	No.	Social background	No.
Orthodox	19 123	Noble and civil servants	18 660
Roman Catholic	4 161	Clergy	974
Protestant	2 430	Urban	5 554
Armenian-Georgian	37	Rural	1 032
Jewish	990	Foreign	569
Muslim	48		
Total:	26 789		

Table 7.2 Students in district schools at 1 January 1865

Religion	No.	Social background	No.
Orthodox	21 119	Noble and civil servants	6 910
Roman Catholic	991	Clergy	505
Protestant	1 339	Urban	13 080
Jewish	323	Rural	3 380
Muslim	180	Foreign	77
Total:	23 952		

Table 7.3 Pupils in girls secondary schools directed by the Ministry of Education at 1 January 1865

Religion	No.	Social Background	No.
Orthodox	7 560	Noble and civil servants	3 242
Roman Catholic	111	Clergy	471
Protestant	1 317	Urban	4 855
Jewish	141	Rural	481
Total:	9 129		

Source: Obzor deyatelnosti ministerstva narodnogo prosveshcheniya v 1862 g, 63 i 64 godakh (St Petersburg, 1865) pp. 274–5; 318–19; 336–7

7.2 EDUCATION AND THE ZEMSTVA

Education was one of the areas to which the Zemstva paid great attention, but it was also an aspect of their responsibility which aroused disquiet amongst the central authorities, as this report by Makov, the Minister of Internal Affairs written in 1880, makes clear.

* * *

Besides participating in charitable, public health and provisioning matters, the Zemstva were also asked to take charge of . . . education. . . . If one can reproach the Zemstva over education, then it is surely over an excess of zeal. The conviction that the ordinary people would reach greater well-being through the help of education would be entirely true only when there existed alongside the consciousness that the people who take on this teaching themselves must be completely firm in the principles of faith and their understanding of their duty. Unfortunately, we have very few of such teachers because demand for them arose suddenly, before life itself had succeeded in preparing them. The Zemstva are now evidently beginning to understand the dangers of randomly selecting teachers and are acting with greater circumspection, giving teachers not only preliminary examinations but also maintaining a watch over them. In this respect the Rybinsk Zemstvo executive stands out prominently: it declared that children who had finished the school course were to assemble on an appointed day in the district town, together with all the village school teachers. At the appointed time, in the presence of an official from the Ministry of Education, a public examination of the pupils took place, being at the same time a check on the work of the teachers. The chairmen of the provincial and district Zemstvo executives reported that these examinations were of substantial benefit.

(L. S. Makov, *Vsepoddanneyshey doklad ministra vnutrennykh del, 8-ogo iyulya 1880 goda* (St Petersburg, 1880) pp. 49–51)

7.3 UNIVERSITIES

Universities were given special attention by the government since they were seen as the breeding-ground for radicals of all persuasions.

Student Unrest, 1857-61

Shestakov, appointed inspector of students in Moscow in 1860, believed that the students had gained overmuch power and that they were being influenced by the works of German materialists such as Feuerbach and Büchner.

* * *

I found myself in what was a new and unknown world: the professors evidently lived in fear of the students, they gave almost all of them good marks, shook them by the hand, and they even . . . missed two or three weeks of lectures without any valid reason. Duplicated lecture notes were much in use, despite the fact that the professors were all against them; but . . . the students want them and so how can they be forbidden? – there is nothing to be done but to allow them. Along with lecture notes, the works of Feuerbach and Büchner are duplicated, of course secretly.

What sort of discipline is there if it is not the professors, but the students who set the tone of the university and give the orders? *O tempora, o mores!* I involuntarily exclaimed. How had such a radical and, to me, incomprehensible change taken place? . . .

Careful observation of the students and continuous contact with them have led me to the conclusion that it is possible to deal with each student individually; to have an impact on them verbally and by persuasion. When they are assembled in a mass, however, when they hold a meeting with some pre-defined aim, then they lose all sense of proportion and decency, then no persuasion can affect them – logic does not exist for them and they are full of confidence in their power as a group. For me this was a completely new phenomenon: in the 1840s there was no sign of student meetings. . . .

The first meeting which assembled in 1857 in Moscow University, on the occasion of some students being beaten up by the police, was the ancestor of student meetings in Russia. From then on . . . students became more and more accustomed to holding meetings. They were actually convinced that their demands, put forward by the student body as a whole, would be implemented and they began to victimise some professors and succeeded in driving them out of the university. Naturally, the professors began to fear the students, and this explained their unnecessary leniency in examinations and other concessions. The tractability of the professors served to increase student pretensions. The students formed a desire to play the role of master in the universities.

Things had got to the stage where the students even demanded the appearance of the vice-chancellor at their court.

(P. D. Shestakov, 'Studencheskie volneniya v Moskve v 1861 g.', *Russkaya Starina*, vol. 60 (1888) pp. 205–7)

The 1863 University Statute

The Official Report of the Ministry of Education for the years immediately following the introduction of the new University Statute argues that it has led to a significant improvement in students' conduct.

* * *

A. The new [University] Statute gives universities independence in their internal running which is vested in the university council. Students are, within the premises of the university, completely subordinate to the council and it has responsibility for the students' moral development. . . .

B. The new law provides that the universities will permanently have an adequate number of professors who are well prepared for their work. . . .

C. Finally, the new law gives the universities an increase in resources for research and teaching. . . .

It is not yet two years since the new law was introduced; and, besides, it is not yet fully implemented . . . but its influence has already been beneficial in many areas.

There is thus no doubt that the students' moral attitudes have changed for the better since the students have been made subordinate to university bodies. Each university has drawn up its own rules dealing with students' duties, discipline in the university, penalties for breaches of discipline, checking on students' studies, etc. As far as is known, these rules have been observed absolutely in all universities and the students have submitted to them willingly. . . . Nothing has been heard of students' disturbances, meetings, mobs, political demonstrations, cases of general insubordination to their superiors and similar such occurrences which several years ago were so usual in our universities and have cast a dark shadow over them for the last two years. . . . In general, since the introduction of the new law, university students have become more zealous than ever in their studies: lectures are attended more diligently than before; students work assiduously in their classes and in the libraries and the laboratories. Such attention to serious work is the best guarantee that the previous disturbances, which in the main were caused by idleness, will not recur.

(*Obzor deyatelnosti ministerstva narodnogo prosveshcheniya v 1862 g, 63 i 64 godakh* (St Petersburg, 1865) pp. 74–7)

Further Student Disorders

This Report written in 1880 by A. A. Saburov, the Minister of Education and D. A. Milyutin, the Minister of War, met with much opposition from the majority of ministers and its only result was that inspectors of students became directly subordinate to the university administration.

* * *

In our opinion, at the present time, the position [of university students] can hardly be considered satisfactory. These young people gather from all corners of Russia amongst a population which is alien to them; they are often without any resources to live on and they look for intimacy and support in friendly groups. Moreover, the existing university statute is aimed at preventing students from coming together and even at destroying their link with the university itself. The present rules do not permit any form of links between students, do not allow welfare funds and other institutions which might serve to help poor students to be set up, and strictly prohibit any attempts at meetings between students about these matters. The consequences of this situation have not been slow to appear.

Despite their being prohibited, meetings, funds etc. do exist, but only in secret and, as a result, free from any inspection or supervision. . . .

Since there are no established rules for student meetings to guarantee order, any meeting becomes a disorderly assemblage of all the students of the university. . . .

The existing order completely destroys that spirit of comradeship between students which served precisely as a powerful means of education in the feelings of honour and dignity and moral principles in general.

The educational significance of comradeship . . . is more than anything else necessary for students at the present time. Most of them now come from an almost uneducated environment and therefore the moral outlook bequeathed to them in their families loses any moral authority. Since after the destruction of comradeship university life cannot develop these moral ideals in the students, they thus remain without any firm principles in life, and this has created the type of people who have received sad notoriety under the name of nihilists. In our conviction, there are only two ways out of this situation. The first is to completely alter the nature of universities by opening them to everybody without limitation or restriction. Courses will thus be turned into simple public lectures and the students into the public, with the police taking care of general external order.

Such a reform of the universities is however hardly desirable since it would inevitably bring with it a lowering of the level of teaching, which would become popular rather than scholarly. Moreover, the admittance of the mass of the public without limitation into the university would lead to disorder with which the police would not always be able to cope.

If this solution is not feasible, then we should directly recognise the undoubted fact that students have common interests, common concerns, a common life and a common intellectual outlook, and in this case it would be more correct and expedient to permit openly what the students do in secret already.

In essence, all the aspirations of the students are produced by one main reason – a fear of the poverty which rules amongst them and a desire to help their less fortunate comrades. They therefore want to set up funds, canteens, organised assistance etc., and the meetings themselves take place for the most part because of the need to discuss matters which concern these subjects relate to the establishment of a court of honour for their comrades who had offended against the dignity of students. . . .

Therefore we would propose:
1. To allow university students to set up funds, cheap canteens and organised assistance in finding work and, in general, means to provide subsidies to needy students, as well as courts of honour among students.
2. To allow them to assemble to elect individuals empowered to manage these institutions and to discuss questions arising both out of these institutions and subjects of academic concern which are suggested by the university administration.

We recognise, however, that too rapid a transition to the new order of things would be awkward in view of the impressionability of the young, who are always ready for any enthusiasms, and we should approach the

matter more cautiously:
1. These regulations should not be published as general rules for students of all universities, but each university should receive permission individually. . . .
2. The heads of the educational districts should be asked to give their views as to whether the students' uniform should be reintroduced, so that the granting of the above-mentioned privileges to each university might coincide with this measure.

This last provision could be useful in view of the fact that in the majority of student disturbances, as is discovered afterwards, the most prominent part is played by individuals who are completely unconnected with the university and a uniform would, to a definite degree, protect the students from these agitators. Besides, a uniform will undoubtedly enable the rebuilding of links and comradship between students.

(G. I. Shchetinina, 'Novyy dokument po istorii vnutrenney politiki Rossii', *Problemy istochnikovedeniya*, vol. 9 (Moscow, 1961) pp. 11–14)

7.4 SECONDARY SCHOOLS

These proposals by the Minister of Education, D. A. Tolstoy, for changes to the 1864 law on secondary schools were approved in 1871.

* * *

The greatest service performed by the 1864 law was the recognition that pupils could only be prepared for university entrance in those educational establishments in which both ancient languages – Latin and Greek – were taught inseparably. . . . It first introduced Greek into the ordinary curriculum of our university grammar schools, and made it a compulsory subject of study for all those aspiring to a university education. . . .

The 1864 law restored serious study in our grammar schools and it also dealt with making adquate provision for it to succeed. In this context it is most important that measures are taken to attract suitable and able people to the teaching profession. With this aim in mind the 1864 law raised salaries and the official status of teachers, tutors, school inspectors and head teachers. As well, the difference between senior and junior teachers which was based not on personal service but on which subjects they taught was abolished. Remuneration more in line with the work involved was introduced, calculated according to the number of lessons each teacher gave: they had earlier been a set salary – one for senior and one for junior teachers, unrelated to the number of lessons they taught. Successful teaching was also to be encouraged by setting the usual number of pupils in a class at no more than forty.... The 1864 law also eased admission to the grammar schools: it abolished the requirement for children belonging to the taxed classes to present a certificate of relief from their community as well as the general requirement for a medical certificate. At the same time, unfortunately, the level of knowledge require for admission into the first year of the grammar school was lowered.... Finally, an undoubtedly useful and important provision in the practical results of the 1864 law was that by which new educational establishment called a pro-grammar school comprising the lower four classes of the grammar schools could be established. This arrangement has already produced very good results and gives great promise for the future.

The 1864 law in all its aspects and especially in the re-establishment of a wide basis of classical education in our university grammar schools, is one of the most useful pieces of legislation of the present reign. But certain disadvantages and inconveniences have been displayed since it came into force....

The insufficient quantity of school time now allocated to the completion of the grammar school course is in itself a significant disadvantage that negates the beneficial results of all the other, completely rational, provisions of the 1864 law. This disadvantage has, however, been intensified – firstly, because the 1864 law reduced the already low entrance requirement for the first year of grammar school. As a result of this the grammar school has had to concern itself with the elementary education of its pupils when too little time was already allotted to the grammar school education. Secondly, the law allowed each individual grammar school council and in reality each individual teacher to prepare their own teaching programmes. As a result of this we have seen the completely natural tendency to widen the scope of each subject, which leads to an increased burden on the pupils....

Although... classical languages and mathematics were recognised as the most important subjects of study through the quantity of time assigned to them, this time was still insufficient for the pupil's minds to concentrate on them and for them to mature as much as possible....

These and other defects were already evident when the law was being implemented and produced representations from the district educational administrators, as well as comments from some Zemstva, gentry assemblies and urban communities and also from some of the more serious organs of our periodical press. . . .

The main conclusions which [my subsequent] investigation arrived at are as follows:

1. For admission to the first year of the grammar school and pro-grammar school, pupils must have a more substantial and better preparation than at present: with this aim a preparatory class should be established in both types of school.
2. The course of study in the grammar school should be increased from seven to eight years to both make it more thorough and to ease the lot of the pupils. . . .
3. The number of lessons in the most important subjects of the grammar school course, especially in classical languages, should be significantly increased, and on the other hand, those in less important subjects should be reduced. . . .
4. The ministry should publish a study plan for each subject which would be compulsory for all grammar schools and pro-grammar schools and would set out precisely the quantity of teaching and its distribution by classes. . . .
8. Identical rules for all grammar schools and pro-grammar schools should be laid down regarding entrance examinations, transfer from class to class and the awarding of the grammar school certificates, as well as disciplinary penalties for pupils. . . .
10. The position of the more deserving and experienced teachers should be improved by their being given higher salaries for the same work.

('Predstavlenie ministra narodnogo prosveshcheniya D. A. Tolstogo o neobkhodimosti izmenenii v ustave gimnazii 1864 g.', *Khrestomatiya po istorii pedagogiki*, vol. 4, pt 2 (Moscow, 1938) pp. 15–20)

7.5 KATKOV ON EDUCATION

M. N. Katkov, an influential conservative journalist, wrote this as part of a letter to the Tsar in July 1879.

*   *   *

. . . In any other area mistakes can be corrected, but in questions of education they have results which are fatal to whole generations. . . .

The state cannot let education slip out of its hands, not only in our troubled and transitional period, but at any time. Education cannot be left to the chance whim or biases of men without responsibility. Our Zemstva, which were not organised for educational aims at all, have, instead of keeping roads and bridges in repair, suddenly conceived a passion for concerning themselves with educational matters. . . . Petitions to give the Zemstva charge of educational matters are usually the work of one or two members, with their own views about this, views often completely different from those of the government. . . .

There is further reason for the intensification of agitation against the Minister of Education – a review of the university statute is on the agenda. If the grammar schools provide students for the universities, so the universities provide the grammar schools with teachers – and the state with all manner of officials. . . . By the 1863 statute the state, why and for whose benefit is unknown, gave up its inalienable rights and its sacred duty in the education of our young people, from whom the state's officials and the educators of the people should emerge. . . .

Our universities are presently described as being 'self-governing'; but the only system which can be called self-government is one in which individuals themselves take care of their own interests. This would be the case if the question under discussion was the autonomy of some scientific society able to determine its own activities, to elect its members, to undertake expeditions, etc. Is that what we see in universities? The professional body, using government authority, determines, unchecked and without responsibility to anyone, not is own affairs, but the fate of a great mass of students who are obliged not only to model their mode of thought in accordance with what this body sees fit to teach them under the guise of science, but it is this body which will also give them the right to enter state service. The most important part of the proposed reform concerns examinations which, according to the proposals, will not be conducted by the lecturers on the basis of their lectures, but by special commissions according to a defined general curriculum, so the examinations will serve not only as a check on the knowledge of the students, but also to regulate the lecture given by their professors. The syllabus for these state examinations will define the content and the extent of the university courses. Professors will have to teach precisely what will be demanded from the students in the state examination and the student, in order to gain the right to work for the state, will have to prove his scholarly knowledge of sciences and not what the professor takes into his head to teach, which may bear no relation either to the demands of scholarship, or of the state. The student, on the other hand, will have the freedom to regulate his studies

... and to choose the lecturers who will be the best and most faithful guide in acquiring the knowledge demanded in state examinations. The professor, in his turn, will be freed from the tyranny of his colleagues who are more expert in intrigues and gain control of the professorial body. They terrorise the recalcitrant with 'students' tales', with a fear of failing to be reappointed at the end of their term of employment and all manner of unpleasantnesses and oppression. There is as a result no freedom of opinion in the university councils and most members silently submit to the intriguers, small in number but strongly united.

('Vozhd reaktsii 60-80kh godov', *Byloe*, 1917, no. 4, pp. 6–11)

7.6 WOMEN'S EDUCATION

This reminiscence of the resurrection of university-level education for women in 1878 indicates the enthusiasm for the courses both amongst the staff of St Petersburg University and among the women of the capital.

* * *

The St Petersburg Women's Higher Courses sprang up again in 1878 with a completely different organisation. The experience of the previous courses had fully demonstrated that women who aspired to higher education were looking for earnest, systematic and absolutely serious knowledge, in both the humanities and pure science. Therefore the St Petersburg Higher Women's Courses were set up to include *three* sections: Humanities, Physics-Mathematical and Special Mathematics. In these circumstances the Minister of Education indicated Professor K. N. Bestuzhev-Ryumin as the individual whom he wished to see at the head of this institution. . . . The old and eminent scholar readily took on the position of 'founder' of the Women's Higher Courses and he, unpaid, carried out these extremely responsible and demanding duties for four years. It was only because of illness which forced him to leave Petersburg in 1882 that he resigned his post.

All the best serious scholars of St Petersburg University at that time agreed to play an active part in teaching the courses. ... The names of these scholars are dear to more than one generation of young women to whom they transmitted a deep love for serious intellectual labour, and developed independence and the habit of systematic and independent work in them.

(V. V. Stasov, *Nadezhda Vasilievna Stasova. Vospominaniya i ocherki* (St Petersburg, 1899) pp. 321–2)

7.7 BOOK PRODUCTION between 1861 and 1877

Year	No. of titles published
1861	1 773
1862	1 851
1863	1 652
1864	1 836
1865	1 863
1866	2 891
1867	3 388
1868	3 366
1869	3 102
1872	2 191
1873	2 668
1874	3 023
1875	4 441
1876	4 331
1877	5 451

Source: M. N. Kufaev, *Istoriya russkoy knigi v 19 veke* (Leningrad, 1927) p. 173

7.8 THE NATURE OF LITERATURE

Saltykov-Shchedrin, a novelist most noted for his work, *The Golovlev Family*, here puts forward his attitude to fiction.

* * *

Literature and propaganda are one and the same thing. However old this truth is, however, it has still so little penetrated the consciousness of literature itself that its repetition is far from superfluous. . . .

Especially important, in the educational sense, is the influence of that branch of literature known as fiction, because this is what is most accessible to the understandings of most people. Of course fiction does not give the reader that totality and certainty of knowledge which science leads to by means of proofs, but the influence of fiction can all the same be beneficial in that it is predisposed to searching for truth and makes the reader approach sceptically those unconscious axioms which he has up to then been guided by. In my opinion, this is a not unimportant service and only people completely devoid of sense can call fiction, as a weapon of propaganda, light reading. These people evidently do not understand that a name is not everything and that it is possible, perhaps, to find light reading in science, work which popularises the fundamental truths, without knowledge of which society cannot however advance further in the field of knowledge. . . .

Each work of fiction, no worse than any learned tract, betrays its author and his whole internal world. Reading a novel, short story, satire or essay it is not difficult to dertermine not only the author's world view, but to what degree he is cultured or ignorant. Those who affirm that the interest of fiction lies solely in its artistic side, or else in the ability of the author to reproduce keenly the attributes of this or that phenomenon are mistaken. The choice of the phenomenon in this case is far from being a matter of indifference, as equally the attitude of the author to it is not indifferent.

(M. E. Saltykov-Shchedrin, 'Ulichnaya filosofiya', *Sobranie sochineniy*, vol. 9 (Moscow, 1970) pp. 62–3)

7.9 ART THEORY: THREE VIEWS

Each of these three opinins on art theory contributed to Russian art in its widest sense during the second half of the nineteenth century.

* * *

Stasov

Stasov, an influential art and music critic, played an active part in the formation of new groups of painters and musicians.

* * *

The content of our pictures is so definite and strong that they are sometimes reproached for being 'tendentious'. What an absurd accusation and what a ridiculous soubriquet! Surely those who make accusations of 'tendentiousness' mean anything which has the force of indignation and accusation, which is filled with protest and a passionate desire to destroy everything which oppresses and burdens the world. If all that is passionate and best in the artist is rejected, many will remain content. But devoid of this, what significance does the artist have? As if everything which is best in the art and literature of all ages and all peoples is not 'tendentious'! . . .

Indifference to one's creations – untendentious art – is now less possible and less conceivable than at any previous time. Up to now art has in this respect lagged too far behind its older sisters – poetry and literature. It is still too slow in making up for this time spent on beautiful and idle trifles. It seems to me that in the future only art which is now called tendentious will remain and all other art will fade away and simply leave the stage. Up to now the best artists have put into this tendentious art everything that is best and most valuable which has arisen flaring in their soul, everything which they have succeeded in seeing, grasping and understanding.

(V. V. Stavov, 'Dvadtsat pyat let russkogo iskusstva', *Vestnik Evropy*, vol. 98 (1882) pp. 254–6)

Ogarev

This attack on the theory of art for art's sake was written in 1859 by Ogarev, a fierce opponent of Tsarism who emigrated to Britain in 1856.

* * *

The very theory of art for art's sake could only appear in a time of social decline. Art, as a discrete activity of man, must attract the attention of thinkers as a particular matter, but one which arises invariably from human life. What is art? Art is the imitation of nature, it has been argued. Subsequently more profound scholarship has looked on this naive definition with a smile of contempt. It defined art as the reproduction of reality. One has to be mad not to recognise the same simple definition in a new academic gown. In reality, art is the imitation of nature, because, apart from nature nothing else exists; in reality, art is the reproduction of reality, because apart from reality nothing else exists. The closer the artist has imitated nature, the more he has achieved that which nature itself has achieved, the better his work, the better he has reproduced reality. But this relates only to the execution, this is a skill, it is almost a technique. Why does the artist need to create something? This is the real question. What are the vital juices which have demanded to be expressed in his works, which have pushed him to creation? There is no doubt that forms should be true to nature; the artist cannot know other forms; but what has shaped this life which compels the artist to produce? This life has arisen from amidst society; the artist only strives to create because all social life breathes through him and gives him no peace. He has to produce, because he must express what he has keenly understood, has felt and has accepted, what social life has filled him with, be that a belief, be it indignation, be it delight or deep sorrow; but outside society and outside one's own opinion of it, it will accomplish nothing. And if you have absorbed nothing from society – neither deep belief, nor a thirst for reform, nor great epic literature, nor deep sorrow, nor passionate hope, nor sobbing laughter – what sort of artist are you? Very likely you will bring art to a highly refined conclusion and you will copy nature and reproduce reality in tiny detail; but you will not breathe life itself into your works. Your work 'for the sake of art' will not be provoked by life in general, life will not run vigorously through you, your work will be abstract or frigid trivia.

(N. P. Ogarev, 'Pamyati khudozhnika', *Izbrannye sotsialno-politicheskie i filosofskie proizvedeniya*, vol. 1 (Moscow, 1952) pp. 297–8)

Kramskoy

National elements were a vital ingredient in the work of Kramskoy, a leading painter during the 1870s and '80s.

* * *

I will declare what sort of art I stand for. I stand for national art, I believe that art cannot be anything other than national. There has never and nowhere been a different art and, if there exists an art which, it is said, is common to all mankind, then this is only by virtue of it being the expression of a nation which stands at the forefront of human development. And if at some time in the distant future, Russia is fated to occupy such a position amongst peoples, then Russian art, being deeply national, will become common to all mankind.

(I. N. Kramskoy, 'Sudby russkogo iskusstva. IV' in I. N. Kramskoy, *Ego zhizn, perepiska i khudozhestvenno-kriticheskie stati* (St Petersburg, 1888) p. 627)

7.10 A NEW SCHOOL OF PAINTING

Stasov here looks back on the birth of the movement which was to become known as the *Itinerants*.

* * *

[The new Russian art] came into conflict with the Academy school. The new and previously unprecedented corporate spirit provided a strong framework for keeping young artists united and strong, rallying together for mutual artistic help. One of the most talented, original and energetic new artists, I. N. Kramskoy, wrote to me that, 'The "artistic cooperative" arose spontaneously. The circumstances were such that this form of mutual assistance created itself. Who first said the word? To whom did the initiative belong? I really do not know. The most prominent feature of our meetings after leaving the Academy in 1863 was concern for each other. This was a wonderful moment in all our lives.' Russian society too viewed the new initiative thus. . . . Only the Academy and censorship were unhappy. The Academy . . . had been ready – to a certain extent of course – to recognise the right to existence of trends devoted to truth in art, to the 'genre', and was ready to give encouragement to such people, to give them awards and assistance, but only if its position of surveillance and its classes in the classical tradition remained completely inviolate. But suddenly – some brave 'protestants' decided to turn everything upside down! Of course, for the Academy this was equal to piracy, to robbery and revolution. An order was immediatley made that nothing should appear in the press about these 'protestants' and their exploits. . . . But the Cooperative itself did not last long. . . . But this powerful growth of the artistic spirit did not die. The Cooperative ceased to exist, but in its place there immediately appeared a new association of artists, made up partly of former members of the Cooperative, partly of new arrivals, but all its members were as a group filled with the same spirit of independence and 'protestantism' against the obsolete forces of art which had created the protest and noble resolution of 1863. In the winter of 1868 – 69 one of the young artists of the new movement, Myasoedov, returning from his scholarship in Italy raised in the Cooperative the idea that a group of the artists themselves should stage exhibitions. The Cooperative looked on this new idea with great sympathy. This was not only a genuine way out of the desperate position which faced the Cooperative, but was a huge step forward for the fundamental and powerful concept itself. . . . The artists of the

Moscow school, Perov, V. Makovsky, Pryanishnikov, Savrasov, warmly took up the idea and at the end of 1869 they suggested to the Petersburg Cooperative that they should both join togther to form a new society. . . . In Petersburg the most energetic and influential supporter of the new idea was, in my view, Kramskoy. I have keen memories of that time, a fruitful time in the history of our art. Perhaps, Kramskoy was the one who was most enthusiastic about the new shape of artistic life and activity in Russia. He called on his comrades 'to give up their stuffy, smoky cottage and build a new house, light and spacious'. . . . The main slogan was: nationality and realism. In this new association (just as in the Cooperative which preceded it) there was no mention of that animal, cowed and senseless life of debauch which had distinguished previous associations of our artists. . . . These new men know how to think and to read books, to discuss amongst themselves, and most of all how to see and sense deeply what was being created around them in life. Art for them could not be an idle indulgence.

All the sympathies of society were with the new bright circle of artists and remained so for an entire decade. What could the wails of backward men, ossified in tradition and without comprehension of the new movement mean against such united strength!

(V. V. Stasov, 'Dvadtsat pyat let russkogo iskusstva', *Vestnik Evropy*, vol. 98 (1882) pp. 635–8)

7.11 THE TRETYAKOV GALLERY

P. M. Tretyakov, a member of a prominent Moscow industrial family, established a picture gallery which was to become the nucleus of the national collection of Russian art.

* * *

I was five or six when Pavel Mikhailovich [Tretyakov] decided to build the first annex to the house – a gallery solely for pictures. He was afraid that there might be a fire in the house and that the pictures would perish.

The gallery was built by a brother-in-law of the Tretyakovs, the architect Kaminsky. Part of the garden was used and in one summer a two-storey building containing two spacious halls was erected. Partitions were put up in the halls as the number of pictures was already too great for the walls. . . .

From 1873 the gallery was open to all: before this the pictures could only be viewed with the special permission of Pavel Mikhailovich. And it was understandably inconvenient to allow everyone in succession into the family apartments of the house.

A sign reading 'Picture Gallery' hung over the wicket-gate which divided the yard from the garden. Each visitor entered from the street into the yard, then passed through the gate into the garden and thence into the gallery. My father met the visitors and admitted them to the gallery. My father already had sufficient to do even though he dealt only with the pictures. And many pictures were bought in these years. Pavel Mikhailovich made one of the three rooms on the ground floor of the house into a workshop for dealing with pictures before they were hung in the gallery. Here the pictures were framed, glazed and sometimes cleaned. . . .

At the end of the autumn of 1880 there was announced the sale by auction in Petersburg of the paintings of the artist V. V. Vereshchagin. Tretyakov always went to such sales and always brought back pictures from them. On this occasion a very large number of Vereshchagin's paintings were being sold, and there were articles about the sale in the newspapers.

Several days after Pavel Mikhailovich's departure for Petersburg my father laughingly told my mother in front of me that in the newspapers they were writing that 'Tretyakov has bought Vereshchagin's whole collection, and nobody else was allowed to get a single picture'. My father brought in the newspaper where Stasov described the auction, 'Tretyakov finished off all his competitors with a ruble. Whatever price his adversaries bid, he invariably squealed, just like a squeaking cart: "a ruble more". And he got the pictures. Thus Vereshchagin's whole collection – from Turkestan and India – is coming to Moscow, to the Tretyakov gallery.'

(N. A. Mudrogel, '58 let v Tretyakovskoy galeree. Vospominaniya', *Novyy Mir*, 1914, no. 7, pp. 139–42)

7.12 RUSSIAN MUSIC

The five composers making up the 'Mighty Handful' – Balakirev, Borodin, Cui, Musorgsky and Rimsky-Korsakov – were the inheritors of both traditional elements of Russian music and of Glinka's work in the early nineteenth century.

* * *

Glinka thought that he was only creating Russian opera, but he was mistaken. He created . . . an entire Russian school of music, a whole new system. In the fifty years since then our music and its school have grown and developed with marvellous and distinctive beauty, talent and strength. For a long period nobody wanted to recognise it; they looked at it scornfully and with disdain. . . .

What forms created the special nature of our school? Which elements gave it its exceptional trend and distinctive physionomy?

Firstly . . . there was the absence of prejudice and of blind faith. Beginning with Glinka, the Russian musical school is distinguished by complete independence of thought and view on music up to that time. Recognised authorities did not exist for our school. It desired to test everything itself, to reach its own conclusions and only then to be agreeable to recognising the greatness of a composer and the importance of a composition. Such independence of though is all too rarely met even today amongst European musicians, and was all the more unusual fifty years ago. . . .

Then, beginning with Glinka, all the best Russian musicians had very little faith in academic study and did not approach it with the servility and superstitious respect which was still common in many areas of Europe. . . .

Another important factor which characterised our new school of music was its national aspirations. This began with Glinka and has continued unbroken up to now. Such aspirations cannot be found in any other school of European music. The conditions of the history of the culture of other peoples have been such that folk song – the expression of direct, ingenuous popular music – has long almost completely disappeared in the majority of civilised peoples. . . . In our homeland, things are quite different. Folk song is still heard everywhere: every peasant, every carpenter, every mason, every yardman, every coachman, every old woman, every laundress and cook, every nanny and wet-nurse brings them with them from their own region to Petersburg, to Moscow, to any city and you hear them the whole year around. They surround you everywhere and all the time. Each working man and woman in Russia, as a thousand years ago, gets on with his work singing through whole collections of songs. The Russian soldier goes into battle with folk songs on his lips. . . . Therefore any Russian who is born with a creative musical soul grows up from the first days of his life among deeply national musical elements. Almost all the most significant Russian composers have been born not in the capitals, but deep inside Russia in provincial towns or on their fathers' estates, and spent their childhood there (Glinka, Dragomyzhsky, Musorgsky, Balakirev, Rimsky-Korsakov). The others spent a large period of their youth in the provinces, away from towns, in frequent and close contact with folk music. Their first and most fundamental musical impressions were national. . . .

Linked to the national, Russian element is another which is a characteristic feature of the new Russian musical school. This is the eastern element. Nowhere else in Europe does it play such a prominent role as with our composers. . . . Some of them have themselves visited the east (Glinka and Balakirev went to the Caucasus); others, although they have not travelled to the east, have all their lives been surrounded by eastern impressions and have thus clearly and brightly passed them on. They demonstrated by this the general Russian sympathy for everything eastern. It is no wonder when such a mass of eastern influences have entered into the make-up of Russian life in all its forms and have given it such a special and characteristic timbre. Even Glinka felt this and wrote in his 'Notes': 'There is no doubt that our Russian song is the child of the north, and has been to some extent passed on by the inhabitants of the east'. As a result of this, many of Glinka's first compositions are filled with eastern elements, as are many of the best compositions of all his contemporaries and successors. To see this only as a strange whim and caprice of Russian composers (as many of our musical critics often have) is absurd and short-sighted.

(V. V. Stasov, 'Nasha musika za poslednie 25 let russkogo iskusstva', *Vestnik Evropy*, vol. 103 (1883) pp. 562–9)

7.13 THE ORTHODOX CHURCH

The Church and Emancipation

This letter from the Minister of Justice to the Chief Procurator of the Holy Synod, written in 1860, makes clear the extent to which the government expected the Orthodox Church to act as its agent.

* * *

I am . . . approaching Your Excellency to ask if you will consider to what extent it would be useful to make it the duty . . . of the provincial parish priests . . . , when the edict and regulations on the improvement in the way of life of landowners' peasants is proclaimed, to instil into the peasants, at any convenient time, that they should in the future diligently and permanently fulfil their duties to the sovereign and authorities established by him. The priests should also explain that the rights and advantages granted to the peasantry will increase their prosperity only with continuous industry, moral behaviour and the precise execution of their obligations to the landowners. The parish priests should as well be very vigilant so that church employees, more often in very close contact with the peasants, do not spread any false rumours about the meaning of the published regulations. On the contrary, in case of incorrect interpretations, they should explain the regulations according to their literal meaning and in the spirit of instructions given by the episcopate.

('Tserkov i reforma 1861 g.', *Krasnyy Arkhiv*, vol. 72 (1935) pp. 183–4)

The Church and Education

The Church was also concerned to maintain its influence over education, as this extract from the Annual Report of the Chief Procurator for 1875 makes clear.

* * *

The clergy has zealously continued to devote itself, through its unwavering work in education, to the intellectual enlightenment of their flock in the spirit of the Orthodox faith and Christian morality. The new ... 1874 regulations on primary education extended the participation and influence of pastors of the Church in this important area. Inspection of the teaching of God's law and of the religious–moral trend of all education in the schools in general was entrusted to the bishops and the teaching of God's law given over to the parish priests. The regulations at the same time allowed the clergy to teach other subjects in schools and gave them the right of participation in school administration through their representatives who were appointed to the school councils....

Many of the bishops were concerned to establish the most reliable means of inspecting schools, and moreover they called on their priests to intensify their activity in carrying out their pastoral duty through the religious and moral education of the Orthodox people. Thus, the bishop of Vladimir instructed clergy members of schools councils to take as close an interest as possible in the progress of education, so that education would go hand in hand with Christian dogma....

The increase in primary schools established by the Ministry of

Education, as well as by the Zemstva, has meant that the number of parish church schools run by the clergy has been reduced; but it still remains significant. Thus, in the Saratov diocese there are 208 church schools with 9817 pupils, in Simbirsk, 191 and 5004 pupils, in Vologda, 190 schools with 2661 pupils in Tula, 168 schools and 4260 pupils in Kaluga 167 schools and 6826 pupils. In view of the undoubted benefits which the church schools have brought to education, especially in those areas where Zemstva have not yet been introduced and school councils not yet opened, bishops and clergy must make an effort to support these schools and increase their number, to attract a large number of pupils and provide them with the best organisation.

(*Izvlechenie iz . . . otcheta ober-prokurora Svyateyshego Sinoda . . . za 1875 g.* (St Petersburg, 1876) pp. 140–4)

8 Nationalities

8.1 THE POLISH REBELLION, 1863

The Tsar's Instructions to his Viceroy

In 1862 the Tsar's brother, Grand Duke Konstantin Nikolaevich, was appointed Viceroy of Poland: these are Alexander's instructions to his brother on taking up his post.

* * *

The main aim of your administration in Poland should be to restore and secure legal order everywhere, on the basis of the institutions I have granted. The unhappy conviction that all our efforts for the good of Poland will never satisfy the impossible aspirations and desires of the extreme patriotic i.e. revolutionary party, should not divert us from this path.

It falls to you to move firmly along this path, not to court popularity and not to be embarrassed by criticism and condemnation of your actions from either our domestic demagogues or from émigrés. You must never forget that Poland, inside its present frontiers, *must always remain Russian property*, but you must not touch on the separate administration and the institutions Poland has been granted.

. . . You should always be guided by the thought that you are serving Russia, and in concerning youself with the interests of Poland, never forget that she must not be a burden on Russia but should bring benefits to her; by virtue of her peaceful development and advanced position, Poland can serve as Russia's link with the rest of Europe.

The mistakes of the past should serve us as a lesson for the future. Your appointment was accepted by right-thinking people as a token of reconciliation, but at the same time it has aroused an almost universal expectation of some new privileges and concessions. *There can be no question of such concessions, in particular no constitution and no national army.* I will not permit either of these *in any form*. To agree to this would be to give up Poland and to recognise her independence, with all its fatal consequences for Russia, that is the loss of everything that was once conquered by Poland and which Polish patriots still consider as their property. . . .

Martial law is all that has restored order and it should be retained in all its strictness under you, especially in the towns, until I consider it possible to lift it. I do allow you however, when you have made closer acquaintance with the position of Poland, to make representations to me about the gradual restoration of normal legal order in individual areas where you consider it feasible and harmless. . . .

It leaves me only to add something about the Catholic clergy. You know how much they have shown themselves to be hostile and have used the mask of religion as a cover for all sorts of political demonstrations. . . .

Show the Catholic Church due respect in all cases, but do not allow the clergy to interfere in any guise in political matters and do not let any such interference remain unpunished.

('Perepiska Imperatora Aleksandra II-go s velikim knyazem Konstantinom Nikolaevichem za vremya pobyvaniya ego v dolzhnosti Namestnika Tsarstva Polskogo v 1862–1863 gg.', *Dela i dni*, vol. 1 (1920) pp. 123–5)

Reports from Warsaw

These two reports written by Konstantin Nikolaevich to the Tsar on the nights of 12–13 and 17–18 January 1863 respectively show the rapid development of the rebellion.

* * *

Everything went satisfactorily and peacefully at first after the levy of conscripts carried out on the night of 2–3 January in Warsaw. The night produced up to 1800 conscripts and there are now over 2400. The police alone, without the aid of troops, succeeded in conscripting this additional number, gradually and with great skill and energy. Moreover we had reliable information that significant numbers of urban inhabitants were fleeing from the city. On the night of 5–6 January we received the first reliable information that a large force was located in the Kampinosskiy forest. A detachment of troops was despatched immediately. . . . There they began a real game of hide and seek in these extensive forests. Many individual prisoners were taken, but we were unable to capture a complete band. . . .

However until yesterday no information of this sort had come from the provinces and everything was being prepared there for the conscript levy assigned for the 15th. Yesterday morning we received the first news of the appearance of armed bands in the suburbs of Plotsk. . . . Yesterday evening, all last night and all today information of the same sort has arrived. On the night of 10–11th, between midnight and 2 a.m. across the whole of Poland a simultaneous attack on the quarters of our troops was carried out. It is now clear that this was intended to be a St Bartholomew's Eve. The rebels burst into the houses where the soldiers were quartered in small groups, killed them in their sleep and seized their weapons. We must thank God that our losses were insignificant. The soldiers were able to rouse themselves, assemble and make strong resistance everywhere. The rebels paid dearly in numbers killed and wounded, and especially in prisoners taken. . . .

After such news we had no doubt as to what action should be taken. This morning I signed a decree placing the whole of Poland under Martial Law. Provincial military commanders were ordered to concentrate and assemble their forces so as to form rapidly flying columns of infantry and cavalry, if necessary augmented by artillery detachments. It is for us to start a small war with these forces to clean up the country and destroy all the armed bands. Now our hands have been untied and everyone is extremely glad of this – both military commanders and troops. . . . You can be absolutely sure that things are not being held up for lack of energy!

The most disturbing feature at present is that the rebels are beginning to destroy telegraph lines and railways. . . .

. . . The troops are in excellent spirit and they are bursting for the opportunity to fight well and avenge their comrades who were so perfidiously killed. . . .

The village clergy supports the rising everywhere and in some places it leads it.

The Warsaw students as a body continue to behave well. People do run off to the armed bands, but these are isolated incidents and the majority is well behaved at the moment. In general as far as can be judged, it is the urban population and petty Polish nobility, landed and landless, who are taking part in the uprising. The great landowners and people, i.e. the peasants, are calm. In many places the peasantry are helping us.

(*Powstanie stycznione. Materialy i dokumenty. Korespondencja namiestnikow krolestwa polskiego styczen-sierpien 1863 g* (Wrocław, 1974, pp. 11–12)

* * *

Our position is not very palatable at the moment, in particular because of the difficulty of communication. The telegraphs are continuously being disrupted. We repair them at one point and they are cut at another. . . . On the roads couriers and the mail are continuously intercepted by various small and separate forces which cannot be pursued. Thus we are never sure that orders have got through, and most importantly that they have got through in time. It is therefore difficult to run military operations from Warsaw. We are trying to give only general orders to the military commanders, to indicate the overall policy and allow them to implement orders in their own areas and to deal with the details. I am afraid that I would otherwise restrict and confuse them and spoil matters by excessive interference. The main thrust of the orders given is to concentrate our forces and to form independent mobile columns. . . .

When the troops are assembled and when mobile columns are established, then the second act will begin, i.e. we will go on to the offensive. This will present its own type of difficulty because of the nature of our opponents. They will obviously try to avoid encounters with our troops and at the approach of troops the armed bands will disperse only to reassemble and plunder in a completely different location. We will have to rush hither and thither like a man possessed. Our columns must not be too weak, otherwise they will fall victim to any trouble. They must not be too large so that they can move quickly. We have too few cavalry and especially too few cossacks for this type of war. I thus foresee that the war will be extremely exhausting and thankless. . . .

The central [revolutionary] committee has now proclaimed itself a provisional government, and the rebels call themselves a people's army. . . .

Warsaw has begun to take on a rather nasty atmosphere and therefore we have renewed all the strict and unpleasant rules from last year; I do not think that the rebels will dare to play any tricks since they know that they will pay dearly for them.

(Ibid., pp. 22–4).

8.2 ROMAN CATHOLICISM

The governor of a province bordering on Poland here describes the influence of the Roman Catholic Church in his area. Muravev had been appointed Governor-General of the western provinces in 1863, becoming known as 'the butcher of Lithuania'.

* * *

The Roman Catholic clergy, made up of 500 priests with a bishop and his suffragan at their head, held complete sway over the population. The bishop was an individual who stood out of the crowd: a man of great intelligence, of iron will, a democrat and an enemy of the Russian government. In the course of a long and unchecked administration of the diocese, he had acquired unlimited influence over it and the clergy submitted, machine-like, to his least indication. By dint of strict discipline he kept the clergy completely dependent on him and punished the disobedient by virtue of his almost unlimited authority. . . . The bishop played an important role at the time of the uprising and he gave it support which was difficult to conceal. When the rebellion had been put down, he continued to carry on a more or less hidden struggle against Muravev's repressive measures, in particular against those which paralysed or made difficult the external manifestation of the Roman Catholic faith, e.g., anointing, religious processions, the activity of the numerous religious orders and the development of Roman Catholic schools. He explained his opposition by the demands of duty, conscience and his responsibilities, explanations which had to be respected by the most zealous adherents of the repressive system. This is the only thing that can explain the fact that he remained unpunished, despite various investigations which exposed him.

The suffragan deferred to his superior in energy, although he was just as unwavering an enemy of the Russian government; but he was more concerned with Polish landowners, who owned more than 18,000 estates in the province. . . . Almost all the clergy subordinate to them were educated in the local seminary, under the influence of its peculiar, systematic and strictly maintained ascetic basis. Isolated from practical life and science, the majority of the seminarists were distinguished by remarkable ignorance and religious-political exaltation. The influence of these pastors on the Roman Catholic population of more than 800,000, in particular on the women, was enormous.

(A. G. Kaznacheev, 'Mezhdu strokami odnogo formulyarnogo spiska', *Russkaya Starina*, vol. 32 (1881) pp. 844–5)

8.3 THE BALTIC GERMANS

This attack on the Baltic Germans was written by M. P. Pogodin, a conservative publicist and earlier, a professor of history at Moscow

University. It exaggerates the spread of Germans throughout the Empire; they were mainly to be found in the Baltic provinces.

* * *

I would like to see a calculation as to the quantity of land and, in earlier times, the number of peasants which in Russian provinces belonged to Germans, Baltic Germans who had received these lands and these peasants as a dowry, as a reward for service, and finally, through purchase.... I foresee that the quantity of land will turn out to be more than is comprised by the whole of the Baltic provinces. One asks why a Russian noble may not enjoy the same rights in the three Baltic provinces as the Baltic nobleman has in all fifty Russian provinces?

German merchants are distributed across the whole of Russia, in Petersburg and Moscow, Archangel and Odessa, Tiflis and Kiev and everywhere they enjoy the same, and in some respects, greater advantages than Russian merchants. There are surely many more of them in Russia than in all the Baltic cities.

No German artisans are interfered with by Russians, but instead they help and cooperate with the Germans with all their strength. Is this the same as the situation of a Russian artisan who by chance finds himself in Riga or Tallinn and is there subject to all possible restrictions?

The idea of the Russian language for the Russians – the question itself is already an insult; a Russian must conceal his ancestry and otherwise cannot be heard in Riga, unless he speaks German! . . . Would this situation be tolerated anywhere else? In Russia I have to speak a foreign language in court!!

As regards landowning, the peasants – Latvian and Estonian will have, of course, equal rights with Russian, Polish and Georgian peasants. . . .

We ask you: what do you want?

You reply: freedom of conscience, German administration, German language, German law. . . .

Freedom of conscience. Enjoy it as you like; remain Protestant, Calvinist.... We have never disturbed you, are not interfering now and will never do so in the future.

But if your slaves who have worked for you for almost seven hundred years ... wish to adhere to our Orthodox Church, then you must also not interfere with them, and allow them the same freedom of conscience as you yourselves have. . . .

German administration. Use your own legal system, as is convenient for you, but if a Russian is subjected to any accusation or penalty, then under a Russian regime he can be tried only by Russian laws and in the Russian language. . . .

German language. We honour and respect the German language. . . .

You do not want to study in Russian and you say 'the Russian language which has been introduced everywhere, will spoil our schools, confuse our administration, threaten our culture. And we are supposed to remain silent'. . . .

The Germans now meet Russians in all branches of administration: military, civil and scholarly; teach them all the Russian language. . . .

The main demands you make are already being strictly observed; you Germans can practise your religion, speak your language and use your own laws.

(M. P. Pogodin, *Ostreyshiy vopros, pismo M. P. Pogodina k professoru Shirrenu* (Moscow, 1869) pp. 6–72)

8.4 FINLAND

Finland was the only part of the Russian Empire to have a parliament. This is Alexander II's speech at its opening in September 1863 in Helsinki.

* * *

Representatives of the Grand Duchy!
Seeing you collected around Me, I am happy that I am able to fulfil My desires and your hopes. I some time ago worked on a series of questions which were subsequently revised and which concerned the most essential interests of the region. The solution to these questions was postponed, since this required the participation of the Diet. Higher considerations, the evaluation of which rests with Me, did not allow me to assemble the representatives of the four estates of the Grand Duchy during the first years of my reign. Nevertheless at the proper time I took certain preparatory measures to this end and since circumstances do not require postponement, I have thus summoned you to take part in business, after hearing the opinion of My Finnish senate on the bills and various administrative measures which you will be concerned with during the present session. Bearing in mind the importance of these laws and measures, I instituted commissions made up of individuals enjoying the

trust of the people to subject them to preliminary examination. The publicity which was given to the speeches in the commissions may already have acquainted you with what will be the subject of your discussions and you may gave given full thought to those bills which correspond to public opinion and the needs of the region. Therefore, despite the significant number and importance of the bills, you will have the opportunity to give them final examination in the period laid down by law. The report on the position of Finland which will be laid before you will show that state revenue has always been adequate for current expenditure and it will show a significant increase in indirect taxation which bears witness to social wellbeing and has allowed the application of more substantial resources to the development of the material and moral needs of the region. . . .

I desire that in the future no loan should be concluded without the participation of the Diet of the Grand Duchy, excluding only sudden attack by enemies or other unforeseen social troubles which would force us to depart from this procedure.

The new taxes I am proposing to the Diet are aimed at implementing various measures which are intended to increase the wellbeing of the region and to make education flourish. You will be asked to decide to what extent these measures are urgent and to what extent they should be fulfilled.

Many provisions of the fundamental laws of the Grand Duchy appear incompatible with the position which has arisen after the unification of the Duchy and the empire and others suffer from a lack of clarity and definition. Desirous of correcting these shortcomings, I intend to instruct that a bill be drawn up which will elucidate and add to these provisions. It will be submitted for the examination of the next Diet which I propose to summon in three years' time. Leaving inviolate the principle of a constitutional monarchy which is part of the customs of the Finnish people and is stamped on all its laws and institutions, I desire to extend through this law the right which the Diet has already of determining the levels of taxation. I also intend to give the Diet the right to propose bills which it enjoyed in previous times, whilst I will retain the initiative in all those questions which concern changes in the fundamental laws.

You are aware of my feelings and you know how much I desire the happiness and prosperity of the peoples entrusted to my guardianship. On my part I have done nothing which could destroy the accord which should exist between a Sovereign and his people.

I desire that this accord will serve in the future as a guarantee of the good relations established between Me and the honourable and trusty Finnish people. It will be of great assistance to the wellbeing of this region, so close to My heart and will serve . . . as a new incentive to summon you at defined periods. You, representatives of the Grand Duchy, must prove by your work, fidelity and composure in decisions, that in the hands of a wise people, ready to act as one with the Sovereign, with practical ideas for the development of their welfare, liberal institutions are not only not dangerous, but are a guarantee of order or prosperity.

(P. N. Maykov, *Finlyandiya, ee proshedshee i nastoyashchee* (St Petersburg, 1905) pp. 523–5).

8.5 THE UKRAINE

Attacks on the Ukrainian language were common, such as the extract from an article by Katkov written in 1863. These attacks culminated in the edict of 1876 which prohibited the use of the Ukrainian language.

The Ukrainian Language

Two or three years ago for some reason Ukrainophilism suddenly ran riot. It went in parallel with all the other negative tendencies which suddenly took hold of our literature, our young people, our progressive civil service and various restless elements of our society. . . . The Polish publicists have begun to prove to Europe with shameless effrontery that Russian nationality is a spectre, that south-western Rus has nothing in common with the remaining Russian people and that it is much closer to Poland in its tribal peculiarities. Our literature, to its shame, has replied to this gross distortion of history with the same ideas of two Russian nationalities and two Russian languages. An astonishing and absurd sophism! As if two Russian nationalities and two Russian languages were possible, as much as if two French nationalities and two French languages were feasible. . . .

The generally accepted Russian language is not some local or, as is said, Great Russian language. It is absolutely obvious that this is not a tribal, but an historical language, and that southern Rus, as much as and perhaps more than northern Rus, participated in the formation of the language. Any efforts to stimulate and develop local dialects to the detriment of the existing general historical language has no logical aim other than the dissolution of national unity.

(M. N. Katkov, *1863 god* (Moscow, 1887) pp. 276–9)

The Ukrainian Language Edict, 1876

In order to halt what is, from the state's point of view, the dangerous activity of the Ukrainophiles, it is appropriate to take the following measures immediately: 1. To prohibit the import into the empire of any books published abroad in the Little Russian dialect [Ukrainian], without the special permission of the Chief Press Administration. 2. To prohibit the printing inside of the empire of any original works or translations in this dialect, with the exception of historical documents. . . . 3. Equally to prohibit any dramatic productions, musical lyrics and public lectures (which at present have the charter of Ukrainophile demonstrations) in this dialect. 4. To support the publication in Galicia of the newspaper *Slovo*, hostile to Ukrainophilism, assigning it a small but permanent subsidy. . . . 6. To strengthen supervision by the local educational administration so as not to allow any subjects in primary schools be taught in the Little Russian dialect. . . . 7. To clear the libraries of all primary and secondary schools in the Little Russian provinces of books and pamphlets prohibited by paragraph 2. . . . 8. To pay serious attention to the make-up of the teaching profession in the Kharkov, Kiev and Odessa educational districts, and to demand from the heads of these districts a list of teachers with a note as to their reliability in relation to Ukrainophile tendencies. Those noted as unreliable or doubtful should be transferred to Great Russian provinces. . . . 9. Note II. It would be useful to establish as a general rule that teachers appointed in the Kharkov, Kiev and Odessa educational districts should be mainly Great Russian and Little Russian teachers should be assigned to the St Petersburg, Kazan and Orenburg school districts.

(F. Savchenko, *The suppression of the Ukrainian activities in 1876,* (reprint of F. Savchenko, *Zaborona Ukrainstva 1876 r.*, Kiev, 1930), (Munich, 1970) pp. 381–3)

8.6 THE JEWS

Jews in the Russian empire lived mainly in the western provinces. Here a Smolensk landowner describes their difficult life.

* * *

Earlier, the Jews were not allowed to live here at all, now they can live only as artisans. But there are Jews whose fathers lived here, who were themselves born here and had produced a clutch of children. . . . The Jews who live here keep mills, pubs, engage in trade and various other matters. This is all forbidden but they all somehow get around this. The Jews are beneficial to the landowners because they pay well and are good at all sorts of things. The Jews mainly cluster together around the wealthy and important landowners. . . . Even if the Jew himself lives legally and all his papers are in order, then it will turn out that some relative, or one of the children's teachers is living illegally, or else some illegal Jews came to some festival or wedding. . . . The Jews are not permanently persecuted, but the situation changes from year to year. Sometimes they are not affected at all. . . .

. . . Sometimes the Jews live peacefully without any artisan certificates for a long period and nothing happens. In such peaceful times there is a multitude of Jews in appropriate places, close to building works, close to distilleries, large timber enterprises, in general where the enterprising and intelligent Jew can handle and gain money. When I came to live in the country, it was just such a peaceful period for the Jews. They were not persecuted and when the railway was being built there were all sorts of business to be done; huts to be built, sleepers to be sawn, stone to be quarried, bread to be provided, and of course vodka. Of course, the peasant cut logs and the peasants quarry stone, and the peasant drinks vodka, but without clever Jews he could not do any of these. There were many Jews here then, Jews occupied even the smallest mills, they kept the pubs and made all sorts of deals, completely taking over the role of the lower middle class, and setting these latter up against the Jew.

Suddenly the Jews began to be persecuted. They were not allowed to stay. They did not have artisan certificates. . . . But the Jews kept quiet and hoped to sit it out. It did not help. They were persecuted, order after order went out to the police; get them out of the district! They pressed the policemen time and again, they slip him something. . . . Again order after order comes! The Jews flew to acquire certificates and asked their 'elders' to help them, to make representations. Some got them, others not and whilst 'their own' were making representations higher up, order followed order. Nothing could be done, and the Jews began to be shifted from district to district. They could not stay long anywhere, the Jew hired carts, collected all his goods, beds, cattle, hens, his wife and children and moved to the next district, settled there and lived until he was driven out anew. Then, depending on circumstances, he either moved to a third district or came back to the first one. Of course such migrations could not go on for ever. The number of Jews decreased, but those remaining lived quite peacefully, and little by little the numbers grew.

(A. N. Engelgardt, *Iz derevni. 12 pisem, 1872–87* (Moscow, 1960) pp. 348–9)

8.7 CENTRAL ASIA

The head of the Governor-General of Turkestan's chancellery here gives a rather self-congratulatory view of the impact of Russian administration on its newly-conquered Central Asian dominions.

* * *

Our battalion arrived in Tashkent four years after Turkestan had been annexed to the empire. Tashkent at that time looked more like a military settlement than the chief city of the region, that is the capital of Russian Central Asia. The majority of the inhabitants were soldiers, either resting after some campaign or else about to go out on a new expedition. Civilians and women were a rarity. Now, thirty six years later, looking proudly at the path we have followed, I can see the colossal results achieved by the Russian government, always humane to the vanquished, but insistently pursuing its civilising mission. Of course, there have been many mistakes, there have been abuses, but this has not halted the rational and expedient intentions of the government. We went into a region which had a population alien to us. The inhabitants of the annexed areas, Muslim without exception, hated all non-believers and heathens, by virtue of the basic principles of their faith. They had for many centuries been accustomed to submitting humbly to the barbaric and cruel despotism of their rulers, but they nevertheless came to terms with their position because their rulers were of their own faith. But there now appeared white shirts, they were chased and beaten by troops and declared to be subjects of the White Tsar. The fanatical mullahs began rumours amongst the mass of the population that, instead of true believer khans, they were to be ruled by heathens who would convert them to Christianity, put crosses around their necks, send them to be soldiers, introduce their own laws, revoke the Sharia (the fundamental law of Islam) and make their wives and daughters uncover their faces.

At first this all agitated the wild and undeveloped natives. Frequent outbursts, uprisings and disorders took place and repression followed. But at the same time the natives saw that the very first steps of the first Governor-General proved the complete falseness of the mullahs. . . . It was announced solemnly everywhere to the local population, that as subjects of the Russian monarch, the population would keep its faith, its national customs, its courts and its judges, that all taxes demanded by the previous collectors were illegal and burdensome in the extreme and would be revoked, and that instead just taxes would be imposed, and that the position of women would remain inviolable. All this of course soon calmed the population and an industrious people settled down to a peaceful life.

(G. P. Fedorov, 'Moya sluzhba v Turkestanskom krae (1870–1906 goda)', *Istoricheskiy Vestnik*, vol. 133 (1913) pp. 803–4)

Selected Bibliography

This bibliography is restricted to works in English.

ABBREVIATIONS
JGO Jarhrücher für Geschichte Osteuropas
JMH Journal of Modern History
SEER Slavonic and East European Review

1. GENERAL WORKS

Mosse, W. E., *Alexander II and the Modernization of Russia* (London, 1958).
Pereira, N. G. O., *Tsar-Liberator: Alexander II of Russia 1818–1881* (Newtonville, Mass., 1983).
Rieber, A. J., 'Alexander II: A Revisionist View', *JMH*, vol. 43 (1971) pp. 42–58.
Seton-Watson, G. H. N., *The Russian Empire, 1801–1917* (Oxford, 1967).

2. POLITICS AND THE STATE

Abbott, R. J., 'Police Reform in the Russian Province of Iaroslavl, 1856–1876', *Slavic Review*, vol. 32 (1973) pp. 292–302.
Atwell, J. W., Jr. 'The Russian Jury', *SEER*, vol. 53 (1975) pp. 44–61.
Balmuth, D., *Censorship in Russia, 1865–1905* (Washington, DC) 1979.
Balmuth, D., 'Origins of the Russian Press Reform of 1865' *SEER*, vol. 47 (1969) pp. 369–88.
Czap, P., 'Peasant Class Courts and Peasant Customary Justice in Russia, 1861–1912', *Journal of Social History*, vol. 1, pt 2 (1967) pp. 149–78.
Emmons, T. and Vucinich, W. S. (eds), *The Zemstvo in Russia* (Cambridge, 1982).
Hamburg, G. M., 'Portrait of an Elite: Russian Marshals of the Nobility, 1861–1917', *Slavic Review*, vol. 40 (1981) pp. 585–602.
Kipp, J. W., 'M. Kh. Reutern on the Russian State and Economy: a Liberal Bureaucrat during the Crimean Era, 1854–1860', *JMH*, vol. 47 (1975) pp. 437–59.
Kipp, J. W. and Lincoln, W. B., 'Autocracy and Reform: Bureaucratic Absolutism and Political Modernization in Nineteenth Century Russia', *Russian History*, vol. 6 (1979) pp. 1–21.
Lincoln, W. B., 'A Profile of the Russian Bureaucracy on the Eve of the Great Reforms', *JGO*, vol. 27 (1979) pp. 181–96.
Lincoln, W. B., *In the Vanguard of Reform: Russia's Enlightened Bureaucrats 1825–1861* (DeKalb, Ill., 1982).
Lincoln, W. B., *Nikolai Miliutin: An Enlightened Russian Bureaucrat* (Newtonville, Mass., 1977)
Miller, F. A., *Dmitrii Miliutin and the Reform Era in Russia* (Nashville, Tenn., 1968).

Orlovsky, D. T., *The Limits of Reform: the Ministry of Internal Affairs in Imperial Russia, 1802–1881* (Cambridge, Mass., 1981).
Pearson, T. S., 'Russian Law and Rural Justice: Activity and Problems of the Russian Justices of the Peace, 1865–1889', *JGO*, vol. 32 (1984) pp. 52–71.
Pintner, W. M. and Rowney, D. K. (eds), *Russian Officialdom* (London, 1980).
Rieber, A. J. (ed.), *The Politics of Autocracy: Letters of Alexander II to Prince A. I. Bariatinskii* (Paris, 1966).
Ruud, C. A., 'Censorship and the Peasant Question: the Contingencies of Reform and Alexander II (1855–1859)', *California Slavic Studies*, vol. 5 (1970) pp. 137–67.
Ruud, C. A., *Fighting Words: Imperial Censorship and the Press 1804–1906*, (Toronto, 1982).
Starr, S. F., *Decentralization and Self-Government in Russia, 1830–1870*, (Princeton, 1972).
Szeftel, M., 'The Form of Government of the Russian Empire prior to the Constitutional Reforms of 1905–06' in J. S. Curtiss (ed.), *Essays in Russian and Soviet History in Honor of G. T. Robinson* (Leiden, 1963).
Wortman, R., 'Judicial Personnel and the Court Reform of 1864', *Canadian Slavic Studies*, vol. 3 (1969) pp. 224–34.
Wortman, R., *The Development of a Russian Legal Consciousness* (London 1976).
Zaionchkovsky, P. A., *The Russian Autocracy in Crisis, 1878–1882* (Gulf Breeze, Fl., 1979).

3. RURAL AND URBAN RUSSIA

Bater, J. H., *St Petersburg: Industrialization and Change* (London, 1976).
Bonnell, V. E. (ed.), *The Russian Worker: Life and Labor under the Tsarist Regime* (Berkeley, Calif., 1983).
Crisp, O., 'Labour and Industrialization in Russia', *Cambridge Economic History of Europe*, vol. VII, pt 2 (Cambridge, 1978).
Crisp, O., *Studies in the Russian Economy before 1914* (London, 1976).
Emmons, T., *The Russian Landed Gentry and the Peasant Emancipation of 1861* (Cambridge, 1968).
Emmons, T. (ed.), *The Emancipation of the Russian Serfs* (New York, 1970).
Field, D., *The End of Serfdom: Nobility and Bureaucracy in Russia, 1855–61* (Cambridge, Mass., 1976).
Field, D., *Rebels in the Name of the Tsar* (Boston, Mass., 1976).
Gerschenkron, A., 'Agrarian Policies and Industrialization: Russia 1861–1917', *Cambridge Economic History of Europe*, vol. VI, pt 2 (Cambridge, 1965).
Rieber, A. J., *Merchants and Entrepreneurs in Imperial Russia* (Chapel Hill, N. Carolina, 1982).
Robinson, G. T., *Rural Russia under the Old Regime*, rev. ed. (Berkeley, Calif., 1960).
Skerpan, A. A., 'The Russian National Economy and Emancipation' in Ferguson, A. and Levin, A. (eds), *Essays in Russian History* (Hamden, Conn., 1964).
Vucinich, W. S. (ed.), *The Peasant in Nineteenth-Century Russia* (Stanford, Calif., 1968).

Zaionchkovsky, P. A., *The Abolition of Serfdom in Russia* (Gulf Breeze, Fl., 1978).
Zelnik, R. E., *Labor and Society in Tsarist Russia: the Factory Workers of St Petersburg, 1855–1870* (Stanford, Calif., 1971).

4. PUBLIC OPINION

Bergman, J., *Vera Zasulich* (Stanford, Calif., 1983).
Berlin, I., *Russian Thinkers* (London, 1978).
Billington, J. H., *Mikhailovskii and Russian Populism* (Oxford, 1958).
Brower, D. R., 'Fathers, Sons and Grandfathers: Social Origins of Radical Intellectuals in Nineteenth Century Russia', *Journal of Social History*, vol. 2 (1969) pp. 333–55.
Footman, D., *Red Prelude* (London, 1964).
Gleason, A., *Young Russia* (Chicago, 1983).
Kelly, A., *Mikhail Bakunin* (Oxford, 1982).
Lampert, E., *Sons Against Fathers* (Oxford, 1965).
Pomper, P., *Peter Lavrov and the Russian Revolutionary Movement* (Chicago, 1972).
Pomper, P., *Sergei Nechaev* (New Brunswick, 1979).
Rogger, H., 'Reflections on Russian Conservatism: 1861–1905', *JGO*, vol. 14 (1966) pp. 195–212.
Thaden, E. C., *Conservative Nationalism in Nineteenth Century Russia* (Seattle, Washington, 1964).
Venturi, F., *Roots of Revolution* (New York, 1960).
Walicki, A., *The Slavophile Controversy* (Oxford, 1975).
Wortman, R., *The Crisis of Russian Populism* (Cambridge, 1976).

5. EDUCATION AND CULTURE

Freeze, G. L., *The Parish Clergy in Nineteenth-Century Russia: Crisis, Reform, Counter-Reform* (Princeton, N.J., 1983).
Frieden, N. M., *Russian Physicians in an Era of Reform and Revolution, 1856–1905* (Princeton, N.J., 1981).
Sinel, A., *The Classroom and the Chancellery: Education under Alexander II* (Cambridge, Mass., 1973).
Stavrou, T. G. (ed.), *Art and Culture in Nineteenth-Century Russia* (Bloomington, Ind., 1983).
Stites, R., *The Women's Liberation Movement in Russia* (Princeton, N.J., 1978).
Valkenier, E., *Russian Realist Art: the State and Society: the Peredvizhniki and their Tradition* (Ann Arbor, 1977).

6. FOREIGN AFFAIRS AND NATIONALITIES

Curtiss, J. S., *Russia's Crimean War* (Durham, N. Carolina, 1979).
Kirby, D. G. (ed.), *Finland and Russia, 1808–1920: Documents* (London, 1975).

Leslie, R. F., *Reform and Insurrection in Russian Poland, 1856–1865* (London, 1963).
Morison, J. D., 'Katkov and Panslavism', *SEER*, vol. 46 (1968) pp. 422–41.
Petrovich, M. B., *The Emergence of Russian Panslavism, 1856–1870* (New York, 1956).
Sumner, B. H., *Russia and the Balkans, 1870–1880* (Oxford, 1937).
Taylor, A. J. P., *The Struggle for Mastery in Europe, 1848–1918* (Oxford, 1954).
Thaden, E. C. (ed.), *Russification in the Baltic Provinces and Finland, 1855–1914* (Princeton, N.J., 1981).

Index

Anarchism, 149–50
Art, 40–1, 190–5
Austria, 51–3, 169–70, 173–4
Autocracy, 3, 61–2, 71–2
Agriculture, 2, 17–30, 99–125

Bakunin, N. A., 45, 149
Balakirev, M. A., 40, 195–7
Balkans, 51–3, 171–3
Belgrade, 56
Borodin, A. P., 40, 195–7
Bureaucracy, 3

Caucasus, 53
Censorship, 16, 94–8
Central Asia, 53, 175–7, 211–12
Chernyshevsky, N. G., 40, 43–4
Chernyy Peredel, 48, 156–8
Committee of Ministers, 6
Consultative Assembly, 74–6
Crimean War, 1, 4, 14, 50–3, 99, 105, 162–4
Crisp, O., 20
Cui, C. A., 40, 195–7
Culture, 178–99

Danilevsky, N. Y., 52
Dostoyevsky, F. M., 40, 50
Duma, 71–2, 74–5, 150–2

Education, 5, 38–53, 178–99
Emancipation, 17–30, 106–22
Exile, 92–4

Fadeev, R. A., 52
Finland, 55, 206–8
Foreign Policy, 50–3, 162–77
France, 1, 7, 29, 51–3, 164–8, 176

Great Britain, 1, 31
Germans, 51–3, 55–6, 204–6
Germany, 166–70
Glinka, M. I., 195–7
Golovnin, A. V., 8, 94

Gorchakov, A. M., 51, 164–6, 170, 175–6

Helsinki, 56
Herzen, A., 42, 140–2
Holland, 176

Ignatev, N. P., 52, 170–1
Industry, 1–3, 31–7, 126–32

Japan, 53
Jews, 55–6, 210–11
Justice of the Peace, 81–2

Karakozov, 145–6
Katkov, M. N., 186–8
Kavelin, K. D., 23, 101–3
Kaznacheev, A. G., 62, 68–9
Koni, A. F., 78
Konstantin Nikolaevich, Grand Duke, 11, 72–4, 200–3
Kramskoy, I. N., 40–1, 192–3
Kvyatovsky, A. A., 158–60

Lanskoy, S.S., 9
Lavrov, P.L., 46
Law, 4–6, 13, 76–82
League of the Three Emperors, 166, 169–70
Literacy, 125
Literature, 39–41, 189–90
Loris-Melikov, L. T., 11–12, 15–16, 58, 74–6

Marshal of the Nobility, 62–4
Medicine, 121–3
Military, 1, 14, 83–8, 136
Milyutin, N. A., 8, 14, 39, 182–4
Musorgsky, M. P., 40, 195–7
Music, 195–7

Narodnaya Volya, 48, 158–61
Nationalities, 53–6, 200–12
Nechaev, S. G., 45, 90–1

Nicholas I, 1, 5, 15, 20–1, 24, 38, 42
Nihilism, 44
Nobility, 2, 103–6

Ogarev, N. P., 191–2
Orthodox Church, 114–15, 197–9

Painting, 193–5
Peasant Commune, 118–21
Peasants
    Household, 118
    Landlord, 2, 17–30, 99–125
    State, 19–30
Pisarev, D. I., 44, 144–5
Plekhanov, G. V., 48
Pobedonostsev, K. P., 50
Poland, 11, 51–6, 144, 162–3, 200–3
Police, 14–15, 88–92
Population, 126, 135–7
Populism, 45–50, 152–5
Poverty, 133–4
Press, 97–8
Prussia, 168

Repin, 40–1
Revolution, 142–4
Rimsky-Korsakov, A., 40, 195–7
Roman Catholicism, 203–4
Rostovtsev, Ya. I, 24

Saburov, A. A., 182–4
Saburov, P. A., 51
Secondary Schools, 184–6
Senate, 6
Serfdom, 2–4, 17–30, 101–3, 105–6
Serno-Soloveich, N.A., 43
Shuvalov, P.A., 90–1, 146–9, 173–4

Slavophiles, 42, 96
Social Elite, 140
Society, 37–50
Sofia, 56
Stasov, V. V., 190–1, 193–5
State Council, 6, 10

Terrorism, 155–6
Tkachev, P. N., 45
Tolstoy, D. A., 38, 184–6
Tolstoy, L.N., 40, 133–4
Tretyakov, P. M., 194–5
Turgenev, I. S., 40
Turkey, 51–3, 169–75

Ukraine, 208–9
United States, 34, 176
Universities, 179–84
Urban Affairs, 31–7, 126–39

Valuev, P. A., 9–11, 15
Vodka, 124–5

Westernisers, 42
Women, 131–2, 135–7, 188–9
Workers, 31–7, 46–7, 93–4, 127–32

'Young Russia', 142–4

Zaichnevsky, P. G., 142–4
Zarudnyy, S. I., 13
Zasulich, V., 13, 48
Zemlya i Volya, 43, 147–50, 154–5
Zemstvo, 9–10, 41, 62–70, 75–6, 179, 184–6
Zhelyabov, A. I., 48
Zürich, 90–1